CHRIST IN THE NEW TESTAMENT

# CHRIST IN THE
# NEW TESTAMENT

## CHARLES M. LAYMON

ABINGDON PRESS    NEW YORK • NASHVILLE

CHRIST IN THE NEW TESTAMENT

Copyright © MCMLVIII by Abingdon Press

Library of Congress Catalog Card Number: 58-9520

SET UP, PRINTED, AND BOUND BY THE
PARTHENON PRESS, AT NASHVILLE,
TENNESSEE, UNITED STATES OF AMERICA

# PREFACE

THE CENTRALITY OF CHRIST IN CHRISTIAN THOUGHT AND EXPERIENCE is both a matter of history and a contemporary fact. Ever since he first made an impact upon the lives of his followers, the significance of his person has been a concern of thoughtful men. Each generation of believers, from the earliest days of the church to the present hour, has inquired who this one might be. More than this, attempts have been made continuously to phrase an answer to this question. Thus Christology may be seen to be inescapable for the Christian.

The roots of the significant statements of the church concerning the person of Christ, as these appear in the historic creeds, may be discovered in the New Testament documents themselves. And behind these writings lies the Christian experience of those who believed in him unto eternal life. The Christology of the New Testament represents an attempt to put into words the thinking of the church concerning Christ, during and shortly after the first one hundred years of its existence. It is informal in character, as compared with the more formal expressions of systematic theology.

In the New Testament, theology where Christ is concerned, and in other areas also, is a developing one. Although in its entirety it takes the high view that Jesus is both Lord and Christ, the Son of God, there are unfolding implications of this conclusion from writing to writing which further Christian experience, broader cultural contacts, and diverse conceptual thought-forms revealed or made possible.

The present volume seeks to delineate the portrayal of Christ throughout the New Testament as a whole, taking note of the continuity and unity of its witness from first to last. On the other hand, it recognizes the diversity of emphasis and perspective which exists from book to book. This unity in diversity and diversity in unity is a distinguishing mark of the revelation of God in the Scriptures. It makes necessary both the understanding of biblical theology and of biblical historical study, and the conversation between the two in recent decades has been significant. Certainly the New Testament itself transmits and interprets the tradition concerning Christ from both points of view at one and the same time.

The portrayal of Christ in the New Testament may be approached in terms of its total witness, summarizing what it says concerning his person in relation to such subjects as the church, salvation, the sacraments, the Spirit, the Kingdom, God, and the end of the Age. A distinctive advantage in this method is the concreteness of statement and the unity of conception which it makes possible.

Another approach is through a consideration of the developing portraiture in the different writings as these are related to the changing background of the church's life and experience. This method is likely to be closer to the historical realities, and is less apt to result in an undue formalization of the portrait. It also opens the way for comparisons of conception, and safeguards the variety in unity which exists in the several representations. By this same rule, however, it may so stress the variety that the unity which is actually present may be neglected. Nevertheless, I have followed the second of these procedures, concluding that the advantages outweigh the disadvantages. The final chapter, "One Lord and One Faith," as well as periodic summarizations, is intended to keep the focus in order.

The possibilities of class use for this book were kept in mind as I wrote, and the level of approach was placed within the range of students already possessing a background of New Testament study. At the same time, it is introductory as far as New Testament Christology is concerned. An extended and representative bibliography is appended in order to encourage supplementary reading in this significant field. In this way a teacher may enlarge and expand the treatment given at any desired point.

It is impossible to give credit to all who have contributed to the writing of this book. The footnotes indicate clearly how numerous are these persons. I wish in particular to express my indebtedness to my professors who first made the great tradition concerning Christ come alive for me. These include William Manson, William J. Lowstuter (in memoriam), Hugh R. Mackintosh (in memoriam), and Rollin H. Walker (in memoriam).

CHARLES M. LAYMON

# CONTENTS

## Background

## Portraiture

## Summation

ONE

# Christk in the New Testament

THE NEW TESTAMENT IS PARTICULARLY IMPRESSIVE IN THE DIVERSITY of its literary offerings. Among its twenty-seven books are to be found Gospels, epistles, a book of history, a homily, and an apocalypse. These writings cover more than one hundred years of experience in the Christian Church. A succession of Roman emperors cast their shadows across its pages, although only three of them are mentioned by name specifically.[1] At least thirteen authors may be singled out; not all can be identified actually, and there were many others who engaged in literary activity behind the scenes.

In the midst of all this diversity there is, however, an impressive unity in the several writings which grows out of the fact that the New Testament as a whole is a book about Christ. Whether it is dealing with his ministry, death and resurrection, concerned with the early history of the Christian movement, applying the faith to current living, or presenting a prognosis of the immediate future, he directly or indirectly is the constant frame of reference.

### The Jesus of History and the Christ of Experience

Because of our modern interest in historical data we have been concerned pre-eminently to know the Jesus of history. Our search for him has taken us back to the Gospels, to Mark in particular, and then back of Mark to the early Christian fellowship, and beyond it to the days of Christ's earthly ministry. During recent decades scholars have not been so confident as they once were that a valid historical portrait could be drawn, mostly because of the realization that com-

[1] Caesar Augustus (Luke 2:1), Tiberius Caesar (Luke 3:1), and Claudius (Acts 11: 28; 18:2). The designation "Caesar" is also found in Mark 12:14 ff.; Luke 23:2; John 19:12 ff.; Acts 17:7; 25:8 ff.; 26:32; 27:24; 28:19; and Phil. 4:22. Many conclude that the Revelation to John comes near to naming Domitian through its numerical reference in 13:18, where the alphabetical value of the figure 666 spells out Neron Caesar, Domitian being regarded as a resuscitation of Nero.

11

munity and personal factors played a large part in forming and transmitting the tradition.[2] On the other hand, it is being felt increasingly that the most direct way to know a person actually is through personal relationships, and that the true dimensions of Jesus of Nazareth are best seen finally through the eyes of those in the Christian community who were transformed in their fellowship with him during the days of his flesh.

For the early church, however, Christ was not only what he was as a citizen of first-century Palestine. He was also what he became in the religious experience of his followers after the Resurrection, particularly during the remaining decades of the first century and the first half of the second, when the faith of the church was being defined and the New Testament written. In other words, the exalted Christ of religious experience was regarded as being one with the Jesus of history, and the final estimate of his person included data from both sources.

In spite of this, New Testament study has sometimes tended to differentiate sharply between the historical Jesus and the Christ as known in Christian experience. The latter involves interpretations and delineations of meaning which the early church found in their experience of him in and following the Resurrection. A volume of several decades ago which drew attention to this distinction between the Jesus of history and the Christ of Christian experience, as interpreted in the Christian community, was Adolph Deissmann's *The Religion of Jesus and the Faith of Paul*. The former was regarded as the original and the latter as the interpretation which modified, if not actually changed, the original into something quite different. It was felt that Paul had turned the religion *of* Jesus into a religion *about* Jesus, thereby diverting the original historical stream.[3]

In the final analysis, however, the New Testament approach is the correct one. Our total view of Christ should include both his historical career and the experiences of him in the early church thoughtfully interpreted. John Knox in writing of these matters has said that "the false assumption that they can be separated and that a purely objective historiography is possible (or could be true even

---

[2] For an indication of the problems involved here and a consideration of attempts to understand and solve them cf. Vincent Taylor, *Formation of the Gospel Tradition*; E. F. Scott, *The Validity of the Gospel Record*; and E. B. Redlich, *Form Criticism*.
[3] Cf. also William Wrede, *Paul* (Boston: American Unitarian Assoc., 1908), ad loc.; Wilhelm Bousset, *Kyrios Christos*, 2nd ed., pp. 120 ff.

if it were possible) partly accounts for the dryness, unreality, and irrelevance which have sometimes characterized biblical scholarship." [4] In his study, *Christ the Lord*, Knox achieves a significant synthesis of the two. And as we have noted, the New Testament itself presents just such a synthesis, and its complete story, as found throughout the writings in their entirety, is needed for a full and adequate portrayal of Christ.

### The Resurrection Perspective

The Resurrection is pivotal in this total New Testament portrait of Christ. Jesus' earthly ministry is viewed in the light of the resurrection fact, and his continuing career as Christ the Lord is seen also as stemming from this same transcendent event. To separate the two would have been unthinkable to a New Testament author, including the writers of the Gospels. While all regarded the human life of Jesus as real, they were certain that his total significance for faith could not be limited to his preresurrection ministry.

When we read the Gospels, it should not be forgotten that even before their authors wrote, they knew the outcome of the story they were telling. They were not surprised to learn of the Resurrection when they came to the end of the account. As a matter of fact, had it not been for the Resurrection and the events which developed from it, the chances are that they would not have written of Jesus in the first place. It is, therefore, all the more remarkable that the Gospels carry such a realistic picture of the earthly activities of the Galilean as they do. From their pages, particularly in the case of the Synoptic Gospels, there emerges a convincing portrait of an actual person. On the whole, theophany,[5] growing out of the Resurrection, does not interfere with historical reality.

And in the Gospel of John, where a supernatural consciousness is basic to the presentation of Jesus, there are genuine down-to-earth touches to the portrayal that are unusual under the circumstances. For instance, Jesus is pictured as being tired, hungry, and thirsty (4:6-8; 19:28). And even if these are regarded as dramatic additions supplied by the author himself, they testify to the fact that he considered Jesus' historical career as genuine.

Although the resurrection perspective does not blind the authors of the Gospels to the reality of Jesus' historical life, it does add to

[4] *Christ the Lord* (New York: Harper & Bros., 1945), p. 3. Used by permission.
[5] Theophany refers to the physical appearance or manifestation of a deity to man.

13

their realization of the significance of the account they are relating. For instance, there is a profound expectancy as they move from reporting one event to another, an overtone of divine meaning. This is *the* great story they are recording. It is not to be handled lightly or treated superficially. This conviction, instead of encouraging it, kept them from the romantic excesses which writers sometimes fall into when describing spectacular events. Their evident adulation of Jesus, while tremendously real, is controlled and restrained. Statements of praise and acclaim are usually quite brief. (Cf. Mark 1:28, 45; 5:42; Luke 13:17; 18:43; Matt. 15:31; 22:33.)

If the Resurrection provided an exalted perspective for viewing the earthly ministry of Jesus, it also cast its light upon the subsequent faith of the church. Paul puts it boldly, if not bluntly, when writing to the Corinthians. He says: "If Christ has not been raised, then our preaching is in vain and your faith is in vain . . . . If Christ has not been raised, your faith is futile and you are still in your sins." (I Cor. 15:14, 17.)

The Resurrection, considered as a fact, is so structually written into the entire New Testament (not just into the Gospels) that the book's total range of meanings is inexplicable without it. James Denney was saying just this when he wrote that the "life that throbs in it [the New Testament] from beginning to end, the life that always fills us again with wonder as it beats upon us from its pages, is the life which the Risen Saviour has quickened in Christian souls." [6]

### Preaching the Resurrection

The kerygma, or preaching message, of the early church further shows how the faith of Christians had been formed in the light of the Resurrection, for it regularly included the raising of Jesus from the dead as a decisive part of its content. Two illustrations, one from Acts (10:38-43) and the other from First Corinthians (15:3-11), will be sufficient to illustrate this point. It is not possible, in my judgment, to state which of the two is the earlier. Both have almost a creedal sound, suggesting frequent usage. Many repetitions had smoothed off the rough edges so that, from a literary standpoint, they seem almost impersonal, lacking the individual accents usually noticeable in a freely composed personal statement.

The first is found on the lips of Peter as he preaches in the home

[6] *Jesus and the Gospel* (Cincinnati: Jennings & Graham, 1908), p. 111.

of Cornelius, the Gentile. This Roman centurion, who had been a God-fearer, had sent to Joppa for Simon in response to a vision that had come to him while in prayer. The apostle came with some hesitation (he himself had needed a vision to prepare him for the visit, Acts 10:9-16), but upon hearing the centurion's story, he began to tell about Jesus to the assembled group. We shall have occasion later to examine the total message of his sermon, but our present concern is with the reference to the Resurrection. It occurs in these words: "But God raised him on the third day and made him manifest; not to all the people but to us who were chosen by God as witnesses, who ate and drank with him after he rose from the dead." (10:40-41.)

At the time of the formulation of this statement by the church, it was accepted that the Resurrection was a major fact, that it had a somewhat corporeal character, and that those who witnessed it were set apart by God for this very purpose. Those who were "chosen by God" had eaten and drunk with the risen Jesus. But more than this, following the Resurrection, and because of it, they were commanded to preach and testify to certain things. Clearly their ministry was based upon the fact of the Resurrection itself.

The second example of the kerygma to which we shall give attention is found in Paul's first letter to the Corinthians (15:3-11). He is reminding them of the terms in which he had preached the gospel to them—which gospel they had received, in which they now stood, and by which they were now saved. And, in what might appear to be an unusual procedure in the case of one who had boasted that he had not depended upon others for his gospel (Gal. 1:11-17), not even upon the apostles, Paul recites the traditional list of witnesses to the Resurrection which he had received, presumably from the church itself.

This list of those to whom Jesus appeared represents in all likelihood the earliest formal enumeration of the original witnesses—at least it is the earliest in the New Testament. That it omits the reference to the women and the Emmaus pair and includes others which may or may not be loosely identified with the tradition in the Gospels is not any more surprising than the fact that these same Gospels individually mention incidents and sayings of Jesus which are not found in all four of them. To the appearances to Cephas, the twelve, the more than five hundred brethren at one time, to James and to all the apostles Paul adds, "He appeared also to me." It would seem that he

15

is referring to his own experience on the Damascus road (Acts 9; 22; 26), which he also probably has in mind in Galatians (1:15-16a) where he wrote: "But when he who had set me apart before I was born, and had called me through his grace, was pleased to reveal his Son to [in] me . . . ." [7]

Whether Paul's listing of himself along with the other witnesses to the Resurrection, and using the same words in doing so, implies that his experience was identical with theirs is difficult to determine. The words "he appeared" (ōphthē) are not finally definitive in this connection, for they may be used to refer both to visionary and non-visionary seeing (Acts 7:26). But from the standpoint of the contention that the Resurrection was basic in the development of the faith as seen in the New Testament as a whole, the nature and character of Paul's experience is not the issue. What is the issue is the fact that in this early kerygma the Resurrection is central in the thinking of the church.

### Other References to the Resurrection

That the Resurrection is basic to the faith of the church throughout the New Testament may be seen further from a succession of references, selected almost at random. They are significant because they appear in connection with different themes and subjects; that is, the Resurrection itself is not being considered as a specific study for its own sake in these instances. Instead, it is assumed to be a fact, and implications of great significance are drawn from it.

In Romans the Resurrection is referred to as Paul introduces himself to the church at the seat of the empire. The apostle speaks of the gospel for which God set him apart as "the gospel concerning his Son, who was descended from David according to the flesh and designated Son of God in power according to the Spirit of holiness by his resurrection from the dead, Jesus Christ our Lord" (1:3-4). It is evident here that the Resurrection is assumed, not argued, as a basic fact which undergirds the gospel.

Again, in speaking of Christ, Paul calls him "the head of the body, the church," and adds that he is "the beginning, the first-born from the dead" (Col. 1:18). The person of Christ, and not the Resurrection, is the subject of discussion in this passage, and the latter is in-

[7] Cf. also I Cor. 9:1: "Have I not seen Jesus our Lord?" This could mean that Paul had known Jesus in the flesh, perhaps during the final days at Jerusalem. Cf. later references to this question, pp. 53-54.

troduced as an accepted fact. The author of Revelation also speaks of Christ as "the first-born of the dead" (1:5). It would seem that this expression had achieved accepted usage.

On occasion a New Testament author will refer to the Resurrection when speaking of God, for this event is a word about the Father, as well as one concerning the Son. He is called "the God of peace who brought again from the dead our Lord Jesus" (Heb. 13:20), and is praised as the Father of the Lord Jesus Christ who mercifully introduced men into a new life of living hope "through the resurrection of Jesus Christ from the dead" (I Pet. 1:3).

These passages are sufficient to indicate further the extent to which the Resurrection had determined the thinking of the early church. As the event which had constituted it a particular kind of fellowship, the Resurrection was definitive in their conception of God, Christ, and the gospel.

### Christ Throughout All

We have seen that the Resurrection is a central fact in the life and faith of the church as depicted throughout the entire New Testament. If it were removed from the account, the very structure of the several writings would collapse. Some kind of picture might be reconstructed, perhaps, but it would not be that which is found in the New Testament. Another way to express it would be to say that without the Resurrection the New Testament would no longer be the *New Testament*.

There are other aspects, however, besides the Resurrection which make the complete New Testament a book about Christ. He is a subject of which all its authors write, as well as the object of their personal faith. More than this, he is also the object of the faith of the members of the church whose story the New Testament relates. The chapters which follow will delineate in detail the full portrait of Christ which is drawn. It is sufficient here to indicate that it is continuous throughout the whole volume of twenty-seven books.

The Gospels are studies in portraiture. The word "portrait" is used in this connection because it suggests both pictorial representation and interpretation, as over against simple photography. They are not purely objective in an abstract sense, since, as we have indicated, their authors have already taken sides in favor of Jesus. This need not, and does not, mean that they are flagrantly prejudicial. It does imply,

17

however, that they approach his portrait from the standpoint both of faith and of fact. At all times, they are the glad bearers of the good news about Jesus the Christ as they tell of his ministry, present his teachings, extol his wonder-deeds, and follow him to Jerusalem, the Cross, and in his resurrected life.

In the case of Luke, the author extends this account beyond the Gospel and into the book of Acts, including both the period of the primitive church and that of the missionary outreach which followed.[8] In the first, sermons are preached in which Jesus is central (10:34-43), visions of Jesus are experienced (7:56), prayers are offered to him (7:59), and in his name the sick are healed (3:1-10). Even when his earthly ministry is not involved in these references, portraiture is present. They etch deeply the character lines of a living personality, the exalted Christ who is at work in the church.

This is true, likewise, of Luke's narration of the missionary movement led by the apostle Paul. Jesus Christ is presented variously through sermons (Acts 13:16-41), church councils (15), guidance (16:7), healing (16:16-18), visions (18:5-11), and teachings (20:35). And even when his name is not mentioned, the events which are described have this mark upon them.

Other New Testament writings continue this presentation of Christ. A few general references will indicate this. Paul justified his advice to the Corinthians concerning marriage and divorce by quoting a remembered word of Jesus (I Cor. 7:10-11), and shamed them for their selfishness by pointing to the sacrifice of Jesus in death for their sakes (11:23-32). He thanked the Father that the Colossian Christians had been transferred "to the kingdom of his beloved Son" (1:13), and urged the Philippians to emulate the divine humility by which Christ Jesus emptied himself of his heavenly prerogatives and took the form of a servant-slave, becoming obedient unto death— even death on a cross (2:5-11).

The author of Hebrews stressed for his readers the example of Jesus, who was tempted as they were being tempted and therefore was able to help them (2:18). And John the seer encouraged the suffering Christians by holding before their eyes a portrayal of Christ as the triumphant King of kings and Lord of lords, who would over-

[8] The assumption here is that the author of Luke-Acts is Luke, the physician, traveling companion of Paul and mentioned in Col. 4:14, Philem. 24, and II Tim. 4:11. Cf. pp. 38 ff.

18

come all evil forces or beings in the universe, including those at whose hands their lives were in constant danger (Rev. 19:11-16).

These references to Christ were selected widely from the New Testament. They bear telling witness to the fact that the Christian community which centered in him, in turn, produced a New Testament whose major theme was himself, and the new life God had brought to men through him.

### Multiple Portraiture

All of the New Testament writings take an exalted view of Christ. He stands on the divine side of life. As has been pointed out, this is no less true of the Synoptic Gospels which present his historical career than it is of the epistles of Paul. And it is as characteristic, also, of the Gospel of Mark as it is of the Gospel of John. But the fact that the entire New Testament is in agreement here does not mean that its authors interpret the pre-eminence of Christ in exactly the same way. Actually, even a casual reading of the book will show that there is considerable variety in the interpretations presented. The references cited already in this chapter leave no doubt about this.

Varied authorship should be taken into account in connection with this multiple portraiture of Christ in the New Testament. A mystic such as the author of the Fourth Gospel must, of necessity, view the story he writes through the lenses of his own personality and experience. And an ecstatic seer such as the author of the Revelation to John, who found himself "in the Spirit on the Lord's day," and who heard behind him "a loud voice like a trumpet saying 'Write what you see in a book'" (1:10-11), such a one will receive a celestial vision of Christ which is different from the portrait of the teacher-preacher of Nazareth.

Not only is there variety in the presentation of Christ, but also there appears to be an enlarging context of interpretation. Although the earliest portrait involved ontological reality, the emphasis becomes increasingly metaphysical as the authors press beyond the earth to the heavenly sphere in explaining his function and person.[9] This will be clearly evident in the chapters which follow.

One factor in particular that will be seen to be responsible for the emergence of these new dimensions in portraiture as the decades pass

[9] The words "ontology" and "metaphysics" are used here as referring to the ultimate nature of being and reality.

is the changing historical background over against which the New Testament documents were written. The old adage that "new occasions teach new duties" may be paraphrased to describe this situation so that it will read "New demands reveal new dimensions." The strains and stresses of later times forced the Christian community to turn to their Lord for wisdom and strength, and as a result they discovered depths and heights in his person which they had not known before. In addition, the spread of the faith, beyond its original Jewish environment, particularly into the Hellenistic world, brought the church into a broader cultural milieu. This gave to it new thought-forms for interpreting its experience, as well as for expressing itself concerning him to whom they were indebted for their salvation. And with the new thought-forms came fuller realizations of the significance of Christ.

The New Testament, then, is a book of multiple portraiture where Christ is concerned. The variety of these representations is the measure of the inspired experiences of the men who wrote the documents, their individual temperaments, and also of the currents of the times—social, political, religious, and theological. Christ is presented variously as rabbi (John 3:2); master (Mark 9:5); prophet (Mark 8:28); teacher (John 13:14); Messiah (John 1:41); servant (Acts 3:26); Son of man (Mark 8:38); Savior (Acts 5:31); mediator (I Tim. 2:5); high priest (Heb. 4:14); Lord (Acts 2:36); judge (Acts 10:42); Son of God (Gal. 2:20); Logos (John 1:1); King of kings and Lord of lords (Rev. 19:11-16). There is a distinctiveness in each of these portrayals even though there is some overlapping of conception.

And yet the authors are not offering their readers several different persons. He is one and the same individual, whatever differences there may be in portraiture. The New Testament knows only a single person where Christ is concerned, and the Christian community is united in this fact. Ernest F. Scott is correct in his contention that "the New Testament writers are careful to lay stress on this unity and to indicate its nature. They address themselves to 'those who call on the name of the Lord,' 'those who are in Christ,' 'those who are called to be saints,' 'all who love the Lord Jesus.' " [10] In this sense they have one Lord and one faith. [11]

[10] *The Varieties of New Testament Religion*, p. 28.

[11] Cf. an extended discussion of the character of this unity in the chapter titled "One Lord and One Faith," pp. 221 ff.

## The Facts of Revelation

The story of the New Testament, which is basically the story of Christ, may be written from a humanistic angle. As such it is seen as the account of the impact of a remarkable person upon other persons, the influence of culture upon culture, and the modification of life and thought by reason. That all of these factors are involved in the situation which the New Testament describes is self-evident.

But, be this as it may, to read the New Testament primarily from this vantage point is to misread it essentially, for this would omit the factor which makes it new, and constitutes it a testament. This would be to disregard revelation in the experience of Christians. When the seer of the Apocalypse of John wrote that he was in the Spirit on the Lord's Day, he was testifying to the ultimate source of his visions. And it was this same Spirit who illumined the thinking of the church as it lived the life which, in turn, brought forth the book.

This new life came upon the church because Christ came to the first century. Call it the divine encounter, the saving event, the existential fact—by whatever appropriate name you choose, it was not something which men got up by themselves as a social and religious contribution to society.

Historicism of the type which interprets New Testament thought as a tapestry woven by reason out of the ideational threads of first-century culture substitutes an artificial rationalism for history. The suggested process is too introspective and subjective to give birth to a movement that was said to have turned the world upside down.

I have always appreciated the expression of this truth by Frederick C. Grant. In his important volume *The Earliest Gospel* he states:

Unless we are prepared to grant the reality of the Spirit, and the valid basis of this primitive Christian experience, I fear that we shall not bring much back with us from our critical forays in the field of New Testament history, literature, and religion. That principle—the primary and indisputable reality of the Spirit, to be apprehended by faith, and genuinely known through direct human experience—is the vital spark of evangelicalism, today no less than it has always been.[12]

To subscribe to this view does not mean the demise of rational thinking; rather, it calls upon reason to accept revelation as a primary fact in interpreting the New Testament.

[12] Pp. 84-85.

# TWO

# The Christian Community

THE CHRISTIAN COMMUNITY AND THE NEW TESTAMENT ARE INSEPA-
rably bound together. Out of this fellowship in Christ came the writings, and the writings, in turn, contributed to the life of the Fellowship. It is the living character of this relationship which unites the
people and the book.

### Epistles and Gospels

The epistles of Paul, for instance, are clearly informal communica-
tions between the apostle and the communities to which he wrote.
In every case but one, the Epistle to the Romans, he had most likely
founded these Christian groups himself.[1] He wrote them as an administrator, a pastor of souls, and a Christian brother. Often he was replying to questions which the young churches had sent him. Sometimes he was sharing with them new insights which he believed would
strengthen their faith in Christ. That these letters were to become
scripture would have surprised Paul, and might even have shocked
him had he contemplated the possibility at the time of their composition. One does not sit down to write scripture in the first place, and
in the second, if one did, his writing would be so self-consciously set
forth that there would be little life to it.

At first glance the Synoptic Gospels appear to be less related to
community life and more formal in character than the epistles. But
this is due largely to the literary process by which the units of the
tradition were brought together. The editorial blending of these
materials gave to the finished product a pattern of arrangement which,
for the casual reader, obscures its living relationship to the Christian
communities from which it came. In the case of the Fourth Gospel,
its sermonic character, the presentation of the material against the

---

[1] Even though Paul had not visited Colossae, it is likely that this church was founded
as a result of his work in Asia. Citizens of this community may have heard him preach
at Ephesus, and carried the word back to Colossae, where they became the nucleus
of a new group of Christians.

background of the great feasts, and the literary style of the author—all these also combine to interfere with our seeing its immediate connections with the Ephesian-area churches, for whom and in whose midst we may assume that it was written.

It is the motive behind the writing of the Gospels which relates them to the Christian community. They, like the epistles, were written to instruct, inspire, and inform. The gathering together of the tradition with its teachings, miracle stories, passion narratives, and so forth in the first instance, even before they were incorporated into a Gospel proper, was undertaken in order to meet the actual needs of the church. These were homiletical, polemical, educational, and missionary. To take one illustration, it seems likely that quite soon after the church came into being, the account of Jesus' death was formulated, and then put into writing. Even though it was an inspiring example of sacrificial love, the Cross remained a stumbling block both to Jews and to Jewish Christians. The Law had stated that all who hung upon the tree were accursed (Deut. 21:22-23). A presentation and interpretation of his death was therefore needed, one that would enable them to see it as an act of God, no less. And this the gospel writers provided by showing that Jesus accepted the Cross as the will of God (Mark 14:32-42; John 12:27-36a).

When the portrayal of Christ in the New Testament is delineated in the chapters which follow, it will be seen at every point how the features of the portrait are related to the needs and nature of the Christian community. This is not to suggest that the Fellowship introduced in large measure, lines which were not actually present, although subjective factors are never totally absent. Rather it is to indicate, as was suggested in the previous chapter, that the concrete experiences of Christian groups progressively revealed and sharpened features in the portrait which had hitherto been missed. The Christian community did not create Christ; Christ created it. Yet it was a medium through which his full stature was to be made known. Because of its significance in this respect we should examine more closely its origin and nature.

## The Origin of the Christian Community

The origin of the Christian community was informal in character. As far as its members were concerned, it was the outgrowth of an experience of Christ rather than the result of a decision. It did not come

23

into being deliberately in order to promote an idea; neither was it formed consciously to perpetuate the memory of Jesus of Nazareth. There is no record of an organizational meeting ever having taken place, in the sense of a coming together of charter members for the considerate purpose of establishing a specific group.

## In the Will of God

In the search for ultimate causes, it may be said that the origin of the Christian community was in the eternal purpose of God. This view can be seen in Paul's letter to the Romans. When the apostle sought to explain the rejection of Jesus, the Jewish Messiah, by the Jewish nation, he turned to the primacy of the will of God in history, and concluded that it was God's purpose for Israel to be broken off "the olive tree" in order that the Christian church, "the wild olive shoot," could be grafted in (11:1-24). God willed it to be so, "in order to make known the riches of his glory for the vessels of mercy, *which he has prepared beforehand for glory,* even us whom he has called, not from the Jews only but also from the Gentiles?" (9: 23-24.) [2]

Whatever one may think of the emphasis on predestination which characterizes this section of Romans, a vigorous sense of the ultimate will of God is found here. Even though it may seem to ride with heavy tread upon human freedom, and needs always to be interpreted in the light of the character of God which Jesus revealed, there is grandeur in this conception of the divine will in history. This may be seen particularly in Paul's conclusion: "For from him [God] and through him and to him are all things. To him be glory forever. Amen." (11:36.)

## In the Commonwealth of Israel

It may be held also that the Christian community had its origin implicitly in the Old Testament congregation of the children of Israel. The very word which is used in the New Testament for the Christian church, *ekklēsia,* is employed also by Luke in referring to the company of Israel to whom Moses gave the living oracles (Acts 7:38). This word in the Septuagint is usually used to translate the Hebrew qāhāl, which as a rule refers to the assembled people of God. Paul

---

[2] Italics mine.

employed this same word when writing of the Christian body as a whole (I Cor. 12:28), as well as when addressing a local church (Rom. 16:1).[3]

In this connection it is interesting to observe that much of the Christian preaching in the book of Acts, particularly that part which reflects the kerygma or message, begins with a reference to the commonwealth of Israel and its leaders. There was an intuitive conviction that the events which they were experiencing in the Christian community were in a direct line of succession from Old Testament history. This continuity was explained sometimes in terms of a prophecy and fulfillment relationship (Acts 2:14 ff.). Again it was regarded as an earlier and a later expression of the work of one and the same God (Acts 3:13).

The relationship of the Christian community to the activity of God in the Old Testament can be seen in yet another reference. All three of the Synoptic Gospels carry the parable of the vineyard and the wicked husbandman (Matt. 21:33-46; Mark 12:1-12; Luke 20: 9-19). This parable represents an attempt of Jesus to interpret his own experience of rejection in the light of God's activity in the past, the present, and of his projected action in the future. It tells of an absentee planter and owner of a vineyard who sent a succession of servants to gather its fruit. These were repulsed and driven out. He then said that he would send his son. Him, they killed. The vineyard was, therefore, to be taken away from its original trustees and given to others. God was the planter and owner of the vineyard; Israel was the original trustee. The prophets were the mistreated servants; Jesus was the Son. The members of the Christian community were the new trustees.

Some would regard the parable as a patent example of first-century Christian apologetics which may or may not rest on a valid tradition; others view it as Jesus' own analysis of the situation. In either case, it relates the experience of the church sequentially to God's redemptive movements in Hebrew history, and undergirds the conclusion

[3] For all practical purposes the expression "Christian community," as used by New Testament scholars, carries the same meaning as the Christian church. Another overlapping and related expression in the New Testament is "fellowship," koinōnia. It is used to refer to the Christian community in fellowship in Acts 2:42. For a formal distinction between ekklēsia as a new society or community, and church as a visible institution, cf. Emil Brunner, The Misunderstanding of the Church (Philadelphia: The Westminster Press, 1953).

that the origin of the Christian community was implicit in the commonwealth of Israel.[4]

## In the Following of Jesus

In a broad sense one might say that the Christian community had its beginnings in the following that Jesus attracted in Galilee and Judea. The response of the people to him was based on the impression he made upon them, both by his teaching and by his wonder deeds. The Gospels speak of them as saying, "What is this? A new teaching! With authority he commands unclean spirits and they obey him." (Mark 1:27.) On one occasion we are told that the people "were all amazed and glorified God, saying, 'We never saw anything like this' " (Mark 2:12). Other reports said that the people "were filled with awe, and said to one another, 'Who then is this, that even the wind and sea obey him?' " (Mark 4:41).

Not all in the large company which responded to Jesus were motivated from the depths of a profound conviction. Some were impressed in the sense of being bewildered or even entertained by his greatness. Others were moved to a temporary attraction and would, according to the explanation of the parable of the sower, wilt and die when the roots touched the rock of tribulation and persecution. But there were those who were deeply drawn toward Jesus, and who actually entered the inner fellowship of the Kingdom. In them the seed would bear fruit, "some a hundredfold, some sixty, and some thirty" (Matt. 13:8).

Among this group of persons who were related to Jesus through an actual experience of the Kingdom at his hands were the twelve disciples, the seventy who volunteered for an evangelistic tour,[5] and the special group of women who provided for him out of their own means. Luke indicates that some of these women had actually been healed by Jesus.

Undoubtedly there were others also whose names are not mentioned but who stayed close by throughout Jesus' entire ministry. It is interesting to note in this connection that when a successor to Judas

[4] "The 'parable' looks more like those in some of the later writers—says Hermas, also a Roman—and is probably best explained as derived largely from early Christian anti-Jewish polemic (cf. Luke 11:49-51), though authentic words of Jesus may survive in it." Frederick C. Grant in *The Interpreter's Bible*, VII, 836.

[5] The sending out of the seventy may be but another version of the sending out of the twelve. Cf. Matt. 10:5 ff. and Luke 10:1-20.

was chosen, and the candidates were required to have been with Jesus from his baptism to the Crucifixion and even to have witnessed the Resurrection, at least two qualified persons were in the company. These were Justus and Matthias, men whose names are never once referred to in the Gospel accounts (Acts 1:21-26). And that there were others besides these two is not an unreasonable assumption.

### In the Resurrection Fellowship

We have seen that the origin of the Christian community may be regarded as implicit in the eternal will of God, in the Old Testament commonwealth of Israel, and in the following Jesus attracted during his ministry. Its beginning, on the other hand, was *explicit* in the Resurrection since it was this experience which his followers had in common that finally welded them into a dynamic union which constituted the actual beginning of the Christian community. Pentecost is often singled out as the birthday of the church, but in the earliest Christian preaching the kerygma invariably stressed the Resurrection and passed over Pentecost. This does not discount the importance of Pentecost, but it does suggest the primacy of the Resurrection.

Paul's recital of the resurrection appearances in First Corinthians (15:3-11) indicates the exclusiveness of this experience. The number of persons who participated in the event, participated in the sense that they were witnesses who responded to it, were relatively few. Some could be listed by name—Cephas, James, and Paul; others are referred to collectively—the twelve and more than five hundred brethren at one time. The Synoptics mention several additional persons. Most of those named, with the exception of Paul, belonged to the inner circle who walked with Jesus during the days when he was proclaiming the advent of the kingdom of God. The five hundred were called "brethren," which suggests close ties of fellowship.

The records imply that the original resurrection experience was known only by those who honored Jesus and believed in him. It was selective, not in the sense that it was open to but a few persons, but that the conditions of love and faith had to be met before Jesus would make his presence known. And the fact that some experienced the Resurrection while others did not resulted in a specific group consciousness. They were witnesses! Others were outsiders.

The resurrection experience, in addition to its exclusiveness, was also transcendent. It was characterized by exaltation and supernal

27

elevation of mind and spirit. The first witnesses knew the radiant presence of Jesus not only individually, but also in company with others (five hundred brethren at one time). These constituted a body of believers who had seen Jesus in his risen glory, and their fellowship together was marked by a warmth and glow, which must have reminded them of the shekinah of Moses when he came from the divine presence to stand before the people. In this sense the Christian community was a community of the resurrection radiance.

We are in error if we think of the Resurrection solely as a tremendous consummation of the kingdom ministry of Jesus. It was this, to be sure, but it was far more. Actually it was a beginning and not an ending. Suddenly there was an arterial highway into the future. The Resurrection meant that the cause of the Kingdom was ready to take a new turn, under the leadership of the resurrected Jesus.

### Pentecost, the Kingdom, and the Christian Community

The exact character of this new turn was not immediately evident. In obedience to the word of the risen Jesus his followers gathered together in Jerusalem, waiting for the promise of the Father (Acts 1:4). As they tarried, in all about 120, they were the Christian community expectant. The Resurrection had set them apart from others and had given them a transcendent consciousness. They were ready for a new manifestation from Jesus. It was pentecost season and, along with their fellow Jews, thoughts of God's revelation in the Law were in their minds. But there was a new dimension in their thinking this Pentecost. The resurrection of Jesus had constituted them a new community, not apart from the past but related to it in a historic succession. What was Pentecost to mean to the new Fellowship of those who would experience it?

Pentecost will be considered later somewhat at length in connection with its contribution to the portrait of Christ in the primitive church. From the standpoint of the Christian community it should be noted here, however, that the coming of the Spirit at this occasion upon the waiting followers of Jesus further solidified the union that the Resurrection had already effected. The two words "presence" and "power" are best suited to carry the high meaning of the pentecost event. It is as Floyd V. Filson states: "What they [the Christian fellowship] needed was for their faith to take fire, their prayer to become realized fellowship, their aspirations to become matched by the power and impulse to act. This Pentecost gave them. Henceforth the Christian group was vigorous, active, and aggressive." [6]

Pentecost with the coming of the Spirit was an event which caught up its participants into a new order of living, one in which ecstasy, power, and great joy predominated. Was this regarded by the church as the beginning of the coming of the Kingdom to which Old Testament prophets and Jesus made reference? By way of answering this question, let us first examine Peter's sermon on this occasion.[7] Here the apostle turns to the "Day of the Lord" conception as found in Joel's prophecy for the framework within which to interpret the pentecost experience. He said:

> And in the last days it shall be, God declares,
>     that I will pour out my Spirit upon all flesh,
> and your sons and your daughters shall prophesy,
>     and your young men shall see visions,
> and your old men shall dream dreams;
>     yea, and on my menservants and my maidservants in
> those days I will pour out my Spirit; and they shall prophesy.
>     And I will show wonders in the heaven above
> and signs on the earth beneath,
>     blood, and fire, and vapor of smoke;
> the sun shall be turned into darkness
>     and the moon into blood,
> before the day of the Lord comes,
>     the great and manifest day.
> And it shall be that whoever calls on the name of
>     the Lord shall be saved. (Acts 2:17-21.)

### The Day of the Lord

The Day of the Lord mentioned in Peter's sermon was a part of Israel's outlook concerning the goal of history. It was to be the time of the nation's triumph to which men looked with eager anticipation (Amos 5:18). At its coming, it was believed that God would establish a victorious rule on the face of the earth. This was to be an eschatological event in the sense that the Eternal's purpose in history

---

[6] One Lord—One Faith, p. 182.

[7] Peter's sermon, whether a free composition, an actual report of his own words, or reminiscences in phrases of the author (cf. pp. 51-52) represents an ideology of the primitive period when eschatology predominated over other teachings such as salvation by faith, and so forth.

would at last be realized. The Kingdom would come, no less, as God's reign was made real.

God's victory in the Kingdom which the Day of the Lord would establish would be a moral one, since it was to be a time of judgment as well as a time of blessing. For this reason Amos warned the people that being Israelites was not enough. They must be ethically righteous as well. And so the prophet said to his nation in their sin:

> Woe to you who desire the day of the Lord!
>> Why would you have the day of the Lord?
> It is darkness, and not light;
>
> .   .   .   .   .   .   .   .   .
>
> Is not the day of the Lord darkness, and not light,
>> and gloom with no brightness in it? (Amos 5:18-20.)

The Day of the Lord and the character of the Lord could not be separated. Sinners would discover it to be a dark hour.

But saints would find in it untold blessings. It will be for them a time of peace (Isa. 51:3) as God's Eden is once more established. Nature will reflect the renewal of all life (Isa. 55:13; 60:13). A new heaven and a new earth will express the re-creation of God's victory over evil.[8] Language pales as it attempts to express the hopes associated with this dream.

> For behold, I create new heavens and a new earth;
>> and the former things shall not be remembered or come into mind.
> But be glad and rejoice for ever in that which I create;
>> for behold, I create Jerusalem a rejoicing and her people a joy.
> I will rejoice in Jerusalem, and be glad in my people;
>> no more shall be heard in it the sound of weeping and the cry of distress. (Isa. 65:17-19).

Seldom has prophetic expectation reached such heights.

The interpretation of Pentecost in Acts places it at the center of this Day of the Lord hope and, therefore, at the heart of the kingdom expectation as well. Pentecost is a kingdom event.

When we return to the question which was asked at the beginning of this section—namely, Was Pentecost regarded by the church as

---

[8] For an effective consideration of the Day of the Lord expectation see John Bright, *The Kingdom of God* (Nashville: Abingdon Press, 1953), pp. 45 ff., 156 ff.

the beginning of the coming of the Kingdom to which the Old Testament prophets and Jesus made frequent reference?—the answer must be in the affirmative. Because the Day of the Lord was bound up with the coming of the Kingdom, and Pentecost was interpreted as an expression of the Day of the Lord, it followed that Pentecost was itself an expression of the Kingdom.

### Pentecost and Jesus' Teaching Concerning the Kingdom

The followers of Jesus during his ministry did not grasp his understanding of the kingdom of God. Their minds were so preoccupied with traditional concepts of a restored Davidic kingdom that Jesus' more transcendent view escaped them. Even at the Last Supper they argued among themselves concerning positions of pre-eminence in the Kingdom (Luke 22:24-27). Although Jesus had tried by precept and parable (Matt. 5:12; Luke 13:20-21; Mark 4:26-29; Luke 17:20-21; Mark 13; Matt. 24; Luke 21:5-36) to modify their thinking in this regard, it would seem that, up to the very end, he did not succeed.

The book of Acts contains a tradition belonging to the resurrection cycle which has bearing here. It reads: "So when they had come together, they asked him, 'Lord, will you at this time restore the kingdom to Israel?'" (1:6.) The traditional view of a restored Davidic kingdom was still in the minds of the disciples. His reply is reminiscent of a statement found in the apocalyptic discourse of Mark. For example: "But of that day or that hour no one knows, not even the angels in heaven, nor the Son, but only the Father." (13:32.) He said: "It is not for you to know times or seasons which the Father has fixed by his own authority" (Acts 1:7),[9] and then added that power would be theirs when the Holy Spirit came upon them. And in Pentecost what he had promised had actually taken place!

What does the inclusion of this tradition in Acts mean? Does it not suggest that following Pentecost the early church discovered in this ecstatic event the basis for understanding the kingdom of God in the teaching of Jesus? What his followers had failed to see during his ministry, because of their traditional bias of thought, they were now realizing in the light of the new experience that had come to them. Certainly Luke must have come to understand it in this way, and there is no reason to conclude that he was not reflecting the views

[9] In the Western text this passage says, "No one can know." This is quite like the reference in Mark 13:32 quoted above.

31

of the church. There is insight and strength in the hindsight that reveals the true significance of historical occurrences. And this, it would seem, is what we have here.

Pentecost meant that the church was living in the "last days." In this sense it was an eschatological community, a community of the kingdom of God.[10] The hopes of the apocalyptists were being fulfilled within its own life. Jesus' message of the Kingdom was being realized among them.

Apocalypticism looks toward the End, the summation of history, and Pentecost was regarded as the beginning of the realization of apocalyptic expectations. The new community in Christ was convinced that it was already experiencing the power and joys of the final time. Greater events were yet to come, but this did not cancel out the fact that members of the Christian community were even now participating in the new life itself, as a kind of first fruits of a later triumphant yield. The speaking in tongues which occurred at this time (Acts 2:4-11), whether it be regarded as the ecstatic glossolalia of Paul and the Corinthians (I Cor. 14), which seems to me most likely, or some other kind of speaking or understanding, was considered to be an evidence of their present participation in the new day, even as it was a promise of the future.

The place of Christ in this experience and expectation will be considered in the next chapter. It is sufficient here to indicate that it was he who was regarded as having sent the Spirit, and that his return in triumph was eagerly anticipated. As Rudolf Bultmann contends, the fact that the earliest church still looked for the Parousia suggests that it did not regard the New Age as having fully come, but "in expecting him as the Coming One they understood themselves as the Congregation of the end of days called by him. For them factually—no matter to what degree it may have been clearly conscious—the old had passed away and the world had become new." [11]

### Living in the Christian Community

We have seen that the Christian community as represented in the primitive Jerusalem church knew itself to have been created

[10] Cf. H. J. Cadbury, "Acts and Eschatology," ad loc. in The Background of the New Testament and Its Eschatology, ed. William D. Davies and David Daube, pp. 300-321.

[11] Theology of the New Testament, tr. Kendrick Grobel (New York: Charles Scribner's Sons, 1951), I, 44. Used by permission.

through an eschatological experience or event which its members shared in common. To belong to the Fellowship was to participate in this experience. It meant that the Spirit had become the possession of "all flesh." Individual lives were lifted above the ordinary human plane as they lived in ecstatic expectation of coming events which would bring history to its final consummation.

Ecstasy, however, was not all. A common round of activities marked their daily living. It was through these that they expressed the ecstasy that was in their souls. There was a life to be lived as they waited in anticipation for the climactic end. Acts carries a summary passage which is revealing in this connection:

And they devoted themselves to the apostles' teaching and fellowship, to the breaking of bread and the prayers.

And fear came upon every soul; and many wonders and signs were done through the apostles. And all who believed were together and had all things in common; and they sold their possessions and goods and distributed them to all, as any had need. And day by day, attending the temple together and breaking bread in their homes, they partook of food with glad and generous hearts, praising God and having favor with all the people. And the Lord added to their number day by day those who were being saved. (2:42-47.)[12]

In the above summary, or summaries, certain characteristics of the life in the new community appear. (1) The apostles are in positions of prominence, both as teachers (of the tradition) and as performers of mighty works, presumably through the Spirit which Pentecost had given them. (2) There was a close fellowship among those who believed. (3) This koinōnia was expressed through common meals, and a common meal, the Lord's Supper.[13] (4) Property was held in common as a reflection of their oneness of belief, and also that the needy might be cared for. (5) The brethren attended the Temple together at the regular hours of worship. (6) And their number was increasing day by day, as the Lord touched others with the new life.

[12] G. H. C. Macgregor (The Interpreter's Bible, IX, 50) suggests that possibly we have doublets here, beginning in vss. 42 and 46. Vss. 42 and 43 would then belong together as a connecting link between the pentecost account and a more ancient fragment, with vss. 44-47 describing the life of the primitive community. The similarities, generally speaking, between the two are striking. The Revised Standard Version introduces a paragraph break between vss. 42 and 43.

[13] Cf. I Cor. 10:16 where koinōnia is used for communion of the body and blood of Christ.

33

To this summary of activities in which the members of the first Christian community participated should be added another which is also found in Acts: "And every day in the temple and at home they did not cease teaching and preaching Jesus as the Christ" (5:42). This is particularly suggestive because it relates teaching and preaching to the home as well as to the Temple. Ample precedents for including the home were to be found in the ministry of Jesus. Luke previously has told of Jesus' informal instruction in the dwelling of Mary and Martha (10:38-42). The Last Supper with its important teaching accompaniments occurred in the upper chamber of a home (22:7 ff.), and it was in this same room in all probability that the disciples and other followers of Jesus met, tarried, and worshiped prior to Pentecost. Later we find the church again gathering in Mary's home as they waited for the outcome of Peter's arrest (Acts 12:12 ff.).

If we were to examine in detail at this juncture these suggested activities of the early Christian community, as found in the opening chapters of Acts, we would move too far afield from our main subject of study. A number of them will be considered in the chapter which follows, as they relate to the portrait of Jesus in the Acts of the Apostles. In any event, our data is more fragmentary than we could wish for. But it is all that we have at many points and, as such, is of great importance. How long the condition depicted in these brief descriptions continued, we have no way of knowing.[14] The Evangelist is putting together the data before him not to prepare an exhaustive history, but in order to convince Theophilus (an individual or all who love God) of the truth concerning the matters of which he (or they) have been informed.[15] His own information was limited, just as his purpose was circumscribed. But, even so, he has opened vistas through which we may peer into a living situation and discover real persons alive with a dynamic faith that made a difference in their lives.

### Commonism in the Primitive Church

The holding of property in common by members of the early Christian community is often referred to as communism. But because

---

[14] We do know that a number of these interests of the primitive Christian community were carried on through the years. For instance, the Pastorals (I Tim. 5:3 ff.) show a concern for helping widows. Cf. also The Shepherd of Herm., Mandate 8, 10.

[15] We are assuming that Luke-Acts is a composite work in two parts, so that the preface of the former (Luke 1:1-4) applies also to the latter (cf. Acts 1:1-2).

this term has in current usage become the proper noun by which to denote a specific economic and political philosophy that is atheistic and materialistic, it seems inappropriate when applied to the practice of the first Christians. For this reason I have substituted "communism."

In the summary of activities already considered it was stated that those who believed had all things in common. In yet another passage Luke says: "Now the company of those who believed were of one heart and soul, and no one said that any of the things which he possessed was his own, but they had everything in common" (Acts 4:32). This particular reference is revealing because it suggests that there was a causal relationship between their spiritual unity and their economic practice. A deep religious experience gave birth to an economic philosophy. The chances are that it was not at any time a formally developed and systematically stated theory such as we have in the writings of Karl Marx or Adam Smith.

Neither does the account of this practice in Acts lead us to conclude that it was a formal requirement codified in a rule of order, such as we find in the Dead Sea Scrolls. The Manual of Discipline of this latter community, in the section which has been named "Entering the Covenant," states:

And all who have offered themselves for his truth shall bring all their knowledge and strength *and wealth* into the community of God, to purify their knowledge in the truth of God's statutes, and to distribute their strength according to the perfection of his ways *and all their property* according to his righteous counsel.[16]

It is clear that this requirement was compulsory for all who became members of this Qumrân community.

As a corollary of this requirement, the Manual of Discipline contained a stipulated punishment for a breach of good faith in reporting one's wealth. It says: "If there is found among them a man who lies about his wealth, and knows it, he shall be excluded from the sacred food of the masters for a year, and shall be deprived of a fourth of his food ration." [17] This is not nearly so severe a sentence as the death which is said to have come to Ananias and Sapphira, who misrepresented their wealth when they supposedly contributed all to the

[16] Translated by Millar Burrows in his volume *The Dead Sea Scrolls* (New York: The Viking Press, Inc., 1955), p. 371. (Italics mine.) Used by permission.
[17] *Ibid.*, p. 380.

Christian community, but held in reserve a part of it. Peter, at this time, said to Ananias: "You have not lied to men but to God" (Acts 5:4d).

In contrast to the Dead Sea community, as we have indicated, the early church did not require that its members sell their goods and contribute all to the Christian brotherhood. Peter said to Ananias at the time of his defection: "While it [the property] remained unsold, did it not remain your own? And after it was sold, was it not at your disposal?" (Acts 5:4.) There was a spontaneity to the practice that marks it as informal.

This suggests that the church did not attempt to copy their contemporaries in the Dead Sea group, for copyists tend to be rigid in the exactness of their copying. Whether or not they were influenced by these Jewish covenanters, as they have been called, is an open question, in my judgment. There was sufficient incentive to economic sharing in the oneness of their spiritual fellowship to account for its rise. A considerate conclusion would be that both groups developed a similar practice from a common root of spiritual conviction rather than that the Christians in Jerusalem borrowed the idea from their Dead Sea neighbors.[18]

It is not possible to say how long the practice of commonism continued in the early church. There is no reference to it in the Pauline epistles. Paul's deep interest in the collection for the saints at Jerusalem is the nearest thing to it in his correspondence (Rom. 15:25-29). But this is not commonism as represented in the Acts of the Apostles. The church may have found it impractical under the environmental conditions surrounding them, since they did not live as an isolated group apart from society. There may have been ascetic tendencies among them, but they were not basically an ascetic group. As their numbers grew and they became scattered throughout Palestine and beyond, such a practice would have been all but impossible to administer. It was difficult to carry through actually within the immediate environs of Jerusalem itself.[19]

We have seen in this chapter that the origin of the Christian community may be said ultimately to have been within the will of God;

---

[18] For a suggestive discussion of a possible relationship between the Essenes of the Qumrân community and the early church, see Sherman E. Johnson, *Jesus in His Homeland*, ch. iv.

[19] Cf. Acts 6:1 ff.

it was also implicit in the Old Testament commonwealth of Israel and in the following of Jesus; in addition it was explicit in the resurrection fellowship. Pentecost further solidified the new company of believers and added others to its fold. This dynamic event was interpreted by Peter in terms of the traditional Day of the Lord expectation of the Jews, and in it the early church found the true basis for their understanding of Jesus' teachings concerning the kingdom of God.

The life of the Christian community was marked by expressions of the power of the Spirit and by great joy, such manifestations as belonged to the anticipated end of the Age. In this sense it was eschatological in character. But the church continued to look for greater things to come when the return of the Lord would usher in the consummation of history and the final reign of God.

There was such unity of spirit among believers in the Fellowship that they held all things in common. Some sold their possessions and distributed them to all, according to their need. And day by day their number increased as the Lord touched others with the new life.

# THREE

# In the Primitive Church of Acts

IN THE PREVIOUS CHAPTER WE WERE CONSIDERING THE ORIGIN AND nature of the Christian community. This is the place to begin, for it was here that the portrait of Christ first emerged. A portrait is more than the physical likeness of a person. It represents his character and significance as well. In this sense the Gospels are portraiture at its best, for they delineate a personality as well as narrate selected events in his life. The meaning of Christ for faith, his place in the experience of believing Christians, and his relation to past, present, and future history are all given to us in these unique documents.

### Portraiture in Acts

The Acts of the Apostles also contains notable portraiture where Christ is concerned. Although it does not cover in detail the phases of his life and ministry which are found in the Gospels, there is a definite representation of him in the account it relates. In fact, the references to Christ in this writing's portrayal of the early days in the life of the church may contain some of the original drawings of the lines of his portrait.

The church during the years immediately following the Resurrection is usually referred to as the primitive church. Its story in Acts is found principally in the first twelve chapters. It is these years with which this chapter is primarily concerned.

There is one marked difference between the Gospels and Acts as they present a picture of Christ. In the Gospels the account is given with his portraiture *mainly* in mind. In Acts the author's primary purpose is to relate the story of the developing church, and the portrait of Christ takes shape as a part of this narrative. In the first instance the approach may be said to be direct; in the second it is indirect.

To state that the portrait of Christ is presented indirectly in the Acts of the Apostles is not to suggest that it is a secondary consideration. If he had not been the Lord of the Christian community, there would have been no story of the church to tell. And this does not refer solely to his earthly life as a kind of prelude to the beginning of the Fellowship; it also includes the fact that as the living and risen one he was an integral part of the experience of those who believed. In relating their story, the writer of Acts must of necessity present Christ also. The one undertaking could not be accomplished without doing the other at the same time.

More specifically, this means that we meet the portrait of Christ in Acts as his living relationship to the life of the church is described. The names by which he is known and called suggest the kind of person he was. His place in the sacraments further delineates the lines of his character. The events in which he plays a part as present Lord also provide occasions for revealing his stature. And, finally, the speeches in this writing contain statements of historical reference, as well as interpretations of Christ's present meaning for life, all of which constitute portraiture of the highest order.

### A Historical Figure

Even though the interests of the early church centered primarily in the living Christ as Lord, there was no inclination on the whole to neglect his earthly ministry. This does not mean that the Fellowship had an academic interest in the Jesus of history. Rather, it was the implications of his life for faith that concerned them. But it was an actual life that possessed these implications. As they met in worship, preached the message, or ordered their conduct, the days of his flesh come into their purview directly.

What is probably one of our earliest examples of typical Christian preaching is found in the message Peter proclaimed at the home of Cornelius, the gentile centurion (Acts 10:34-43).[1] Whether this brief sermon, if it might be called such, be regarded as presented in its original form on the lips of Peter, or as modified by Luke who recorded it here, its primitive character remains.[2] And the references to the historical Jesus are particularly impressive. Brief and terse as they are, they point, nevertheless, to his earthly ministry.

[1] Cf. C. H. Dodd, *The Apostolic Preaching and Its Development* for a critical analysis of early Christian preaching in which the kerygma as the message of the church is distinguished from the didache, its ethical instruction.

[2] The expression "Lord of all" (Acts 10:36) may be a Lucan adaptation to a gentile situation as over against the "Lord and Christ" (Acts 2:36) of the pentecost sermon with its Jewish cast. But this does not materially alter the sermon at the point of its reference to the Jesus of history.

When we analyze this sermon, we discover that many facts concerning Jesus are present in it, facts which constitute portraiture: (1) Jesus proclaimed "the word" throughout all Judea, beginning in Galilee. (2) He undertook his ministry following his baptism, which John preached. (3) The Holy Spirit with its attendant power came upon him—presumably at the time of his baptism, although this is not expressly stated here. (4) He performed a series of good deeds; particularly noteworthy was the healing of the demon-possessed. (5) In this activity he gave the impression that God was with him. (6) His ministry was in Jerusalem as well as "in the country of the Jews." (7) The Jews killed him. (8) Crucifixion was the method used. (9) God raised him from the dead. (10) The Resurrection occurred on the third day following his death. (11) God made Jesus' presence known to specially chosen witnesses. (12) These ate and drank with him after he rose from the dead. (13) The risen One commanded these witnesses to preach to the people. (14) Their message was to be that the risen Jesus was chosen by God to judge the living and the dead.[3]

As we consider the words in this sermon, we tend to read into them the details of the gospel accounts with which we are familiar. These were also known to Peter, and it would be logical to assume that he enlarged upon the outline from point to point. But, be this as it may, there emerges here a portrait in which certain characteristics are definitely drawn.

Even within this poverty of detail we can see a person of strength and power, one who exercised authority over the world of demons, who lived close to God, and who was considerate of the needy. The triumph of his life over his enemies and the death they forced upon him climaxes the portrait, together with the commission he gave to his disciples to proclaim his message.

### The Pentecost Portrait of Jesus

In the sermon attributed to Peter at Pentecost (Acts 2:14-36) there are also references to the Jesus of history which constitute portraiture. Although they are brief and limited in scope, they are nonetheless specific. Here are to be found the facts out of which the meaning emerges and apart from which the pentecost message is with-

---

[3] I have included the resurrection ministry as a part of the portrait of the Jesus of history because it occurred within a historical context.

40

out support. The very brevity of the reference suggests familiarity with the details. It was not necessary to belabor the events of his life. Broad statements would suffice.

Jesus is pictured in this sermon as a man of Nazareth (2:22). The home community supplies an address by which he can be related to a certain place. Floyd Filson is correct in taking issue with certain biblical scholars who have supported the idea that it makes little difference whether or not Jesus ever lived, now that we have the teachings and the ideals. He asserts that the early church had no such view: "Not so the disciples of Jesus. Not so the earliest preachers. Not so the church. The entire Christian gospel disintegrates when deprived of the historical existence of Jesus as a real human figure." [4] The mention in Peter's address of the village in which Jesus was reared provides basic support to this view.

Not only was Jesus a man of Nazareth; he was also a person who had done mighty works, wonders, and signs (2:22). These are the words (dunamis, teras, sēmeion) which are used in the Gospels to refer to Jesus' activity.[5] It is not suggested here that Jesus performed these on his own. God was at work in them attesting him before the people.

Without offering further details, Peter states that Jesus was "crucified and killed by the hands of lawless men" (2:23). Even as his mighty deeds were interpreted as an attestation by God, so his crucifixion is regarded as fulfilling a divine plan. According to this same purpose, Jesus was raised from the dead (2:24). As elsewhere in the New Testament, the religious meanings of the events in Jesus' life are invariably a part of the portrait. He was the kind of person in whose being and activity it was logical to conclude that God was at work. This suggests a definite quality of character and a personality accent that is distinctive. There was a religious impression which he made upon his own generation during his lifetime as well as after his death.

### Portraiture in the Account of the Healing of the Lame Man

As was stated earlier, much of the portraiture of Christ in Acts is indirect; it is not drawn for its own sake but appears as a part of a

[4] *Jesus Christ the Risen Lord*, p. 45.
[5] Cf. Matt. 11:20; John 4:48; 2:11.

41

larger context that involves it. The healing of the lame man, together with the situation that results from it, is one such portrait-event (3:1 ff.).

In commanding the man to be made whole, Peter invokes the name of Jesus Christ of Nazareth. This is an unusual reference. It contains the familiar term "Jesus Christ," which means *Jesus Messiah*. An exalted title this! So frequent was its usage that it came to be regarded as a personal name. But to the ascription of messiahship are added the words "of Nazareth," thus relating the significant *name* to the historical Jesus who had lived in this Galilean community. The very act of commanding healing in this name says certain things about the one to whom it belonged. He had been, and still was, such a person as would be interested in and powerful to perform merciful acts of healing. And it should not be forgotten that behind Peter's use of the name was his knowledge of the healing ministry of Jesus.

When word of the restoration of the lame man was circulated throughout the Temple area, a considerable group of people gathered about Peter and John. In addressing them, Peter refers to Jesus in terms that constitute portraiture. He calls him God's *servant* whom they (the Jews) had "delivered up and denied in the presence of Pilate, when he had decided to release him" (3:13). With the gospel account of these happenings before us, even as a knowledge of them was in the mind of Peter as he spoke, this brief reference takes on added meaning. Peter then continues to tell them that they had denied "the Holy and Righteous One" and killed "the Author of life, whom God raised from the dead" (3:14, 15).

When Peter referred to Jesus as God's servant, it is possible that he had in mind the suffering-servant passage or conception of Isaiah (52:13–53:12). We know that later in Acts (8:32-35) the meaning of Jesus' death is interpreted by Philip in terms of this reference. And there is good reason also to conclude that Jesus had likewise identified himself with the servant.[6]

In calling Jesus "the Holy and Righteous One," it would seem that this same Isaiah passage was also in Peter's thinking. There it is said of the servant that "by his knowledge shall the righteous one, my servant, make many to be accounted righteous" (53:11b).[7] And

---

[6] Cf. Mark 10:45; Luke 4:17 ff.

[7] Cf. also Acts 22:14 where Jesus is called "the Just One." Enoch (38:2) uses this term with a messianic connotation.

since the early church interpreted the servant passage messianically, we may conclude that we have here a messianic portrait of Jesus. There are reflections of this expression, though they are not messianic, in the Gospels where Pilate's wife is represented as calling Jesus a righteous man (Matt. 27:19), and the centurion, looking at Jesus in death, pronounced him an innocent man (Luke 23:47).

The expression "Author of life" (archēgon tēs zōēs) which Peter used in speaking of Jesus to the people may be translated—the "originator of life." It is used in Hebrews (2:10) in referring to Jesus as the "pioneer" of salvation. Another passage in Hebrews (12:2) employs archēgos in relation to Jesus also. He is the pioneer of faith in this case. But from both usages in Hebrews, as well as in Peter's words to the assemblage which gathered following the healing of the lame man, the expression would seem to refer to the new life which came into the Christian community and into the lives of Christians through Christ. And this is portraiture since Christ must have been a life-giving person if his influence was such as the expression implied.

The religious authorities arrested Peter and John because of the disturbance associated with the healing. In making his defense, Peter again referred to Jesus Christ of Nazareth whom they had crucified, but whom God had raised from the dead. After warning them to speak no more in this name, the pair was released. Upon gaining their freedom, they went to their Christian friends. So overjoyed was the church that they prayed with triumphant gratitude, and in their prayer referred to God as stretching out his hand to heal and perform signs and wonders through the name of his "holy servant Jesus" (Acts 4:30). God was at work, but at work through Jesus. It would seem that the early church regarded the healings that occurred in their midst when the name of Jesus was invoked as a continuation of the healing work of the historical Jesus. He was still alive with healing power in his presence.

### Portraiture in Early Christian Experience

Christian experience in the early church also became a source of portraiture where Christ was concerned. For these first believers, he was not solely the teacher and preacher of Galilee. He was this person, as we have already seen, but he was more—much more. He

43

was also what they discovered him to be through their religious experience in and following the Resurrection.

The awakening at Pentecost has already been considered, particularly in its reference through Peter's address to the Jesus of history.[8] But the Christ of present power and authority is also delineated in this sermon. And he was known thus through the experience which had come to those who participated in the outpouring of the Spirit.

Following his mention of the Resurrection, to which the followers of Jesus had been witnesses, Peter continues: "Being therefore exalted at the right hand of God, and having received from the Father the promise of the Holy Spirit, he [the Jesus God had raised from the dead] has poured out this which you see and hear . . . . God has made him both Lord and Christ, this Jesus whom you crucified." (2: 33-36). These words suggest dimensions in the person of Jesus, now known as Lord and Christ, which go beyond the original experience of him as the carpenter-preacher of Galilee.

This advance in portraiture was the result of a spiritual experience which centered in the living Christ. No longer was he just a rabbi or teacher. The Resurrection and Ascension had changed all this. Reference has already been made to the significance of the Resurrection in the enlarging of the portrait of Jesus.[9] More needs, however, to be said concerning the Ascension.

Whatever the experience which is referred to by this name might have been, its essential nature does not lie in physical levitation. Location in space is altogether beside the point in this regard; instead, it is a matter of exaltation of being and person. Although Luke alone among the gospel writers refers to it (Acts 1:9-11 and possibly Luke 24:51), there should be little doubt as to its historicity. Apart from the Ascension, or another similarly transcendent experience, it would be difficult to account for the frequent references to the exalted Christ in the primitive church.[10]

The Resurrection brought to the disciples the assurance that Jesus had survived the grave and overcome death. But this tremendous fact does not explain the conviction of the early church that Jesus was stationed at the right hand of God (2:33; 7:55). The Ascension does account for it. The expression "at the right hand of God" suggests

[8] Cf. pp. 40-41.
[9] Cf. pp. 13-17.
[10] Cf. Oscar Cullmann, *Christ and Time*, p. 151.

the authority of God in Christ's rule over men. It is symbolical of the exaltation and sovereignty which the ascended Christ enjoys. And this is portraiture of a high order, portraiture which grew out of the experience of the Ascension.

In the pentecost sermon Peter declares that it is Jesus exalted who pours out the Spirit upon the waiting disciples. It is suggestive that the Fourth Gospel also represents Jesus as bestowing the Spirit upon the disciples: "He breathed on them, and said to them 'Receive the Holy Spirit' " (20:22). There is this difference, however, between the Johannine and Lucan accounts. In the former the *resurrected* Jesus gives the Spirit; in the latter the *ascended* Jesus bestows the Spirit. Separate sources might explain this variation. It is also possible that in the Fourth Gospel's transcendent portrait, Jesus is already viewed by the author with such exaltation that he does not consider the Ascension as a background for this mighty and authoritative act.

### An Exalted Messiah

Peter closed his sermon at Pentecost by saying that God had made the crucified Jesus both Lord and Christ (2:36). This is a suggestive combination of titles. The term "Christ" (*Christos*) is the Greek equivalent for Messiah. The tradition of the primitive church is clear in its ascription of messiahship to Jesus, as are also the Gospels. As a matter of fact, it may be argued impressively that the early church discovered in Jesus' own words the basis for their conviction that he was the Messiah. This would not mean that the Resurrection and Ascension did not further undergird their conclusion; it suggests only that the original incentive toward taking this view came from Jesus. The Resurrection and Ascension confirmed it and further defined it.

Among the Jews the traditional view of the Messiah was that of a royal ruler.[11] Modifications of this conception appeared from time to time, one such being found in the servant passages of Deutero-Isaiah.[12] For the most part he was considered to be an earthly figure. During the century and a half prior to Jesus' birth, however, a new dimension entered the picture, and the Messiah was thought of as a heavenly being, the transcendent Son of man. In Daniel the phrase referred to the messianic reign of Israel,[13] while in the similitudes of

[11] Isa. 9:7.
[12] Isa. 42:1-7; 49:1-6; 52:13–53:12; 61:1-3; 62:1, 6-7.
[13] 7:13-14.

Enoch it stood for an individual.[14] Jesus applied this expression to himself, although it should probably be concluded that he gave his own particular interpretation to it, combining it paradoxically with the suffering-servant conception of Isaiah.[15] The Resurrection and Ascension provided a new perspective for interpreting Jesus' words concerning himself, and the primitive church now focused its attention upon the exalted character of the Messiah. At the same time it insisted that, as the Christ, Jesus was one with the promised deliverer of the Old Testament messianic hope.

The interpretation of Jesus as the exalted messianic figure which resulted from the Resurrection and Ascension adds new lines to the portrait of Christ. It is of this development that A. E. J. Rawlinson writes with such cogency when he notes:

> On the one hand His exaltation [and he was from henceforth the exalted Messiah] betokened already his enthronement as King. He was reigning in majesty at the right hand of God, in the unseen world of heavenly reality and glory, and the "Kingdom of the Messiah," which for the Jews had been an object of hope and expectation, was for the disciples of Jesus already begun. On the other hand, it was clear that the Kingdom of the Messiah was not destined to be a "kingdom" of the political sort at all. It was "not of this world." It lay on the further side of the cleavage between "this Age" and "the Age to come." [16]

### Christ as Lord

The risen and ascended Jesus was not only the Christ, the exalted Messiah; he was also the Lord (kurios). As such he drew from his followers an allegiance and dependency all but equal to that given to God. Actually this relationship came to have the full religious value of loyalty to God, so that the church finally ascribed a unique divinity to the person of Jesus, a divinity which, in time, made the trinitarian formula inevitable.

Much consideration has been given to the question as to whether the title "Lord" was ascribed to Christ during the days of the primitive church, as Acts indicates, or later, upon Greek soil under Hellenistic cult influences. Bousset has urged the latter view, concluding that the expression "Lord" in the early period was the vocative form

[14] I Enoch 37–71.
[15] 52:13–53:12.
[16] The New Testament Doctrine of the Christ (New York: Oxford University Press, 1949), p. 32. Used by permission.

of address (*kurie*) rather than a personal title.[17] This view has not been universally accepted since it was first urged.[18] For one thing, Paul's use of the Aramaic *Maran* ("Our Lord") suggests a Palestinian source for the title (I Cor. 16:22). In the form in which it is used, *Maranatha*, it is a prayer-petition addressed to the exalted Christ whose glorious return was eagerly anticipated.

Another factor also opens the possibility of a Palestinian use of the title "Lord." The Hebrew *Adonai*, as used in Jesus' day, referred to God as "Lord." It was employed as a substitute for *Jahve* whenever the Scriptures were read, and this would serve as a background for the early Palestinian church's use of the title "Lord" when referring to the exalted Christ. The word already had an association with divinity, just as the experience of the Christians with Christ had begun to move into a more-than-human category. The title would therefore come naturally when referring to Christ.

Gustaf Dalman, however, regards the translation from the divine name *Jahve* to the divine name *Lord* as a peculiarity of Jewish Hellenism, rather than of Hebraic Judaism.[19] But with the constant traveling of the Jews between the Hellenistic and Hebraic worlds which took place at the time of the making of the primitive faith of the church, we should not rule out the possibility of the influence of the use of the Hebrew *Adonai* upon the languages of the early Christians. In any case, as a prime consideration in this discussion, it should be remembered that it was the experience of the lordship of Christ, rather than any specific word within reach, which necessitated the finding of a proper title by which to refer to him.

### Prayers Offered to Jesus Christ as Lord

The developing portrait of Jesus, the Christ, as found in the primitive church, clearly shows that he was regarded as one to whom believers turned with the same gratitude, hope, and expectation that they customarily felt toward God. He had been sent by the heavenly Father in accordance with his purposes, revealed in history and scripture. Following the Resurrection and Ascension, he, in turn, had bestowed upon them the Spirit, and as they looked to him, they were caught up into an ecstatic life which was a foretaste of the New Age, soon

[17] Cf. *op. cit.*, pp. 98, 99.
[18] Pro: cf. Bultmann, *Theology of the New Testament*, I, 51-52. Con: cf. Rawlinson, *op. cit.*, pp. 231-37.
[19] *The Words of Jesus*, pp. 179 ff.

47

to come. Through the power of and by faith in his name mighty acts had been performed. They continued to trust him for the eschatological future which he would bring. Christ all but filled their sky.

Even though the early Christians were monotheists, and remained so to the end, we would expect such religious values as these, when centered in a particular person, to result in prayers directed to him. This we find to be the case in connection with the martyrdom of Stephen. As Jesus had prayed to the Father in death, so this faithful follower prayed to his Lord while being stoned.

The prayers of Stephen to Christ, as presented in Acts, impress us with their similarity to the prayers of Jesus from the cross. Both asked forgiveness for their persecutors, and both committed their souls to heaven.[20] It would almost seem that Stephen had been thinking of how his Lord had died in the midst of his suffering, and that he was moved to follow his example. There was strength and courage in remembering.

But it was not to the Jesus of history that Stephen prayed. Instead it was to the historical Jesus, *now exalted as Lord*. This was appropriate, for Stephen had just seen Jesus as the Son of man standing at the right hand of God. In the midst of the angry clamor at his trial, when he was charged with saying that Jesus of Nazareth would destroy the Temple and change the customs of Moses, Stephen had been granted this vision. To the exasperation of his enemies he said: "Behold, I see the heavens opened, and the Son of man standing at the right hand of God" (7:56). It was this portrait of Christ which called forth the prayer from the soul of the dying Stephen. He was not praying to a human spirit, as such, but to the transcendent Lord, God's exalted Messiah.[21]

We must not conclude that prayers to Christ took the place of prayers to God in the primitive church.[22] And it is my judgment that they were at a minimum. But that they did occur is a reasonable conclusion.[23] Cullmann is probably correct in holding that the oldest liturgical prayer is the Aramaic Maranatha.[24] This, as we have seen,

---

[20] Cf. Acts 7:59-60; Luke 23:34, 46.

[21] Prayers continued to be addressed to Christ beyond the primitive period. Cf. I Clement 59:4-5.

[22] Cf. Acts 4:23-31.

[23] Bultmann, however, agrees with Bousset that prayers to Jesus were not likely in the earliest church, and holds that Jesus was not cultically worshipped. Cf. op. cit., p. 51.

[24] Cf. I Cor. 16:22; Rev. 22:20.

is addressed to Christ the Lord and is a prayer for his speedy return. The Didache (The Teaching of the Twelve Apostles) indicates that it was said at the close of the meal.[25] In commenting upon its significance, Cullmann says: "The fact that this prayer is handed down by Paul untranslated and that it continued in that original form until the time of the composition of the *Didache* shows the extraordinarily important role which this earliest liturgical prayer of the early Christian community must have played." [26] And Jesus as Lord is at the heart of it. This fact constitutes portraiture.

### The Sacraments and Portraiture

The account of the primitive church as presented in Acts makes some mention of the sacraments of baptism[27] and the Lord's Supper[28] from time to time. They are referred to as a part of the ongoing narrative with a bare minimum of interpretation. In connection with the Pauline, Synoptic, and Johannine portraits of Christ more detailed attention will be given to their contribution, an attention commensurate with the treatment they receive in these documents.

They appear as a definite part of the early period in the church's life. The worshipers at Pentecost are urged by Peter to be baptized in the name of Jesus Christ.[29] This act is more than a perfunctory gesture such as a handshake of welcome to members of the new community. Baptism is for the forgiveness of sins and will bring to them the gift of the Holy Spirit (2:38). What had been at the hands of John the Baptist a preparatory rite for the coming Kingdom was now associated with the gift of the Holy Spirit.

Significant from the point of view of this study is the fact that these tremendous experiences of forgiveness and the coming of the Spirit were available to believers "in the name of Jesus Christ." Just as the healing of the lame man at the gate of the Temple was made real through the *name*, here also the benefits of baptism are brought home to the individual through his *name*. The question, then, becomes, "What kind of person would introduce men into such newness of life, such redemptive quickening through baptism in his name?"

[25] Cf. the Did. 10:6. This may well be the first formal treatise on church order and should probably be dated around A.D. 100 or shortly after.
[26] *Early Christian Worship*, p. 13.
[27] 2:38; 8:12, 16, 35-36; 10:47-48; 11:16.
[28] 2:42, 46.
[29] For the earliest description of Christian baptism cf. the Did. 7.

The sacrament of the Lord's Supper does not loom large in the Acts of the Apostles by way of being lifted up or singled out for special consideration. This need not suggest that it was regarded lightly; on the contrary it probably implies that it was established procedure and not a subject of controversy.

In the summary Luke gives (Acts 2:43-47) of the activities of the church, he says that the believers broke bread in their homes and ate together "with glad and generous hearts." The expression "breaking bread" calls to mind Luke's account of the meal in which the resurrected Jesus made himself known to the two of Emmaus in the breaking of bread (Luke 24:28-35). It likewise is reminiscent of the story of the feeding of the five thousand, in which special mention is made of the fact that Jesus broke the bread before the feast (Luke 9: 16). Notice also should be taken that it was the custom in Palestine to break the bread at the beginning of a meal rather than to cut it with a knife.

All of this may seem to indicate that Luke's reference in Acts to the breaking of bread in the home and the eating of food with glad and generous hearts implies the partaking of a fellowship meal only and not the Eucharist. In view of the tradition Paul reported as coming to him (I Cor. 11:23-26), and the Synoptic accounts of the Lord's Supper (Mark 14:22-25; Matt. 26:26-29; Luke 22:14-23) where mention is made of the breaking of the bread, we should probably, however, interpret the account in Acts as referring to the Eucharist.[30] The absence of a reference to the cup need not imply otherwise, especially in the face of the positive reasons for this conclusion.

It is also likely that the Lord's Supper in the summary passage in Acts was celebrated in conjunction with a love feast, the Agape, where the poor were cared for and Christian brotherhood prevailed. At such times a vivid sense of the living Christ was experienced, and great joy in the expectation of his return was felt. There is some reason to conclude that the daily gathering gave way later to a weekly celebration due to practical considerations, and that worship on the Lord's Day centered in the Eucharist.[31] As a matter of fact, it is known that the Lord's Supper in time was separated from the Agape. A developing

[30] For the use of the new term, "Eucharist," cf. Ignatius, To the Philadelphians 4, and the Did. 9 and 10.

[31] Cf. "On the first day of the week, when we were gathered together to break bread, . . ." (Acts 20:7.) Cf. the Did. 14:1; Justin Martyr Apology I. 67. 3.

sacramental interest contributed to this separation, as well as practical considerations such as the difficulty of finding homes of sufficient size to accommodate the enlarging church membership.

### A Note on Sources

We have been considering the thinking of the primitive church concerning Christ as it is found largely in the first twelve chapters of Acts. The assumption has been that, in the main, this source is trustworthy. Outside of a few conclusions based upon other New Testament writings and reached by implication, the first chapters of Acts remain our sole canonical source for this information.

As it stands, this material at least represents at the time of its writing the outlook of the church which produced it (circa A.D. 90). And in this sense it is a valid source for discerning the New Testament portrait of Christ. But there is also some basis for holding that it rests upon earlier tradition which is to be trusted as correctly representing the views of the primitive church.

Assuming that Acts is the second part of a larger work, Luke-Acts, and that it has a common authorship with Luke, it follows that the same ideals of procedure which underlie the Gospel also apply to it. These are listed in Luke 1:1-4, and include such factors as dependence upon eyewitnesses, care in sifting the tradition for accuracy, the preparation of an orderly account, and concern for the truth. This does not make of Luke a scientific historian in the modern sense, but it does suggest a workman who was not insensitive to truth and fact.

Luke had ample opportunity to contact sound sources in preparing his material. His relationship to the apostle Paul—who was in a position to be informed concerning the beginnings of the faith—as well as his connections with others at Antioch, Jerusalem, and Caesarea, no doubt brought much information to him. By the time he wrote, the church was firmly established in its catechetical teaching, and the early tradition had probably found a more or less fixed form so that the facts involved were readily available for his use. Nor would he feel free to veer much from them without giving good reasons to the church which was familiar with them, and had already accepted them as valid.

More questions have probably been raised concerning the trustworthiness of the speeches in Acts 1–12 than about any other part of the book. It is too much to expect stenographic reports of what was actually said on these occasions, and there is a kind of verbal similarity to them that suggests a single mind at work in them. Yet there are differences among them which imply different individuals as their source. R. B. Rackham has stated that he thinks this to be particularly true of the speeches delivered at the council, and when Peter, Stephen, and Paul are speaking. Certainly they are appropriate to the situations within which they occur.[32]

The practice of authors in that day to express their own ideas in the speeches of their characters has been cited as evidence of the questionable character of Luke's speech material. At best, such an argument in this particular case when viewed over against other facts, such as mentioned above, is not finally determinative. A statement of Thucydides is sometimes referred to in this regard. He explained his method of writing speeches, pointing out particularly that after using the language which he thought the speaker would employ, he also adhered as closely as possible to the general sense of what was actually said.[33] This does not represent a total lack of concern for historical fact. May not there be a similar process behind sermons and speeches in Acts? [34]

Torrey's suggestion that Acts 1-15 is based upon an Aramaic original, if true, would imply an early date for the source, which might possibly further add to its historical credibility. This hypothesis, for such it is, has not met with wide acceptance. Aramaisms which appear here and there in Acts do not require it to explain them, and the historicity of the book does not ultimately depend upon this view.

In this chapter we have been considering the portrait of Christ in the primitive church of Acts. He was seen here as one with the historical Jesus. His portrait emerged in the pentecost sermon and in the healing acts of the disciples. His character as exalted Lord was also delineated in the accounts of the religious experiences of his first followers, particularly in connection with the Ascension and the coming of the Spirit at Pentecost. The prayer life of the early church and its practice in regard to the celebration of the sacraments of baptism and the Lord's Supper further revealed portraiture where Christ is concerned.

[32] Cf. The Acts of the Apostles, pp. xliii ff.
[33] History of the Peloponnesian War I. 22.
[34] Cf. H. J. Cadbury, The Book of Acts in History, pp. 128 ff., where the author compares Acts with a reconstructed history of the early church, reconstructed on other bases, and finds that Acts presents a number of suggestive correspondences.

# FOUR

# In the Pauline Epistles: Sources

THE ACCOUNT OF THE PRIMITIVE CHURCH IN ACTS WHICH WAS CON-
sidered in the previous chapter presented the portrait of Christ which
was held by the earliest Christians. As the Fellowship grew, Christ
the Lord continued to remain at the center of its life, and their conception of him determined what they thought and did. The Pauline
letters make this abundantly clear.

In many ways Paul's portrait of Christ dominates the New Testament. Its details are not so closely drawn as in the Synoptics, but the
framework of his life which gives meaning to Paul's gospel is here
nevertheless (Rom. 1:1-4; Mark 1:1; Matt. 1:1; Luke 9:20). There
are affinities also between his presentation of Jesus and that of the
Fourth Gospel (Gal. 5:22-23; 2:17; I Cor. 6:11; Phil. 3:1; II
Cor. 4:14; Rom. 8:11; John 16:7 ff.). This is true especially in the
latter's emphasis upon Jesus as the Christ who brings the new birth
and both sends and makes his presence felt in the lives of believers
through the Spirit. There are passages, furthermore, in Paul which
foreshadow the apocalyptic portrait of Christ in the Revelation to
John (I Thess. 4:13-18; I Cor. 15:51-56; Rev. 19:1 ff.; 21:22–22:5).
For these reasons it might be said that Paul's presentation dominates
the total New Testament portrait of Christ. Although this is not immediately evident with a surface reading of the epistles, a closer study
will bear it out.

### Paul's Knowledge of Jesus Christ

In considering Paul's portrait of Jesus Christ, the question of his
sources must be faced. How did he come to know him; from what
data did he construct his conception? Luke is careful to tell us that
his own information concerning Jesus came from eyewitnesses (1:1-4).
Was Paul an eyewitness? Did he know intimately any persons who
had seen or been with Jesus?

It is difficult to reply to the first of these questions, while the answer to the second is obvious to anyone with a minimum of knowledge of the relationship among the personalities of the New Testament. About all that we can say as to whether or not Paul was an eyewitness to Jesus' ministry is in the realm of possibilities. The apostle was a contemporary of Jesus in Jerusalem. If he were a student of the Law at this time under the distinguished Gamaliel, it is reasonable to assume that he might have shown some interest in this person called Jesus who was creating such a stir in the capital city. Curiosity alone might have commandeered his attention, causing him to seek out Jesus of Nazareth. Theological students then were undoubtedly like theological students today, interested in ideas and issues which are lively and in any way controversial. And this the teachings of Jesus were definitely. It is quite likely, therefore, that Paul had seen and heard Jesus while a student in Jerusalem.[1] But this conclusion remains conjectural.

In one of his letters Paul makes an interesting statement which has sometimes been held to say, or at least imply, that the apostle had known Jesus in the flesh. It reads: "From now on, therefore, we regard no one from a human point of view; *even though we once regarded Christ from a human point of view*, we regard him thus no longer." (II Cor. 5:16.)[2] Taken by itself, this passage may suggest a knowledge of the Jesus of history. Its main emphasis, however, is upon a spiritual knowledge of Christ who makes "new creations" of men (II Cor. 5:17). The use of the plural "we" may be purely rhetorical rather than autobiographical on Paul's part. In any case, Paul's personal knowledge of Jesus in the flesh, if he possessed any such at all, would seem to have been external in character. He probably was an observer who was conscious of passing events only.

To the second question as to whether Paul knew well any who had been closely acquainted with Jesus in the flesh, the answer must definitely be in the affirmative. He did. Outstanding among these was Peter. Although they did not always see eye to eye (their differences can be exaggerated and often are),[3] there was likely a genuine rapport

[1] Cf. C. Anderson Scott, *Foot-Notes to Paul*, p. 143 and Johannes Weiss, *The History of Primitive Christianity*, I, 162, for a confirming view. Cf. John Knox, *Chapters in a Life of Paul*, pp. 123-24, and Paul Feine, *Theologie des Neuen Testament*, p. 259, for a contrary view.

[2] Italics mine.

[3] Cf. the Tübingen School with its theory of the tension between Pauline and Judaic thought.

between them. Paul once said that he saw Cephas for fifteen days and on the same visit, met James, the Lord's brother (Gal. 1:18-19). This occurred in Jerusalem, where, no doubt, there were many unnamed Christians who had kept company with Jesus during the days of his flesh. In addition there was Paul's close association with Luke who wrote the Third Gospel. In all probability Luke had begun to gather together the tradition which he later compiled in his Gospel during these years of association with Paul. Surely this would have been the case at the time of the apostle's two-year imprisonment at Caesarea, when Luke was free to follow his bent in this direction.

One with Paul's alert intellect and native sensitiveness to situations could be expected to inquire concerning the known details in the life of the Person who had come to mean salvation to him. Only a limited judgment of the personality and mind of the apostle could conclude that he was completely disinterested in the Jesus of history, now that he had been laid hold of by the resurrected and exalted Christ. In the New Testament as a whole there is no separation of the two; even in an apocalyptic writing such as the Revelation to John, the Jesus of history is basically one with the King of kings and the Lord of lords (11:8). It is not forgotten that he had been crucified at Jerusalem.

### The Record Speaks

When it comes to the extent to which Paul was familiar with the teachings of Jesus (and his teachings are a part of the portraiture), the record speaks for itself. He is not unaware of what Jesus said, even as he is acquainted with what he did. One of the factors which assured Paul's knowledge of the words of Jesus was the practice of the early church to justify its decisions and actions by reference to the teachings of Jesus.[4] On one occasion he specifically identifies his recommendation with such a teaching: "To the married I give charge, not I but the Lord, that the wife should not separate from her husband . . . and that the husband should not divorce his wife" (I Cor. 7:10-11). In connection with this same situation he gives further advice, but disclaims that it is based on a known word of Jesus (I Cor. 7:12, 25).

The fact that there are only a few such instances where Paul specifically indicates that he either has or has not a statement of Jesus

---

[4] Cf. previous reference to this practice, p. 18.

to buttress his point of view does not imply that these represent the sum total of his knowledge of what Jesus said. Overtones of the teachings of Jesus can be found throughout Paul's writings. To take one illustration, the echoes of our Lord's instructions, especially in the Sermon on the Mount, that appear in Rom. 12 are marked. The reprinting of one section (vss. 14-21) of this chapter will indicate the relationship:

Bless those who persecute you, bless and do not curse them. (Matt. 5:44; Luke 6:28.) Rejoice with those who rejoice, weep with those who weep. Live in harmony with one another; do not be haughty, but associate with the lowly (Luke 14:12-13); never be conceited. Repay no one evil for evil, but take thought for what is noble in the sight of all. (Mark 9:50.) If your enemy is hungry, feed him; if he is thirsty, give him drink; for by so doing you will heap burning coals upon his head. (Matt. 5:44; Luke 6:27.) Do not be overcome by evil but overcome evil with good. (Luke 6:35; Matt. 5:9.)

Not only are the sentiments in this passage representative of Jesus, but in some cases the words employed, the expressions used, and the references indicated suggest a knowledge of the tradition that appears in the Synoptics.[5]

It is unlikely that Paul actually read Mark's Gospel, and his use of Matthew and Luke is out of the question, unless a date is assigned to them much earlier than most scholars allow today. But when it comes to the tradition which lies behind these Gospels, that is another matter.[6] It was coming into form at such centers as Jerusalem, Caesarea, Antioch, and Rome at the very time that Paul was in these communities, and it is unthinkable to conclude that he would have turned a deaf ear to it.[7] Whether or not the Pauline epistles are "dominated by the gospel tradition," [8] as Deissmann contends, surely the great apostle was not unacquainted with it, and as such, it is an important source for his portrait of Christ.

[5] "One of the things Paul learned from the Jerusalem believers was the oral gospel, that Aramaic summary of Jesus' ministry and teaching which primitive Christians gladly learned by heart, and taught new converts." Edgar J. Goodspeed, *Paul* (Philadelphia: The John C. Winston Co., 1947), p. 27.

[6] Was Paul familiar with the sayings of Jesus (*Logia*) which both Matthew and Luke draw upon heavily? Cf. Goguel, *The Life of Jesus*, p. 126.

[7] Cf. C. H. Dodd, *The Epistle of Paul to the Romans*, pp. 208, et al.

[8] *Paul* (New York: George H. Doran Co., 1926), p. 197.

## The Earthly Career of Jesus Christ

In addition to an acquaintance with the synoptic *tradition* concerning the teachings of Jesus, Paul also reveals considerable knowledge of the synoptic *tradition* concerning his personality and spirit, as well as of some facts about his career. The man Jesus whom he knows was a person who was steadfast in the face of opposition (II Thess. 3:5); he was obedient to the will of his heavenly Father and through that obedience has opened the way for others to draw near to God (Rom. 5:19). To this steadfastness and obedience was added a quality of meekness coupled with gentleness (II Cor. 10:1). The supreme characteristic which he possessed, however, was love (Rom. 8:35).

It is not unlikely, as some have suggested, that in several of the heroic passages where Paul describes Christian character, he has the figure of Jesus of Nazareth before him as his ideal.[9] Take such a statement as he makes in Second Corinthians when he describes true servants of God. He says that they commend themselves to others

through great endurance, in afflictions, hardships, calamities, beatings, imprisonments, tumults, labors, watching, hunger; by purity, knowledge, forbearance, kindness, the Holy Spirit, genuine love, truthful speech, and the power of God; with the weapons of righteousness for the right hand and for the left; in honor and dishonor, in ill repute and good repute. We are treated as impostors, and yet are true; as unknown, and yet well known; as dying, and behold we live; as punished, and yet not killed; as sorrowful, yet always rejoicing; as poor, yet making many rich; as having nothing, and yet possessing everything." (6:4-10.)

This could well be a character sketch of Jesus. The same may be said for the classic statement on love found in First Corinthians:

Love is patient and kind; love is not jealous or boastful; it is not arrogant or rude. Love does not insist on its own way; it is not irritable or resentful; it does not rejoice at wrong, but rejoices in the right. Love bears all things, believes all things, hopes all things, endures all things. (13: 4-7.)

All of this fits the portrait of Jesus which is given us in the Synoptic

[9] John Baillie, *The Place of Jesus Christ in Modern Christianity* (New York: Charles Scribner's Sons, 1929), p. 81.

Gospels so perfectly that it is difficult not to conclude that Paul had Jesus in mind when he wrote.

Certain facts concerning Jesus appear in the writings of Paul which further indicate that he possessed considerable knowledge of his life among men. He knows, for instance, that Jesus was "descended from David according to the flesh" (Rom. 1:3), and that the Jews had a right to claim him for their own (Rom. 9:5). There can be no doubt that Paul believed in the genuineness of Jesus' life in the flesh, in spite of the exalted and transcendent factors which he also ascribed to him. This can be seen when he contrasts him with Adam, saying, "For if many died through one man's trespass, much more have the grace of God and the free gifts in the grace of that one man Jesus Christ abounded for many" (Rom. 5:15). The point of the contrast is lost if Jesus' humanity were unreal. Paul even goes so far as to say that Jesus was "born of woman, born under the law" (Gal. 4:4c). He also notes that he had a brother named James (Gal. 1:19).

While we do not have a detailed description in the writings of Paul of the ministry of Jesus, there are sufficient references to certain facts to indicate that Paul was informed about it. He knows that there were twelve disciples, because he mentions this group as one which had seen the risen Christ (I Cor. 15:5). Furthermore, he notes that Jesus' ministry was among the Jews, where he "became a servant to the circumcised" (Rom. 15:8). And as we would expect from the early Christians, Paul was familiar with the instituting of the Lord's Supper. It occurred, he says, on the night of the betrayal, although he does not mention Judas by name (I Cor. 11:23-26). Crucifixion followed, after which there was a burial. But this was not the end, for on the third day Jesus was raised from the dead "according to the scriptures" (I Cor. 15:4). In a moving statement Paul says, "For he was crucified in weakness, but lives by the power of God" (II Cor. 13:4). Rawlinson believes that there would have been a fuller delineation of details in the career of Jesus, except for the fact that Paul was addressing himself to converted believers who were already familiar with the facts, as they had been expounded to them in missionary preaching and the catechetical instruction which followed.[10]

At the heart of one of the great christological passages in the New Testament, one which there is good reason to regard as coming from the pen of Paul, is a statement that further implies Paul's knowledge

[10] Op. cit., p. 118.

of the earthly life of Jesus, such knowledge as may well have stemmed from the synoptic *tradition*. When we read it, we inevitably fill in the details, and it is quite likely that Paul did also. Surely he expected his readers to do this, counting upon their store of information that had come to them through the Christian preaching they had heard. And much of this message they had first received from his own lips.

This passage is found in Phil. 2:5-11, and is known as the "kenosis passage" because of its use of the verb *kenoō* which is here translated "to empty." There are many technical questions regarding it which need not concern us at this point.[11] Paul's purpose clearly was to urge an attitude of humility upon the Philippian Christians, and he sought to do this by referring to Jesus as an example. Although he possessed a pre-existent life "in the form of God," he surrendered it temporarily by coming to earth "in the likeness of men" and "taking the form of a servant." In this human form he further humbled himself by accepting death, such death as that of the accursed cross. Because of this, however, God has highly exalted him so that his name is above every other name, except that of God the Father.

We shall have occasion later to consider more fully this important piece of portraiture, for that is what it is essentially,[12] but for the present we turn to it for its realistic portrayal of the earthly life of Jesus. To all appearances he was lowly, as lowly as a servant or slave (*doulos*). But humbler still was his death on the cross. The Law had branded all such as accursed (Deut. 21:22-23).

Whether Paul had in mind the suffering servant of Isaiah in saying that Jesus had assumed "the form of a servant" is a much debated question.[13] The community of ideas between the two representations would suggest at least a general relationship. But in our present consideration this is not the issue. What we are concerned to note is that Paul is clearly informed of the suffering which came upon Jesus of Nazareth. It was not only that Paul regarded Jesus as identifying himself with humanity. He was doing this, to be sure, but he was also experiencing voluntarily and temporarily a humble descent to the level of a crucified slave. This was the supreme indignity and ultimate glory.

[11] Cf. the commentaries.
[12] Cf. pp. 95-97.
[13] Cf. H. W. Robertson, *The Cross of the Servant*, pp. 73-74, favors this identification. Cf. also Benjamin Bacon, *Jesus and Paul*, pp. 108 ff. For a contrary view cf. W. L. Knox, *St. Paul and the Church of Jerusalem*, p. 16.

## Paul and the Primitive Christian Portrait

In the preceding chapter the portrait of Jesus as it was known in the primitive church was considered. The question which now confronts us is the extent to which Paul made use of this representation in coming to his own understanding of Jesus. Was he influenced by these earlier conceptions which grew out of the first experiences of the Jerusalem church?

The portrait of Jesus in the primitive church, as we have seen, presented a person who had lived a genuinely historical existence within the framework of the religious system and ideas of first-century Jews. He had come to his own as God's Messiah. Although he knew and accepted himself as such, his people would not concur. Instead, they crucified him as an enemy. But in his death he was expressing the ideal of the suffering servant of Isaiah. Then God raised him on the third day by an act of resurrection, declaring thus that he was an exalted Messiah, greater by far than Hebrew traditional expectations.

Not only did God bring forth Jesus from the grave, but also he elevated him to a position of unparalleled power at his right hand. This conclusion came to the first Christians through an experience of Jesus in his ascension into heaven. As the exalted and ascended Messiah, he sent the Spirit upon his followers at Pentecost, thus inaugurating the beginning of a new order of life which looked toward a final consummation with his return in triumph at the end of the Age. The worshiping Fellowship now regarded Jesus as Lord and Christ, by whose power and in whose name healing and other mighty deeds were performed. Through these experiences, which had contributed to the making of the portrait, Jesus had come to have in their religious life the value of God himself, and on occasion prayers were directed to him personally. This was not a denial of monotheism and the supremacy of God, for Jesus was considered to be God's Son, and in these moments of worship the focus was upon one divine reality rather than two.

Paul had ample opportunity to become familiar with this portrait of Jesus in the primitive church, both before and following his conversion. We can only surmise what the nature of this contact might have been before this dramatic event on the Damascus road, which not only changed Paul's personal life, but also modified all human history eventually. He was at this time an arch persecutor of the followers of the Way. The usual interpretation is that Paul was under a conviction of conscience when he laid waste the church, imprisoning both men and women and voting (or giving assent) for their death (Acts 26:9-11). What gave rise to these pangs of conscience that drove him to such lengths in an attempt to silence the accusing voice? Was it not that the knowledge of Christian claims concerning Christ and the example of Christian living and dying had made him unsure of his own religious experience as a Pharisee? And one such as Paul would not have developed a conscience on the basis of sentiment alone. Only some acquaintance with the facts concerning Jesus and his followers would have disturbed his spirit so greatly as to cause him to become a persecutor of Christians.

Some, however, hold that it was not a matter of conscience that drove Paul to his acts of opposition. They suggest instead that it was a question of disposing of a contrary viewpoint by crushing the opposition. The church was claiming that Jesus was the Jewish Messiah. All of this ran counter to the traditional teaching which we may assume that Paul, as an orthodox Pharisee, subscribed to. In some respects what the Christians were saying and doing was blasphemous in spirit, if not actually in act. Stamp out the false doctrine! Persecute those who hold it! If this analysis is correct, it presupposes some knowledge by Paul of the Christian portrait of Christ in the primitive church; and considerable knowledge too, if Paul's act is to be in line with his temperament as shown later in his life as a Christian missionary. He was thorough always both in thought and in deed.

### Paul's Conversion and the Primitive Church's Portrait of Jesus

The conversion of Paul was a pivotal event in the history of the early church. Not only did it catapult an energetic figure into its ongoing life; it also perpetuated a portrait of Jesus which had already taken form in the primitive period. The claim that Paul personally turned Christian thinking concerning Christ into *altogether new directions* can hardly be substantiated in the light of our knowledge of the early church, as it shines through both the Acts of the Apostles and the Gospels. That he pointed it up and gave it new vigor, however, because of the character of his conviction is evident from a thoughtful reading of the epistles.

Joseph Klausner, in speaking of Paul's contribution to the conception of Christianity, gives a proper place to this inheritance which Paul received. He states:

There were days in which Paul was considered to be "the inventor of Christianity" to use the expression of Nietzsche. At present those holding this opinion are growing fewer. Almost all scholars occupied with Christian origins have come to the conclusion that Paul depended in large measure not only upon the opinions and teachings of Jesus, but also upon the "primitive church" of Jerusalem—this "primitive church" being the immediate transmitter of the known facts about the life and teachings of Jesus.[14]

To these facts should be added the interpretation of Jesus which grew out of the religious experience of the early church at his hands.

The importance which Luke attached to Paul's conversion may be seen in the fact that he gave three detailed accounts of it in Acts (9:1-19; 22:3-16; 26:2-18). In spite of certain variations in detail, the three accounts agree that it was an ecstatic experience in which Jesus Christ as exalted Lord appeared to Paul. The exact *form* of the appearance, whether objective or subjective, need not be discussed at this point. It is the impression concerning Jesus Christ which lay at the heart of the conversion that concerns us. And in this regard the record is clear.

In the Damascus-road event Paul personally discovered that Jesus was alive as exalted Lord.[15] He was so closely related to the Christian church that to persecute its members was to persecute him personally (Acts 9:5; 22:8; 26:15). More than this, he was directing its course and would guide Paul in the days immediately ahead and beyond.

The accounts in Acts are not primary evidence for the nature of the conversion of Paul, although we may hold that in part at least they go back to Luke, who was his close companion. But this does not mean that they are without value, especially when they are corroborated by statements from Paul's own hand. For instance, in writing to the Galatians, the apostle to the Gentiles is interested in validating his own apostleship. And as one of the major supports to his claim, he insists that his gospel came through a revelation of Jesus Christ. He says:

[14] From *Jesus to Paul*, p. 580.

[15] Hugh R. Mackintosh in *The Person of Jesus Christ* (p. 54) says, "He [Paul] habitually conceives of Christ as clothed in the *doxa* or Divine Radiance in which he first beheld him at Damascus."

For I did not receive it from man, nor was I taught it, but it came through a revelation of Jesus Christ. For you have heard of my former life in Judaism, how I persecuted the church of God violently and tried to destroy it; and I advanced in Judaism beyond many of my own age among my people, so extremely zealous was I for the traditions of my fathers. But when he who had set me apart before I was born, and had called me through his grace, was pleased *to reveal his Son to me*, in order that I might preach him among the Gentiles, I did not confer with flesh and blood, nor did I go up to Jerusalem to those who were apostles before me, but I went away into Arabia; and again I returned to Damascus. (1: 12-17.) [16]

Of particular interest in this recital is the reference to the fact that God had revealed his Son "to" or "in" Paul.[17] The experience of Christ in this revelation was so transcendent that from this time forward he thought of him in heavenly terms and became his eternal slave (Rom. 1:1; Phil. 1:1). The primitive church had already taken this lofty view of Jesus, and it may be assumed that Paul had often heard its members express themselves accordingly. In the conversion, however, he became assured of its truth for himself. General information became personal knowledge. To doubt it would be to doubt himself, and this such a one as Paul could not do.

### Participation in the Fellowship and Paul's Portrait of Christ

Paul's portrait of Christ was not an intellectual construction. We are not to think of him as systematically putting it together as an architect designs a building.[18] Instead, its features came into bold relief as he experienced Christ within the Christian community. And as this experience deepened or moved in new directions, the features in the portrait were more fully defined.

A close study of the Pauline correspondence indicates that throughout it all there is a transcendental view of Christ. His earliest letters, First and Second Thessalonians (or Galatians?), show clearly at this time Paul regarded Jesus in the highest terms. It is therefore difficult to diagram a development in outlook and to discover an ascendancy in conception based upon an analysis of Paul's writings. New situations bring to the fore new perspectives and emphases, to be sure, but one

[16] Italics mine.
[17] Cf. T. R. Glover, *Paul of Tarsus*, p. 67: "If, with some historians, we say that this is all that can be said as to his conversion, and decide to suspend judgment on Luke's data [in Acts], Paul's statement here is enough."
[18] Cf. H. F. Rall, *According to Paul*, p. 120.

cannot say that the apostle did not hold these views of Christ prior to his recording of them.[19] And yet only a most static view of personality and an unusually rigid understanding of Paul could lead one to assert that there was no modification in his portrait of Christ through the years.[20] Perhaps the greatest development in Paul's portraiture came during the time between his conversion and his letter-writing period. His own reference to spending three years in Arabia following the Damascus-road experience suggests an opportunity for thoughtful consideration of the full meaning of Christ. And that this full meaning came to Paul gradually during this retreat is a reasonable assumption, although impossible to document.

Paul's Christology, which is essentially portraiture, was dynamic rather than formal in character. He refers to it, not for its own sake, but in relation to his purpose in writing. For instance, as he introduces himself to the Christians in Rome, he has occasion to speak of his gospel as one that concerns God's Son. Then follows a segment of portraiture by way of explanation:

. . . the gospel concerning his Son, who was descended from David according to the flesh and designated Son of God in power according to the Spirit of holiness by his resurrection from the dead, Jesus Christ our Lord, through whom we have received grace and apostleship to bring about obedience to the faith for the sake of his name among all the nations, including yourselves who are called to belong to Jesus Christ. (1:3-6.)

Again, when writing to the Colossians, Paul reminds them of the great deliverance which was theirs in the kingdom of God's Son. This leads him to comment further on Christ, and the portrait is presented:

He is the image of the invisible God, the first-born of all creation; for in him all things were created, in heaven and on earth, visible and invisible, whether thrones or dominions or principalities or authorities—all things were created through him and for him. He is before all things, and in him all things hold together. He is the head of the body, the church; he is the beginning, the first-born from the dead, that in everything he might be preëminent. For in him all the fullness of God was pleased to dwell, and through him to reconcile to himself all things, whether on earth or in heaven, making peace by the blood of his cross. (1:15-20.)

[19] Cf. Phil. 2:5 ff.; Col. 1:15-20.

[20] Pro development: cf. Bacon, op. cit., pp. 208-9. Elias Andrews, The Meaning of Christ for Paul, pp. 242-43. Con development: cf. A. E. Garvie, Studies in Paul and His Gospel, pp. 20 ff.; R. H. Strachan, The Historic Jesus in the New Testament, p. 32.

Later he warns this same church against false doctrines of human tradition, urging that they should turn, instead, to Christ. And a verbal vignette follows:

For in him the whole fulness of deity dwells bodily, and you have come to fulness of life in him, who is the head of all rule and authority. In him also you were circumcised with a circumcision made without hands, by putting off the body of flesh in the circumcision of Christ; and you were buried with him in baptism, in which you were also raised with him through faith in the working of God, who raised him from the dead. And you, who were dead in trespasses and the uncircumcision of your flesh, God made alive together with him, having forgiven us all our trespasses, having canceled the bond which stood against us with its legal demands; this he set aside, nailing it to the cross. He disarmed the principalities and powers and made a public example of them, triumphing over them in him. (2: 9-15.) [21]

It should be noted that portraiture in these references is drawn in terms of what Christ has done both in the universe and for persons.[22] He is such-and-such a person because he has done such-and-such a thing. Abstraction gives way to concrete presentation in statements likes these. There is no making of theology for the sake of theoretical speculation. Instead, it is the interpretation of Christian experience which is basic to the emerging portrait.

In this chapter we have suggested that Paul was considerably acquainted with both the teachings of Jesus and the major events of his life. These were available to him in the synoptic *tradition* which the primitive church possessed. Furthermore, it was indicated that Paul was likely to have begun an inquiry along these lines at the time he was persecuting the church, at least with sufficient thoroughness to justify his acts of violence. In addition, we have taken note of the contribution his conversion experience made to his portrait of Christ. The exalted Lord whom he discovered personally in this event now came into the foreground of his life. Ever after, as he lived within the Fellowship, he was to think of him in the highest possible terms, both in his relation to God and the universe, as well as in his relation to persons.

[21] Cf. also the portraiture in Phil. 2:5-11 already considered (p. 59) where Christ is presented as an example in humility which his followers should emulate.

[22] Cf. also II Cor. 5:21; 8:9; Gal. 4:4; Rom. 15:3.

# FIVE

# In the Pauline Epistles: Salvation

WE HAVE SEEN THAT PAUL'S PORTRAIT OF CHRIST WAS DYNAMIC IN character; it was related to the new life which he and other believers experienced as they turned to him in faith. In large measure the apostle's conviction that salvation centered in Christ determined his conception of his Lord.

### Christ and the Law

The struggle of the Jew as he attempted to please God was rooted in his inability to keep the Law.[1] And when Paul presents Christ to the church, he lifts him up as one who brings victory in this undertaking. The "Law" (*nomos*) in his writings refers to the Old Testament Law or to the Old Testament as a whole (Rom. 4:13-15; I Cor. 14:36). In daily living the ethical demand of the commandments laid its insistent hand upon men, calling them to obedience so that they might become righteous before God (Rom. 2:1–3:20). Certain aspects of the Law were cultic and ritualistic, such as the Sabbath requirements and the offering of sacrifices at the Temple; others were ethical, such as the commandments against stealing, lying, and covetousness.

During his ministry Jesus encountered considerable opposition from the Jewish religious leaders, particularly the scribes and the Pharisees, because he opposed what he regarded as their legalistic insistence on keeping the letter of the Law, regardless of what it did to persons. So basic was this issue that one of the first sections of the tradition concerning his ministry to be collected had to do with it (Mark 2:1–3:6).[2]

Before his conversion, Paul's problem with the Law was personal.

[1] Paul's statement in Phil. 3:6 that he was blameless under the Law should be discounted in the light of Rom. 7:5 where he refers to his sinful passions as being aroused by the Law and bearing a fruit for death.
[2] Cf. pp. 128-30; 141-42.

66

His writing is autobiographical when he says, "I was once alive apart from the law, but when the commandment came, sin revived and I died; the very commandment which promised life proved to be death to me" (Rom. 7:9-10). By defining the ideal of righteousness, the Law not only made Paul conscious of his sin; it also contributed to his sinning. But looking back upon his experience, as a mature Christian the apostle concluded that the commandments were holy, just, and good (Rom. 7:12). Actually, the Law was spiritual since it summoned men to righteous living (7:14). It was even ordained by angels (Gal. 3:19). And yet there was a tragic weakness in the Law; it did not empower men to keep it. On a literal or legalistic basis it was impossible to do so. Even though the Jews would probably have disagreed with him, Paul held that a failure to keep one of the commandments is, in principle, a failure to keep the entire Law. Death before God is the final impasse in such a system.[3]

What, then, is the purpose of the Law? It is here that Paul's portrait of Christ emerges. He sees the Law as a custodian until Christ came (Gal. 3:24). In a sense it was a tutor to bring men to Christ. At the heart of this great moral impasse where man's standing before God is at stake and where he is helpless to act for himself, Christ alone becomes his hope and his salvation. He is such a one as can bring deliverance in an issue that determines man's final destiny. Thus the full significance of Christ shines forth against the background of the Law with its moral demands, on the one hand, and man's inability to meet them, on the other. This significance constitutes portraiture, no less.

### Christ and Salvation

At the heart of Paul's portrait of Christ is his claim that through him righteousness becomes available to man and, therefore, the demands of the Law are met and salvation is possible. The term "righteousness" in this context (*dikaiosunē*) is used in a legal or forensic sense as meaning to be pronounced or declared righteous before God

---

[3] Since no one is able to achieve righteousness before God through the Law, however, it may be questioned as to whether it was ever in God's plan that he should (Gal. 2:16). And besides, it would be false to assume that in his creaturehood man could attain salvation by himself, so that he could boast before God of his achievement. If any boasting is to be done, Paul concludes, "Let him who boasts, boast of the Lord," not of himself (I Cor. 1:28-31).

(Rom. 2:13). The verdict is that man is recognized as innocent, particularly at the final judgment (Gal. 5:5). In this latter sense righteousness is an eschatological hope, and may become an eschatological fact.[4]

But righteousness may also be a present reality (I Cor. 6:11; Rom. 9:30). "We are justified by faith, [and] we have peace with God through our Lord Jesus Christ," Paul writes to the Romans (5:1).[5] The future declaration of acquittal at the Judgment is already realized as taking effect in the present. This does not mean the achievement of sinlessness on man's part in an ethical sense, but rather that if anyone is now in Christ, God does not count his sins against him (II Cor. 5:19); reconciliation has already taken place.

It should be noted that in the references quoted already in this section, Christ plays a determinative role, but this is only because God was at work in and through his Son. In this sense the portrait of the Son involves a portrait, so to speak, of God. It is this fact which gives meaning to such expressions as a "Christlike God." In the great creeds of the church this likeness means more than similarity; it actually stands for a metaphysical reality.

The question immediately before us, however, in delineating Paul's portrait of Christ, is to determine just how the apostle conceives of Christ's place in man's salvation, in his being declared righteous before God. In answering this question, we shall discover that Paul frequently uses languages metaphorically, first reaching into one area and then into another for illustrations by which to interpret Christ's work in salvation.[6] To press for a literal interpretation of Paul's language would do violence to the meaning he intends. Paul is more of a preacher-poet in these passages than he is a technical theologian, systematically constructing a logically coherent theology. He writes in the tradition of Jesus, who was always inquiring, "To what shall I liken . . . ?" But because Paul's figures of speech are to be taken suggestively rather than literally, it should not be assumed that they are not to be regarded seriously. The apostle is deeply in earnest as he writes. Christ actually made a destiny-deciding difference in the

---

[4] Eschatology is the study of final things and involves such subjects as the Judgment and the end of the Age.

[5] Italics mine.

[6] Cf. Deissmann, op. cit., p. 167. "To this one object [Christ] the confessor bears witness in a continually new variation of figurative words of similar meaning and often with the parallelism of prophetic emphasis." Cf. also pp. 200 ff.

68

salvation issue. Because of his life, death, and resurrection the situation was changed.

Rall distinguishes five different approaches in Paul's presentation of the work of Christ in salvation: that is, reconciliation, satisfaction, sacrifice and propitiation, deliverance and redemption, and the mystical-ethical.[7] Each of these is concerned with the same central reality, namely that Christ made a saving difference in man's salvation. Elias Andrews considers Christ's place here as being that of the redeemer from sin, the revealer of God's righteousness, the vanquisher of evil, the creator of a new life, and the inaugurator of a new humanity.[8] Bultmann, in this connection, speaks of what he calls "the salvation-occurrence" (the incarnation, death, and resurrection of Jesus) which Paul interprets in terms of Jewish sacrificial practice, vicarious sacrifice, redemption through ransom, the death of a divinity of the mystery religions, and the gnostic myth.[9]

John Knox presents Paul's interpretation of Christ's work in saving men in a statement containing five propositions. As we have indicated previously, since these are concerned with something that Christ did, they are a part of his portrait:

1. *Jesus paid a ransom on our behalf and thus secured our release from the slavery of sin.*

2. *He satisfied the requirements of the law for us; he paid a penalty we could not pay.*

3. *He offered an adequate sacrifice for sin, which we were not able to offer.*

4. *He met and defeated sin and the powers of evil which had mastered us and which we had not strength to overcome.*

5. *He offered a perfect obedience and thus became the New Man, undoing the results of Adam's transgression and making possible our incorporation into a new and sinless humanity.*[10]

Other scholars present still different analyses of Paul's thought in this connection, but all are concerned with the same idea. Paul's portrait of Christ includes the fact that he was such a one that through him God could accomplish a deliverance which affected the destiny of the human race.

[7] *Op. cit.,* pp. 94-108.
[8] *The Meaning of Christ for Paul,* pp. 41-105.
[9] *Op. cit.,* I, 292-306.
[10] *Christ the Lord,* pp. 118-19. Used by permission.

## Some Classic Verses

Although it is not possible within the limits and purpose of this chapter to examine in great detail Paul's theory of the atonement and of salvation, certain classical verses which contain this teaching should be considered. From one standpoint it might be said that the apostle gives us several theories of the atonement (a type of presentation of how Christ saves men). From another and more considerate judgment it should be stated that Paul is dealing with a single fact of deliverance from sin, evil, and their consequences, interpreted first in one way and again in another.

For instance, in Rom. 3:21-26 Paul uses three metaphors—one from the legal system of the day, another from slavery, and still another from practices in religious sacrifice. Yet the apostle is referring to but one act on God's part for man's salvation. The passage follows:

> But now the righteousness of God has been manifested apart from law, although the law and the prophets bear witness to it, the righteousness of God through faith in Jesus Christ for all who believe. For there is no distinction; since all have sinned and fall short of the glory of God, they are justified by his grace as a gift, through the redemption which is in Christ Jesus, whom God put forward as an expiation by his blood, to be received by faith. This was to show God's righteousness, because in his divine forbearance he had passed over former sins; it was to prove at the present time that he himself is righteous and that he justifies him who has faith in Jesus.

When Paul states in these verses that men are "justified [dikaioumenoi] by his [God's] grace as a gift" (3:24), he is turning to the realm of jurisprudence for his illustration. Because of his love, freely given (grace), God has acquitted sinners who look in faith to Christ. They are declared innocent, even though actually they are not sinless; God's judgment no longer rests upon them.

The second metaphor comes from the practice of liberating slaves who were military prisoners: "Through the reaemption [apolutrōseōs] which is in Christ Jesus" (3:24). Moffatt makes this passage read: "Through the ransom provided in Christ Jesus." Sometimes in the Greco-Roman world the payment of a ransom would bring the release of captives taken in combat. But with Paul the word "ransom" should not be pressed too literally.[11] It may mean simply emancipation, in

---

[11] The word may be used without the idea of money to be paid.

70

the sense that the Hebrews were delivered from bondage out of Egypt.[12] Interpreted thus, the teaching there could be that in Christ men are freed, emancipated from their enslavement to sin.

Finally, in this message Paul finds his third illustration in the area of religious sacrificial systems: "Christ Jesus, whom God put forward as an expiation [*hilastērion*] by his blood, to be received by faith" (3:25). It is sometimes suggested that "expiation" as used here means to propitiate, in the sense of placating an angry god. Instead, it probably refers to an act of annulment of sin, available through faith, which God initiated by sending Jesus Christ. Placating an angry god is pagan, not biblical. In doing this, he was motivated by love, as in Rom. 5:8: "But God shows his love for us in that while we were yet sinners Christ died for us."

The reference to blood in Romans 3:25 should probably be understood in the light of the Old Testament emphasis upon blood as the seat of life (Gen. 9:4; Deut. 12:23). The shedding of Jesus' blood was equivalent to the sacrificing of himself. Christ was "obedient unto death, even death on a cross" (Phil. 2:8). This does not necessarily carry with it the idea that Christ was a substitute victim in connection with the payment of a penalty.[13] Nor need it be taken ritualistically, often the case in primitive religion, as referring to Christ's death as blood shed to remove defilement.[14] Instead we should, in my judgment, realize that here as elsewhere Paul is concerned with the actual deliverance which comes to man as he responds by faith to Christ crucified, and that he is illustrating it figuratively by referring to an area of life known to his readers.

When Paul says that Christ "died for all" (II Cor. 5:15), he meant every word of it. This is the supreme stroke in his portrait at this point. As a Jew, he is thinking within the conception of solidarity or unity, in which the group is regarded as being just as real as an individual.[15] In his death, Christ represents all humanity. By faith in him men enter into his death for them. His act of obedience becomes theirs; his love for God becomes their love for God. When Paul's

[12] Cf. Gal. 3:23–4:7 where the idea of the Christian's deliverance from bondage is central.

[13] Cf. Anselm (A.D. 1033-1109) and the satisfaction theory of atonement.

[14] In the Old Testament, rituals are provided for the cleansing of both persons and things. Cf. Lev. 13-16 ad loc.

[15] Cf. Achan's sin and the group's indictment (Josh. 7; 22:20). In our discussion of Pauline mysticism more will be said along this line.

71

view of Christ's death for men is interpreted in this light, the idea that his death was a substitute for man's own death, due him because of sin, is seen to misrepresent the apostle's thinking as a whole.

### Christ—Salvation—Deliverance

It is difficult for a modern man to sense the tragedy of a life lived under the shadow of belief in evil spirit-forces and demons. But this was the view of the first-century world in Paul's time, and the apostle's portrait of Christ takes on new dimensions when studied against the background of this outlook. Paul accepted the existence of these forces, and his conception of Christ was formed, in part, from his conviction that his Lord was victor over them, and would, in turn, bring a similar victory to all who put their trust in him.

There was a background for this belief in the accounts of Jesus' ministry prior to his crucifixion. It was said of him that "With authority he commands even the unclean spirits, and they obey him" (Mark 1:24-27). And it was recorded specifically that he had cast seven demons out of Mary Magdalene (Luke 8:2), exorcised many others from a Gerasene demoniac (Mark 5:1-20), and successfully commanded an unclean spirit to depart from an epileptic boy (Mark 9:14-29). Reports of Jesus' activity along this line were widespread, so that the claim that the exalted Christ was Lord over the kingdom of demons fell upon prepared ears. The people were eager to believe it because their need for deliverance was great.

Paul employs various titles for the evil spirits. These include "angels," "thrones," "principalities," and "powers." Again, they are referred to as "world rulers of this present darkness" and "spiritual hosts of wickedness in the heavenly places." The apostle speaks also of "elemental spirits of the universe" (the sun, moon, and planets under the control of spirits), "the prince of the power of the air," and "the prince of this world." Sometimes this "prince" is called the "Devil," "Belial," or "Satan," different names for the same personal evil spirit who was considered to be the chief of demons. Whereas individual men may be demon-possessed, the entire human race was regarded as subject to these high and unseen spirit-forces. They represented a hierarchy with the Prince of Evil at the top, intermediate beings next (powers, principalities, thrones, and so forth), and finally the myriads of lesser demons. Similar hierarchies were found in contemporary gnostic systems. They were also known to the

72

Jews as far back as their Babylonian enslavement (586 B.C.), when they came into contact with ancient astrology.

The need for deliverance from these hostile cosmic spirits was particularly felt in the Gentile world. Instead of the moral impasse which a failure or inability to keep the Law created among the Jews, it was the thraldom caused by fear of enslavement at the hands of evil powers in the universe that made the message of salvation in Christ a welcome one to Gentiles in Greco-Roman society.

It would, however, be faulty to assume that the Jews were wholly without concern in this regard. Even their own priests practiced the exorcising of evil spirits (Matt. 12:27). And in times of crises, when men's souls were stirred, it is not unlikely that they too would turn for help to such conceptions as fate and a belief in unseen evil forces. When Paul writes, "So with us; when we were children, we were slaves to the elemental spirits of the universe" (Gal. 4:3), he may be referring to his own temptations at this point.

Concerning the deliverance which Christ brings to those who are enslaved by the fear of evil forces or spirits (in Paul's day and wherever accepted in ours) a passage from Warneck is exceptionally pertinent, in my judgment:

> The insurmountable wall which rises up between the heathen and God is not as among ourselves (not in the first place at least); it is the kingdom of darkness in which they are bound. That bondage shows itself in the fear that surrounds them, fear of souls, fear of spirits, fear of human enemies and magicians. The Gospel comes to unloose the ignoble bonds. It stands forth before their eyes, a delivering power, a redemption. They see Jesus certainly as the self-revelation of God, but they see him chiefly and most clearly as the conqueror of demons and the Devil.[16]

My own acquaintance with the testimony of present-day missionaries from countries where animistic beliefs still hold would confirm this view.

### Portraiture Present

Our purpose in considering the outlook of the first century in regard to evil spirits is to show that it contributed to Paul's portrait of Christ at the point where he pictures his Lord as victor over them. To the question "How think you of Christ?" Paul would reply that

---

[16] *The Living Forces of the Gospels*, p. 232. Quoted by C. Anderson Scott, *Christianity According to St. Paul*, p. 32.

Christ was such a one as brought, among other things, all evil cosmic forces under his control. The question "How did he accomplish this?" inevitably follows.

The answer to this inquiry is that Christ did it actually through his death on the cross, followed as it was by the Resurrection, and that he will do it finally at the end of the Age. The evil forces are being destroyed where Christ continues his work in the world and faith is active. Already Christ has "disarmed the principalities and powers and made a public example of them, triumphing over them in him" [17] (Col. 2:15).

There is more here than a simple historical reference to the Jewish and Roman authorities whose human activities brought about the crucifixion of Jesus. These agencies are seen, instead, as the unconscious instruments of higher evil spiritual powers. And as E. F. Scott says: "Christ is conceived as doing battle with the great captains of that supernatural host which had enslaved the human race. He has beaten them down and stripped them of their armour, and then exposed them by making a public spectacle—exhibiting them to men and angels as his captives." [18] In all of this it should not be forgotten that God was at work through Christ; it was a part of the divine plan for salvation. But at the same time it is actually a portrait of Christ, for it was he who went to the cross and thus prevailed over these cosmic hostile powers, just as by this same cross he had achieved a salvation where the Law had only condemned, but was powerless to aid.

Final victory over these evil forces of spirit, however, must await the end of the Age when Christ will destroy "every rule and every authority and power. For he must reign until he has put all his enemies under his feet." (I Cor. 15:24-25.) Death itself is the final enemy, and it shall be utterly vanquished.

A characteristic touch in Paul's portrait of Christ is this belief in his Lord's return at the end of time. In line with the eschatological expectation of the primitive church, Paul looked for the second com-

---

[17] Moffatt translates *en autō* with the words "in the cross." A literal translation is "in it" or "in him." The Revised Standard Version prefers "in him," that is, in Christ. Another possible translation of this verse is that he (Christ) "stripped off from himself the Principalities and the Powers. . . ." This suggests that in death Christ shed his flesh (*sarx*) which had brought him unsuccessfully under the domination of the evil forces of spirit. In this way he broke from them and, by rising from the dead, became victor over them.

[18] *The Epistles of Paul to the Colossians, to Philemon and to the Ephesians*, p. 48.

ing of Christ within his own life span (I Cor. 7:29). He never gave up this anticipation, although his later references to it are not quite so vigorous as the earlier statements. As is true of the Gospel of John, present spiritual (mystical) experiences of the living Christ more and more fill the horizon and take away the emphasis from the final coming. Yet the hope is never wholly absent from Paul's thinking, as Col. 3:4 ("When Christ who is our life appears") and Phil. 3:20-21 ("But our commonwealth is in heaven, and from it we await a Savior, the Lord Jesus Christ, who will change our lowly body to be like his glorious body, by the power which enables him even to subject all things to himself") clearly testify.

### Christ—Salvation—The Spirit

Paul's portrait of Christ as presented in his writings has such a variety of facets that one is in danger of losing it in the discussion necessary to interpret each facet. His Lord is presented against the background of salvation, and this theme is developed from so many different perspectives that the portraiture may become lost in the analysis. Actually this need not be the case if we keep in mind the fact that all lines converge upon the same Figure whether the apostle is talking about the Law, righteousness and justification, sacrifice, ransom, evil spirit-forces, or mysticism. Like a multicut diamond which scatters light rays in all directions, while remaining a single stone, so is Paul's portrait of Christ.

For this reason we must constantly recall what has previously been stated, namely, that when the apostle considers Christ, he is not concerned with abstract definition, but with concrete representation as known in experience. Christ is such a one that in him and through him certain life-giving events have occurred—and still do. Paul's classic expression of this is to be found in his statement to the Corinthians that "if any one is in Christ, he is a new creation; the old has passed away, behold, the new has come. All this is from God, who through Christ reconciled us to himself and gave us the ministry of reconciliation." (II Cor. 5:17-18.)

This truth is nowhere more evident than when Paul is considering the experience of Christ which is made known through the Spirit. It is helpful to recall that following his Damascus-road conversion Paul was visited by a much venerated Christian, Ananias. Upon entering the house where the new convert had been taken, after he had been blinded by the "light from heaven," Ananias laid his hands upon him, and said, "Brother Saul, the Lord Jesus who appeared to you on the road by which you came, has sent me that you may regain your sight and be filled with the Holy Spirit." (Acts 9:17.) In the account of this experience Luke notes that immediately "something like scales fell from his eyes and he regained his sight" (vs. 18). After this he was baptized. The passage clearly implies that Paul received the Holy Spirit even as the first Christian converts at Pentecost. Henceforth he was to speak of these high concerns on the basis of personal experience.

The existence of the Spirit had long since been a familiar belief among the Jews. As far back as the Genesis account of creation it was written that "the Spirit of God was moving over the face of the waters" (Gen. 1:2). Mighty deeds were sometimes attributed to the visitation of the Spirit, as when it was recorded that Samson killed a lion with his bare hands. In this case the author wrote that "the Spirit of the Lord came mightily upon him" (Judg. 14:6). Prophets also spoke out of spirit-filled minds. At Jesus' baptism the Spirit came upon him (Luke 3:22), and it was this same Spirit that impelled him to go into the wilderness of temptation (Luke 4:1). We have noted already that at Pentecost the Spirit was given to those who believed. What was new in this situation, however, was that the resurrected and exalted Jesus was credited with sending the Spirit. Henceforth the experience of the Spirit had a Christ content or relationship which was completely new in the Hebrew tradition.

### The Spirit of God—The Spirit of Christ

The relation of Christ to the Spirit may be further seen in Luke's account of Paul's second missionary journey. The author reports that Paul was eager to preach the word in Asia (Ephesus), but that he was forbidden by *the Holy Spirit*. Then it is stated that the apostle attemped to go to Bithynia, but *the Spirit of Jesus* did not allow it (Acts 16:6-7). Here are two separate expressions, but they stand for the same religious fact. There is a common experience represented in these references to the Spirit. The "Holy Spirit" and the "Spirit of Jesus" seem to be used interchangeably.

The wording in the above reference comes from Luke. It is paralleled, however, in Paul's own writings. For instance, when the apostle sought to explain the new life in the Spirit, he unwittingly equates the experience of the Spirit of God, the Spirit of Christ, and the indwelling Christ. "But you are not in the flesh," he writes to the Romans, "you are in the Spirit, if *the Spirit of God* really dwells in you. Anyone who does not have *the Spirit of Christ* does not belong to him. But *if Christ is in you*, although your bodies are dead because of sin, your spirits are alive because of righteousness." (8:9-10.) [19] Again, there is a single religious reality in experience behind the references to the Spirit of God, the Spirit of Christ, and the indwelling Christ.

Strictly speaking, Paul does not here identify the Spirit of God with the Spirit of Christ, as though they were a single being. What he is saying in this passage is that when one experiences the presence of God's Spirit in his life, he is conscious of the indwelling Christ, and that when the Spirit of Christ is within the heart, God's Spirit is felt to be present also. Each brings a consciousness of the other. Even though the relation is close, very close indeed, the two are not actually identified as one.

On one occasion, however, Paul seems actually to identify Christ with the Spirit. This is when, in writing to the Corinthians, he says: "The Lord is the Spirit, and where the Spirit of the Lord is, there is freedom" (II Cor. 3:17). When this is coupled with a portion of the next verse, identification appears likely. For example: "For this comes from the Lord who is the Spirit." And yet even here there are grounds for uncertainty. The verb (*eimi*) "is" may stand for "means" (representation) as well as for identity.[20] It is best, therefore, to interpret this verse in the light of Paul's total reference to the relation of Christ and the Spirit. Each exercised the same function in Christian experience, and each brought the consciousness of the reality and presence of the other, and yet they remain separate entities to the end.

### Pauline Mysticism

We have seen that one facet of Paul's portrait of Christ was that his Lord was regarded as an indwelling Spirit. Once the apostle put it this way: "Thus it is written, 'The first man Adam became a living being'; the last Adam [Christ] became a life-giving Spirit" (I Cor. 15:45). Because of this fact Paul could speak of Christians as those

---

[19] Italics mine.

[20] Cf. Gal. 4:24. Cf. also Moffatt's translation of I Cor. 11:24: "This *means* my body broken for you."

77

who were "in Christ." Deissmann has figured that this expression, together with its cognates, appears 164 times in Paul's writing, not including Colossians, Ephesians, and the Pastorals.

To be "in Christ" may be interpreted in terms of mysticism. Some suggest that Christ was a kind of atmosphere within which the Christian lived.[21] Others decry such a pantheistic interpretation of being "in Christ" and insist that Paul's mysticism was of the "I-Thou" type. Rawlinson is of this opinion, and states that "the distinction between believers and Christ is invariably maintained: St. Paul can use the language of mutual indwelling: he never uses the language of pantheistic absorption." [22] With this latter view I personally agree. Much that the apostle says concerning the relation of the individual believer to Christ cannot be interpreted on the basis of a pantheistic type of mysticism.

There is a sense in which Paul regards "being in Christ" as an ethical experience. When he writes to the Philippians to "have this mind among yourselves, which you have in Christ Jesus" (2:5), he was thinking in these terms. Accordingly, Christ's love motivates the life of the Christian, just as his will comes to have the authority of God in man's decisions.

In addition to the mystical and moral or ethical interpretation of what it means to be in Christ, there are those who explain Paul's view of the experience eschatologically. Bultmann takes such a position. When one is in Christ, even as when he is in the Spirit, he has come into a new "eschatological existence." He writes: "As the eschatological existence can be called a 'being in Christ,' so it can also be called a 'being in the Spirit' (Rom. 8:9), and the locutions 'to have the spirit of Christ' or 'Christ in you' (v. 9 f.) can take its place with no difference in meaning." [23] Dodd supports a related view with his emphasis upon a *realized eschatology*. He believes that Paul thought of the new life in Christ as a future experience, not too distantly in the future, yet one which was still to come. Later, however, he considered it to be already realized in the life, death, and resur-

[21] Cf. Gunkel, *Die Wirkungen des heiligen Geistes*, pp. 43 ff.; also Albert Schweitzer, *The Mysticism of Paul the Apostle*, ad loc.

[22] *Op. cit.*, p. 157. Used by permission. Cf. F. C. Porter, *The Mind of Christ in Paul*, p. 283.

[23] *Op. cit.*, I, 335. Used by permission.

rection of Christ. There was still to be a final consummation, but a present possession was already had.[24]

However one interprets Paul's view of "being in Christ," according to pantheistic mysticism, I-Thou mysticism, ethical union, or eschatological existence, this experience was the heart and core of his being. For this reason he could say: "I have been crucified with Christ; it is no longer I who live, but Christ lives in me: and the life I now live in the flesh I live by faith in the Son of God, who loved me and gave himself for me." (Gal. 2:20.) And any representation of Paul's portrait of Christ which omits the fact that he is such a one who brings this experience is truncated and incomplete.

We have further examined Paul's portrait of Christ in this chapter. The apostle sees his Lord as bringing salvation to man in relation to the keeping of the Law, in connection with being declared righteous before God, and in finding deliverance from the thralldom of the world of evil spirits. In addition, we have considered Paul's conception of his Lord's relation to the Spirit, and the mystical life "in Christ" which Christians were experiencing. All of this constitutes portraiture, for Christ is seen as such a one through whom and in whom this great salvation was being known.

[24] *The Apostolic Preaching and Its Development*, pp. 146 ff.

# SIX

# In the Pauline Epistles: The Church and Its Sacraments

PAUL'S INTERPRETATION OF THE CHRISTIAN FAITH WAS SO CHRISTO-centric that in considering his portrait of Christ it is necessary to examine his total thought. We have seen already how this is true in relation to the Law, salvation in its several aspects, and the Spirit. It remains for us to look into the apostle's views regarding the church, the sacraments, the cosmic order, history, and the end of the Age, by way of determining what these areas in his thinking contribute to our understanding of his conception of Christ.

### Christ and the Church

In the preceding chapter it was noted that when the Spirit indwelt the life of a believer, when he was "in Christ," he was, as Paul put it, a "new creation." In this experience no sharp distinction was drawn between the Spirit of God and the Spirit of Christ, although they were not formally and finally identified metaphysically as one and the same. So transforming was this being "in Christ" that from one standpoint it constituted salvation itself. Although there was at the heart of the experience a mystical union with Christ, it was our conclusion that the believer did not lose his identity as the Spirit of his Lord entered his life. He still remained as one who looked in faith to Christ; there was always both a subject and an object in the transforming relationship.

But just as Christ was a spiritual presence in the lives of a single follower, he was also an indwelling spirit in the hearts of all other disciples. Thus was created a fellowship of believers, the Fellowship in the Son, Jesus Christ the Lord (I Cor. 1:9). This constituted them a koinōnia in Christ.

We noted previously that this early Christian community was also known in the primitive church as the Fellowship. Luke describes it as such in Acts when he summarizes its life as one which included instruction, the breaking of bread, and prayers (2:42). It has been suggested that the use of the name "Fellowship" is even earlier than the primitive church, that it goes back to the Chabūra (Aramaic) of the Jews which referred to those who came together as friends to celebrate the Passover. And Anderson Scott even suggests that probably "if the group of followers whom Jesus gathered most closely around Himself, took or had given to it some distinguishing name, that name would naturally be 'The Chabūra of Jesus.'" [1] Be this as it may, it is certain that with Paul, the Christian community was known as the Fellowship of the Son, Jesus Christ our Lord.

Since Christ was a life-giving Spirit, the new fellowship in him was likewise a fellowship in the Spirit. Paul calls it a "participation in the Spirit" (Phil. 2:1), and speaks of it as characterized by encouragement, love, affection, and sympathy. This constitutes portraiture, since it is most surely a reflection of the character of Christ. The imprint of his own personality is upon and within the Fellowship which bears his name; it is his own character writ large.

It is immediately apparent that what Paul has in mind in these references is not a formal institution or a concrete organization, although it may express itself through such. Instead it is a dynamic organism which Christ as indwelling Spirit creates. The apostle frequently refers in his letters to the fruits of the Spirit and also to the gifts of the Spirit, the charismata. Although the statements in which these are mentioned suggest that they come from the Spirit of God, it should not be forgotten that it is Christ who is represented as sending the Spirit at Pentecost, and that, in experience, the Spirit of God brings the consciousness of the presence of the Spirit of Christ. Because of this, both the fruits of the Spirit and the gifts of the Spirit are associated with Christ, and no adequate presentation of Paul's portrait of his Lord can pass lightly over this association.

The fruits of the Spirit and the gifts of the Spirit are manifested in the Christian Fellowship which Christ indwells. It is not surprising, therefore, that we recognize the former as characteristic of the personality of Christ, and the latter as representative of the Lord at work in the world through the Fellowship. The fruits are named as love, joy, peace, patience, kindness, goodness, faithfulness, gentleness, and self-control (Gal. 5:22-23). And the gifts are listed as the utter-

[1] *Christianity According to St. Paul*, p. 160.

81

ance of wisdom, the utterance of knowledge, faith, the gifts of healing, the working of miracles, prophecy, the ability to distinguish between spirits, various kinds of tongues, and the interpretation of tongues (I Cor. 12:8-10). These are given to members of the Fellowship individually, but they are intended also to quicken the whole community in Christ.

## The Body of Christ

Since the Spirit is active within the fellowship of believers, Christ may be said to indwell the church, even as he indwells individual persons. In this sense Paul refers to the church as "the body of Christ" (Eph. 4:12).[2] All those who are "in Christ" are included in a corporate relationship. This collective expression, however, is not a matter of statistics, such as the sum total involved in a numerical count. It is a corporate reality in itself. Individual believers are constituted one body through mystical union in Christ.

It is difficult for us who are accustomed to think of groups as an aggregate, composed of an association of individuals, to grasp Paul's thought of the church as the body of Christ. What the apostle has in mind is an organic entity which is metaphysically as real as a single person. The body is more than a metaphor; it is a reality itself.[3] In interpreting Paul's thought as to how it was that Christ's death made a saving difference in the lives of his followers, reference was made to the concept of solidarity by which the group was regarded as having an existence as real as that of the individuals composing it.[4] Somewhat along this same line of thinking, Paul regards the church as the body of Christ. This solidarity is mystical (spiritual) in character.[5]

Since Christ indwells the church so that it can be spoken of as the body of Christ, in a very real sense this church can be regarded as an

---

[2] Pauline authorship is not assumed here for Ephesians as a whole. The passage quoted is regarded, however, as essentially Pauline.

[3] E. F. Scott considers that the early idea of the church as the body of Christ, as in I Cor. 12, was figurative. Only in the later epistles does it become the mystical reality, "a larger incarnation of Christ." *The Epistles of Paul to the Colossians, to Philemon and to the Ephesians*, p. 24.

[4] Cf. p. 71.

[5] Schweitzer believes that Paul's thought of the mystical body of Christ starts from "the conception of the predestined solidarity of the Elect with one another and with the Messiah." As the Elect participate with Christ in the same corporeity, they become a part of the body of Christ. (*Op. cit.*, p. 117.) Rawlinson thinks its origin is found in the language of the Eucharist (cf. *Mysterium Christi*, ad loc.); Dodd takes a related view (*Epistle of Paul to Romans*, p. 194); Bacon finds its beginning in Stoicism (*The Story of Paul*, p. 259).

extension of the person of Christ. Thus, through the church, Christ continues to work in the world. But how does he become active through the church? Paul does not provide a detailed answer to this question, but his scattered references are suggestive. As we have noted, he taught that the Spirit-filled believers who comprise the church have been granted spiritual gifts. And, like the several members of the human body which make up the whole, these who possess the spiritual gifts are one body in Christ (I Cor. 12:12). In expressing these gifts, the body (church) and Christ through it are at work.

When Paul wrote to the Corinthians, he told them that they were the body of Christ and individually members of it. Then he added, "And God has appointed in the church first apostles, second prophets, third teachers, then workers of miracles, then healers, helpers, administrators, and speakers in various kinds of tongues" (I Cor. 12: 28).[6] These functions, when compared with the gifts of the Spirit in this same chapter (vss. 8-10), are seen to correspond to them. As the functions are exercised, therefore, spirit-filled (Christ-filled) activity results, and Christ is at work.

Actually Paul does not spell all of this out with detailed or calculated precision. In the final analysis, it is a mystical conception which is intuitively grasped rather than logically deduced. For this reason any attempt to systematize it is apt to do violence to Paul's portrait of Christ, expressed in terms of the mystical body. It is, therefore, not to be wondered that Schweitzer should have written: "In the whole literature of mysticism there is no problem comparable to this of the mystical body of Christ. How could a thinker come to produce this conception of the extension of the body of a personal being? How can Paul regard it as so self-evident that he can make use of it without ever explaining it?"[7]

It is one thing to refer to the church as the body of Christ, and even to consider it in a mystical sense as an extension of the person of Christ, so that through it the work of Christ continues. But it is another, and quite a different, thing to suggest that Paul actually identified Christ's being with the church. Scholars like Schweitzer who regard the "in-Christ" experience as a quasi-physical reality tend

---

[6] Cf. Rom. 12:4-5: "For as in one body we have many members, and all the members do not have the same function, so we, though many, are one body in Christ, and individually members one of another."

[7] Op. cit., p. 116.

to make the identification complete, but others, more properly in my judgment, do not hold that Paul ascribed to Christ and the church a metaphysical unity. He assumed as he wrote that individuals maintained their identity within the body when they were "in Christ." Pantheism on this basis is ruled out, making a metaphysical identification of Christ and the church all but impossible.

### Christ, the Head of the Body

Not only was Christ related to the church in such a way that it could be said to be his body; he was also regarded by Paul as its head. In writing to the Colossians, the apostle put it this way: "He [Christ] is the head of the body, the church" (1:18). As the head of the body (the church), Christ is its most important member, for it is from the head that all the other parts of the body are governed. By its direction all the members of the body function as an organism.

Reference to Christ as the head is also found in Ephesians. Here Christians are told to "grow up in every way into him who is the head, into Christ" (4:15). The author then moves into a description of the relationship of the head to the body, a description which suggests early medical science. At that time it was believed that not only was one part of the body in contact with another part, but also that all were bound into a single whole by the tissues and nerves which act as media to convey nourishment. Just so the individual followers of Christ who have received the Spirit and the gifts which he brings are bound together and fed from Christ, who is their head.[8]

This representation of Christ as the head of the church is yet another aspect of Paul's portrait of his Lord. It is more than a description or a sketch, however; it is a basic interpretation of the meaning of Christ for the church. Henceforth the church and Christ are so inseparably bound together that they cannot be divorced in Christian thought. There is more involved here than the simple statement that Christ founded the church. In a very real sense he *is* the church, because his life is related to it organically, and apart from this relationship the church would cease to exist. It is because of this fact that through the centuries in its highest hours the church has insisted that it is not simply *another* institution such as the state. Christ is its life, and its life is Christ.

[8] Cf. E. F. Scott, *Epistles of Paul to Colossians, to Philemon and to Ephesians*, p. 214, for a further development of this idea.

Paul's thought of Christ in his relation to the church has other aspects to it than that of the body and its head. For instance, he is the shekinah of the church conceived as the temple of God (I Cor. 3:9). He is also the maker of the New Covenant which constitutes the congregation of Israel the true and new people of God.[9] Thus the ancient ekklēsia is made new (II Cor. 5:17; Gal. 6:15).[10] The use of the word "ekklēsia" for the church ties together the Old Testament idea of the congregation of Israel as God's people, for this is the word by which it was known in the Septuagint, with the New Testament conception of the church as God's people. Only the church was now the true Israel.[11] And it is God who made them this in Christ.

### Christ and Baptism

We have seen throughout this discussion that Paul's interpretation of the Faith is Christocentric. For this reason there is portraiture in relation to nearly every theme he develops. This is no less true of his thinking in regard to the sacraments than it has been in his presentation of the other areas we have already considered. They occur "in Christ" and unite the believer to him in the closest spiritual relationship. For this reason Christ is seen through them as the source of a new life that redeems. In baptism and the Lord's Supper he is creatively present.

The fact that Paul expresses satisfaction over not having baptized many at Corinth, and that he asserted that Christ had not sent him "to baptize but to preach the gospel" (I Cor. 1:14-17) should not mislead us into concluding that he regarded this sacrament lightly. These remarks were made as a corrective in a situation where Christian preachers were being placed above Christ himself, so much so that Paul felt it necessary to inquire, "Were you baptized in the name of Paul?" (vs. 13). And it is within this context that they should be evaluated; they are not formal statements of his position concerning baptism.

Paul did not originate baptism within the Christian community. It was well established already when he met Christ on the Damascus

[9] The covenant at Sinai constituted Israel as God's people. Just so, the New Covenant ("This cup is the new covenant in my blood." I Cor. 11:25) of Christ (cf. Jer. 31:33) constituted the church the new and true people of God.

[10] Cf. the view of the Damascus group (The Zadokite Document, Charles' Corpus II. 802) and the Qumrân community (Dead Sea Scrolls).

[11] Rall, op. cit., pp. 152-53.

road. John the Baptist had made use of the rite in his dramatic preaching of the advent of the Day of the Lord. Jesus had himself been baptized at the hands of John, and on this occasion had experienced his call to be the Messiah. His followers, in turn, baptized new converts during the days of his own ministry, although Jesus himself presumably did not perform the act (John 4:1-2). And within the primitive church baptism was customary. At Pentecost, Peter urged those who heard him to be baptized in the name of Jesus Christ (Acts 2:38), and in the desert area toward Gaza, Philip baptized the Ethiopian eunuch as the caravan stopped at an oasis by the side of the road (Acts 8:36-38). The apostle himself was baptized following his conversion. All of this means that baptism was an accepted procedure long before Paul became a follower of Christ.[12]

Although Paul did not instigate baptism among the first-century believers, he did bring to it a significant interpretation which related Christ personally to the sacrament, and added new dimensions to its meaning. He accepted and asserted the traditional idea of cleansing which had been customarily associated with the rite. When addressing the Corinthians, Paul said: "But *you were washed*, you were sanctified, you were justified in the name of the Lord Jesus Christ and in the Spirit of our God" (I Cor. 6:11).[13] It is not claimed here that all three—cleansing, sanctification, and justification—are made real in baptism, but that baptism is a beginning step in experiencing the fullness of salvation in Christ. And in yet another way baptism is introductory; by it the convert becomes a member of the body of Christ. Through the Spirit known in the sacrament the believer is "baptized into one body" (12:13).

We err, however, if we conclude that Paul thinks of baptism as though it were only a vestibule through which entry into the larger dwelling is made. It is this, to be sure, but it is also a great deal more. By it the Christian dies to his old self and the past, while rising to a new life in Christ.[14] In baptism Christ unites himself with the believer; and the believer is joined in union with Christ so that it may be said: "We were buried therefore with him by baptism into death,

---

[12] Ablutions, including immersion, were also practiced by the Qumrân community of the Dead Sea Scrolls. Cf. Burrows, *op. cit.*, p. 236.

[13] Italics mine.

[14] "Paul saw in baptism not merely a rite of admission, but the incomprehensible reality of God's saving action in every baptized person." Martin Dibelius and Werner G. Kümmel, *Paul* (Philadelphia: The Westminster Press, 1953), p. 122.

so that as Christ was raised from the dead by the glory of the Father, we too might walk in newness of life" (Rom. 6:4). This is an allegory, but it is also a fact in experience. In saying that Christians are buried with Christ in baptism, Paul is also asserting that they have been crucified with him.

The new life into which we are raised through baptism, Paul sometimes refers to as a putting on of Christ: "For as many of you as were baptized into Christ have put on Christ" (Gal. 3:27). This again is based upon the idea of solidarity, mystically conceived, to which reference was made in interpreting the death of Christ, and also the church as the body of Christ. Christ is the head as well as the body of a corporate community. Baptism unites the believer with this body, and thus he may be said to have "put on Christ."

In all of this it should not be concluded that Paul thinks of the rite of baptism in a magical or strictly sacramental sense.[15] Here as elsewhere it is always faith which quickens the new life into being through the Spirit. At the heart of a significant reference to baptism as a burial with Christ, the apostle speaks of being "raised with him *through faith* in the working of God" (Col. 2:12).[16] In this sense baptism is a kind of recognition of belonging to Christ and an expression of the faith that already existed prior to it.

Cullmann has summarized the relation of faith to baptism in this way:

(1) *After* Baptism, faith is demanded of *all* those baptized;
(2) *before* Baptism, the declaration of faith is a sign of the divine will that Baptism take place, demanded from *adults* who individually come over from Judaism or heathenism, but in other cases lacking;
(3) *during* the baptismal act, faith is demanded of the praying *congregation*.[17]

The faith of which Paul speaks, and to which Cullmann refers, is centered in Christ as the one through whom God is at work in saving men. And this fact contributes strong features to Paul's portrait of Christ.

---

[15] For the suggestion of a sacramental view see I Pet. 3:20-21: "During the building of the ark, in which a few, that is, eight persons, were saved through water. Baptism which corresponds to this, now saves you, not as a removal of dirt from the body but as an appeal to God for a clear conscience, through the resurrection of Jesus Christ."
[16] Italics mine.
[17] *Baptism in the New Testament*, p. 55.

That baptism does not automatically (*ex opere operato*) bring a person into the perfection of life in Christ is made clear in another passage of Paul's, where he urges baptized Christians to "seek the things that are above" (Col. 3:1 ff.). In the section of Colossians where these words occur, the apostle is dealing primarily with Christian ethics. Uppermost in his mind is the thought of a life free of immorality, impurity, passion, evil desire, and covetousness. These he urges Christians to put away, since they have "put off the old nature [in baptism] with its practices and have put on the new nature, which is being renewed in knowledge after the image of its creator" (vss. 9-10). The new life, begun in baptism, should be deliberately pursued within the church, the body of Christ.

### Christ and the Lord's Supper

Just as baptism occurs "in Christ" and therefore has a bearing upon Paul's portrait of Christ, so also does the Lord's Supper. Christ is definitely known in this sacrament of the church as a specific kind of Lord and Savior, one whose character and deeds are an extension of his ministry on earth.

It is interesting to note that Paul gives us the earliest written account of the Lord's Supper, one which considerably antedates that of the Gospels (I Cor. 11:23-26). And in presenting it, he makes it clear that he is passing on a tradition which he had received. The data upon which his statement rests had already become tradition (accepted) before he had put it into his epistle.[18] Paul says that he received this "from the Lord," meaning that his statement goes back directly to the historical Jesus, rather than that he had a special revelation.

In presenting the work of Christ in the Lord's Supper, Paul is not a strict sacramentalist, even as he was not in his view of baptism. He makes this clear when, in comparing the supernatural food of the Israelites in the wilderness with the life-giving elements in the Eucharist, he notes that the act of eating the manna did not preserve the ancient Hebrews from the punishment due them because of their idolatry (I Cor. 10:1-13). Just so, there was no magic in the rite of the Lord's Supper itself whereby the Christian who sinned was delivered

---

[18] Because of Aramaisms in Mark's account, it is possible that it represents an earlier tradition than that which Paul uses, but this does not mean that the apostle's sources are untrustworthy.

from judgment. By taking the wrong attitudes toward it, and failing to discern "the body [Christ]" when partaking of the elements, Paul held that one may eat the bread and drink the cup of the Lord in an unworthy manner. This would bring upon him the judgment of the Lord himself (11:27-32).[19]

We have already considered Paul's teaching on the church as the body of Christ.[20] This conception is basic to his view of the sacraments. In baptism, by faith one is joined to the body, while in the Lord's Supper, by faith one is incorporated into the Fellowship which is his body. And just as when in baptism one is buried with Christ and participates mystically in his Lord's death and resurrection, so when one partakes of the Eucharist he enters into his Lord's death by which the new Fellowship was constituted.

This is what Paul has in mind when he inquires of the Corinthians: "The cup of blessing which we bless, is it not a participation [communion] in the blood of Christ? The bread which we break, is it not a participation [communion] in the body of Christ?" (I Cor. 10:16.) Fellowship with the cup unites the Christian with Christ in his death, and fellowship with the bread unites him with Christ in the church, which is the body.

In the light of Paul's *total* thought concerning the Lord's Supper, it seems clear that the apostle does not hold that the bread and the wine are the body and blood of Christ in a literal sense. It is as A. B. J. Higgins states when he writes: "They are a means of sharing in the body and blood of Christ, and are not equated with them." [21] But this does not indicate that Christ was not actually present with the believers who partook of the elements. As they thought of him, contemplated his death for them, and looked to him in faith and trust, his spiritual presence was brought home to their consciousness and consciences, so that they knew they had really communed with him. This is the true presence in the Eucharist.

Paul makes certain unique emphases in his presentation of the

[19] At first (cf. chap. III) the Lord's Supper was observed as a closing part of a real meal in which the brotherhood shared their food. It was thus in the Corinthian situation as found in I Cor. 11:17 ff. Later it was celebrated as a self-constituted sacrament apart from the social meal. It is difficult to say just when the Eucharist was divorced from the broader context, familiarly called the Agape or love feast. But by the time of Justin it had been combined with the preaching of the word. Cf. *Dialogue with Trypho* 41:4.

[20] Cf. pp. 82-84.

[21] *The Lord's Supper in the New Testament*, p. 70. Cf. also Vincent Taylor, *Jesus and His Sacrifice*, pp. 134 ff.

Lord's Supper which also constitute portraiture.[22] In the tradition he presents in I Cor. 11:23-26, in contrast to Mark's account, he represents Jesus as saying that his body was "broken for them." Mark has only: "This is my body" (14:22). The reference to his dying for them may be implied in the evangelist's version, or in the tradition which underlies it, but the words "broken for you" do not appear in his Gospel. Paul regarded them as true to the intent of Jesus, and as a self-interpretation of his death.

Another particular Pauline touch is that he considers the cup as the seal or sign of a new covenant. He quotes Jesus as saying: "This cup is the new covenant in my blood" (I Cor. 11:25). This is in line with Paul's frequent references to the new covenant in Christ (cf. Gal. 3:15 ff.; 4:24 ff.; Rom. 9:4; 11:27). It is held by some scholars, and with considerable justification, that we have no evidence that Jesus spoke of a covenant *in connection with the cup* at the Last Supper, even though the *idea* of such may have been in his mind. In any case, it was Paul who brought it out and made it central.[23] This view of Christ as the maker and effecter of a New Covenant adds dimensions to the portrait which are distinctive. It implies that Christ has a determinative relation to history which affects the destiny of the human race. More will be said of this later;[24] it is sufficient here to note that Paul finds this teaching at the heart of the Lord's Supper itself.

In yet another Pauline emphasis, the apostle stresses the Eucharist as a commemorative meal to be repeated regularly. Mark does not give this interpretation in so many words. This has led to a suggestion by Lietzmann that it was Paul who tailored the original passage in line with the memory feasts of the Greeks which relatives held on the anniversaries of their deaths. But since the Last Supper was probably recognized as the Passover meal by the early church, and the latter was a memorial supper, it is more likely that Paul's stress upon the Eucharist as a memorial to be repeated regularly is due to Hebraic influences.[25] Jesus may or may not in so many words have called upon

[22] In this section I am indebted particularly to Higgins, op. cit., pp. 28-37.

[23] Cf. ibid., pp. 29-34. Martin Dibelius, From Tradition to Gospel, p. 209. Cf. also W. D. Davies, Paul and Rabbinic Judaism, p. 251.

[24] Cf. pp. 102-5.

[25] Cf. Exod. 12:14; 13:3; 13:9; Deut. 16:3. The common meals of the Qumrân Community as found in the Dead Sea Scrolls, while possibly patterned from Jewish practice, do not carry the full meaning Paul finds in the Eucharist. Cf. Burrows, op. cit., pp. 332-33.

his followers to repeat the act. To do so, however, would be in line with his purpose and intention on the night of the Last Supper, and Paul's view of Christ includes the conviction that he did so direct his disciples. This would mean that believers were not only experiencing Christ in the Lord's Supper; they were also obeying him in celebrating it.

One final accent in Paul's portrait of Christ as found in his teachings on the Eucharist is that the sacred meal proclaims the Lord's death "until he comes" (I Cor. 11:26). It is an expression not only of the reality of his presence now in the church, but also of the faith in his return in the future. In this sense the Lord's Supper is an eschatological act. No doubt Paul was influenced in this view by the reported words of Jesus in Mark (cf. also Luke 22:18): "Truly, I say to you, I shall not drink again of the fruit of the vine until that day when I drink it new in the kingdom of God" (14:25). By this fact the Lord's Supper becomes a Kingdom supper and involves a view of Christ as messianic King. It is interesting to note that there is also an eschatological element in the description of a sacred meal found in the "two columns" in the Palestine Museum, probably representing an early phase of the Qumrân Movement. Here the "Messiah of Israel" is present, but he is given a place lower than the priest who blesses the bread.[26]

In this chapter we have been considering Paul's portrait of his Lord as it emerges in his conception of the church, and the sacraments of baptism and the Lord's Supper. Each centers in Christ, not only historically, but also organically. The "new life" which occurs in the souls of those who are members of the church and partake of these two sacraments comes from Christ himself, and therefore portraiture is definitely present in Paul's presentation of them.

---

[26] Cf. Burrows, op. cit., p. 237. For a contrary view cf. Theodore H. Gaster, The Dead Sea Scriptures (Garden City: Doubleday & Co., Inc., 1956), pp. 19-20.

# SEVEN

# In the Pauline Epistles: God and Eschatology

In the preceding chapter paul's portrait of christ was considered in respect to the church and the sacraments of baptism and the Lord's Supper. It remains for us to examine his conception of his Lord's relation to God, the universe, and the final consummation of history.

Paul did not live in an intellectual vacuum. In his epistles he gives every evidence of being alert to his environment. Since he was reared in the Greco-Roman world, it is logical to assume that he was familiar with its ongoing life and conversant with the ideas which were current coin among its citizens. For this reason it has long been the practice of scholars in the Pauline field to attempt an assessment of the contribution of this environment to the apostle's thinking. And this has been particularly true in respect to the Mystery Religions.[1]

### The Mystery Religions and Paul's Conception of
### Salvation in Christ

Not only as a matter of general consideration, but also as a result of Paul's use of specific words and conceptions, the conclusion that he owed much to the mysteries has been advanced. The words often cited include *mustērion* (mystery), *teleios* (full grown, fully accomplished), *sōtēria* (salvation), *sophia* (wisdom), and *gnōsis* (knowledge). The ideas and practices frequently referred to in this connection include rebirth, the dying and rising of a savior-god, divination, ablutions, and sacred meals. Myths involving Attis, Osiris, and Adonis are pointed out as contributing to Paul's thought in this regard. Among the other mysteries which come under consideration are those at Eleusis and the cults of Mithras and Dionysius.

[1] The bibliography here is large. Cf. H. A. A. Kennedy, *St. Paul and the Mystery Religions*; Samuel Angus, *The Mystery Religions and Christianity*; Frederick J. Foakes-Jackson and Kirsopp Lake, *The Beginnings of Christianity*; William Fairweather, *Jesus and the Greeks*; Bousset, *op. cit.*

Several considerations have led recent scholars to minimize earlier claims of the determinative influences of the mysteries upon Paul's thought of Christ and the salvation that was known in him. Even though he was reared in a Hellenistic world, he was born and taught in the home of a Jew, and this implies a firm monotheistic background. And it was from the ranks of the strictest sect of the Jews, the Pharisees, that he entered the Christian Fellowship.

In addition to this, it is now believed that many of the mysteries did not fully develop into popular religions, widely accepted, until after Paul's time. Because of this, as Schweitzer writes: "Paul cannot have known the mystery-religions in the form in which they are known to us, because in this fully-developed form they did not yet exist." [2] And, it is further significant to note that among Christian writers down to the close of the second century, marked references to the mysteries are conspicuous for their absence. These include Clement, Hermas, and the apologists as a group. This fact argues against their influence upon Paul.

Our purpose here does not warrant a detailed study of his subject. But there are certain facts that should be pointed out which are pertinent. (1) Paul stressed moral regeneration; the mysteries did not place their emphasis here. (2) He was not a pantheist; some aspects of the mysteries involved this outlook. (3) His use of similar words does not carry the meaning assigned to them in the mysteries. For example, the word "mystery" for Paul customarily does not mean a kept secret, but rather a revealed one. (4) The apostle was not a strict sacramentalist; salvation in the mysteries assigned magical powers to the rites. (5) For him salvation was contingent upon faith; the mysteries did not teach this. (6) And finally, Paul at all times took a firm stand against syncretism with pagan cults; this would rule out an interest in borrowing from the mysteries.

The heart of Paul's religion is Christ, as known in history, present in the primitive church, realized in his own religious experience, and interpreted within the framework of the Christian Fellowship itself. What may appear to the surface reader or to the academic theorist to be borrowing from the mysteries, may usually best be explained as a general reflection of the language and outlook of the Greco-Roman world in his time. As a religious writer today might introduce,

[2] Cf. Schweitzer, *Paul and His Interpreters* (New York: The Macmillan Co., 1951), pp. 191-92.

now and again, scientific terminology which was familiar to his readers, without subscribing himself to a specific scientific theory or conclusion, just so, Paul employed the language of his day in presenting Christ to the Greco-Roman world. And as a part of this language, phrases and expressions from the Mystery Religions were present.

### Christ Pre-Existent

In view of the singular features in Paul's portrait of Christ which have been interpreted in these chapters, it is not surprising that he also ascribed pre-existence to his Lord. Much speculation has occurred concerning the source of his teaching, it being felt that it must bear some relationship to the thought-forms of the first century. This approach has merit as long as it is not assumed that Paul merely borrowed the idea from his environment in order to round out an abstract system of thought.

Actually, the initial incentive in the direction of this conclusion concerning Christ is to be found in the salvation which came to Paul as he looked in faith to him as Lord, participated in the sacraments, and lived within the Fellowship which was his body. The experience of God which the apostle knew "in Christ" pointed toward conclusions concerning his Lord that were distinctive and exalted. His pre-existence was one of these. As God was eternal, so must this one be, through whom he was so transcendently known.

Once this truth was intuitively grasped, it was inevitable that Paul should discover that it was involved in and confirmed by the thought-forms of his own time. For instance, basic to his conception of Christ's pre-existence is the fact that the Jews customarily ascribed this characteristic to both men and things, for example, Moses, Jerusalem, the Law, the Sabbath, the Temple, and the Tabernacle. Why not then of Christ?

More specifically, Christ's pre-existence as interpreted by Paul may be said to be explained by his identification of Jesus with the pre-existent eschatological "Son of man." This idea was probably held in an individualized form by Jesus himself,[3] and the early church looked for his early return in glory from heaven. We know also that Paul expected the second advent of his Lord (I Cor. 7:29; 15:47; Rom. 13:11 ff.).

Another possibility is that Paul identified Christ with *the heavenly*

---

[3] Cf. my *Life and Teachings of Jesus*, ch. XIV.

94

man of the current Hellenistic myth. This conception, which had its origin in Persia, interpreted the origin of man by referring to the descent from heaven of a Primal Man.[4] Paul's knowledge of this myth may be questioned, however, on the ground that the apostle's background was essentially Hebraic and his thought-forms biblical.

A further explanation of Paul's specific formulation of his idea of Christ's pre-existence may be sought in the Hebrew conception of Wisdom. In a Colossian passage the apostle associates his Lord with the divine Wisdom of the Old Testament (1:15-17) which was pre-existent and participated in the act of creation.[5] When Christ is thus related to Wisdom, his pre-existence is logically accounted for. The same is true when he is associated with the divine glory (I Cor. 11:7; Eph. 1:17), and the divine word (John 1:1). Each of these is also represented in Hebrew thought as pre-existent.

### A Significant Pauline Passage
### Phil. 2:5-11

The pre-existence of Christ is taught in several significant Pauline passages. When it is claimed that the Lord Jesus Christ was once rich and became poor in order that he might make others rich (II Cor. 8:9), it is implied. This is likewise true of the passage which equates the supernatural rock from which the Israelites drank with Christ (I Cor. 10:4), and the statement in Romans that God sent his Son "in the likeness of sinful flesh" (8:3). These references are found in what may be regarded as the letters from Paul's middle period, suggesting that acceptance of this idea was not in the apostle's thinking solely at the close of his ministry.

It is in the letters from the later period, however, that the pre-existence of Christ receives its fullest exposition. For instance, the kenotic passage from Philippians, already referred to,[6] has this to say of Christ:

Who, though he was in the form of God, did not count equality with God a thing to be grasped, but emptied himself, taking the form of a servant, being born in the likeness of men. And being found in human form he humbled himself and became obedient unto death, even death on a

---

[4] Cf. Bousset, op. cit., 2nd ed., pp. 140 ff. Also Reitzenstein, Poimandres, pp. 81 ff.

[5] Cf. Prov. 8:22 ff.; Sirach 24:3 ff.; 42:21 ff.; 24:19, 22; Enoch 30:8. The Colossian passage will be considered in greater detail later in this chapter.

[6] Cf. p. 59.

cross. Therefore God has highly exalted him and bestowed on him the name which is above every name, that at the name of Jesus every knee should bow, in heaven and on earth and under the earth, and every tongue confess that Jesus Christ is Lord, to the glory of God the Father. (2: 6-11.) [7]

Not only does this passage say that Christ was pre-existent; it also indicates that in this state he was "in the form of God." This expression should be read correlatively with the phrase "in the form of a servant" which also occurs in the passage. Christ was not actually a servant, although he appeared to be. He was without sin, despite the fact that he was born into sinful humanity. In this same sense Christ was not originally God, although he appeared from all eternity to be divine. Paul is probably contending that the existences of God and Christ were of the same kind, but it is to be doubted whether he had a fully developed metaphysics in mind.

The reference to "equality with God" as "a thing to be grasped" by Christ in this Philippian passage may be interpreted either as a state already possessed,[8] or as a prize to be seized or clutched in the future.[9] When the latter (to me the preferred) view is taken, the prize is not to be grasped by force or violence; instead it is to be possessed through self-humiliation.

I have referred already to this humiliation when I discussed Paul's interest in the historical Jesus. By coming to earth in the form of a slave (doulos) and being born as a man, the sacrifice of his former glory began. But there was more; in accordance with the Father's will, Christ accepted the Cross. He was obedient unto death. Throughout all of this, including his pre-existent life "in the form of God" and his earthly life "in the form of a servant," Christ was self-determinative. He chose his course and pursued it through his own free will. It was not forced upon him.

It is here that the moral significance of the Incarnation, from the standpoint of Christ himself, emerges in Paul's portrait. Sometimes

[7] Ernst Lohmeyer regards this as a pre-Pauline hymn, a psalm of the Kyrios originating not on Hellenistic but on Palestinian soil. Héring thinks it was first written in Aramaic to be used in the churches of Syria. In any case, its ideas seem to be Pauline, and its inclusion here by Paul implies assent to its views.

[8] Cf. Joseph B. Lightfoot, St. Paul's Epistle to the Philippians, p. 110; Gifford, The Incarnation: A Study of Philippians 2:5-11.

[9] Cf. James Robertson, "Philippians," Abingdon Bible Commentary (Nashville: Abingdon Press, 1929), p. 1244.

it is assumed that the apostle is a theologizer, and that Christ is but a factor in a theological formula instead of a moral person making real decisions in his presentation. The Philippian passage should dispel this notion. It is the fullness of Paul's thought about Christ, the varied character of his approach, and the depth of his understanding that may give this misleading impression. No other biblical writer has sounded the significance and meaning of Christ from as many different angles as has Paul. And basic to each representation is the Christ who as a moral person became obedient to God, obedient unto the death on the cross.

Because of this obedience to the Father, God highly exalted Christ, and "bestowed on him the name which is above every name, that at the name of Jesus every knee should bow, in heaven and on earth and under the earth, and every tongue confess that Jesus Christ is Lord, to the glory of God the Father" (Phil. 2:9-11). Behind the writing of these words are more than two decades of Christian experience. The Resurrection and Ascension have taken place. The Spirit has been sent. The primitive church has known Christ as exalted Messiah and present Lord. Paul himself has entered the new life in Christ in answer to his summons on the Damascus road. Therefore what the apostle is saying concerning the exaltation of Christ is not speculation but a matter of history and autobiography. It has already occurred.

Through obedience Christ has been exalted to a place even higher than that which he had held before coming to earth. The prize to be clutched or seized in the future is his. He also holds a more elevated position than he knew on earth before his resurrection. And at the mention of his name divine honors are to be accorded him throughout the universe. Now he may be said to have both the name and the nature of Godhead, whereas before he had only the nature.

### An Additional Pauline Passage
### Col. 1:15-20

Another significant passage in relation to Christ's pre-existence, also from Paul's later period, is found in Col. 1:15-20:

He is the image of the invisible God, the first-born of all creation; for in him all things were created, in heaven and on earth, visible and invisible, whether thrones or dominions or principalities or authorities—all things were created through him and for him. He is before all things, and in him all things hold together. He is the head of the body, the church;

97

he is the beginning, the first-born from the dead, that in everything he might be preëminent. For in him all the fullness of God was pleased to dwell, and through him to reconcile to himself all things, whether on earth or in heaven, making peace by the blood of his cross.

As in the statement from Philippians, these verses imply not only that Christ was pre-existent, but also that he possesses a cosmic significance and holds a unique relation to God. He was the agent of creation, sustains its existence, and is the image of God.

Dodd has paraphrased this passage thus:

Christ is the divine Agent both of the original creation of the universe and of its ultimate unification under the rule of God. In the former aspect, he is the "image" of God (spoken of in Gen. 1:27); he is prior in time and therefore in dignity to all created beings; by his energy not only the visible world, but its unseen rulers were brought into being; and as he existed before the universe so he maintains it in being. In the latter aspect, the totality of Godhead resides in him, so as (through his sacrificial death) to reconcile all warring elements in the universe, including the warring powers of the unseen world.[10]

This Colossian statement strikes the reader as being highly speculative and philosophical, but its purpose was intensely practical. The ever-present danger of weakening the Christian Faith by combining it with other beliefs in the environment, including the worship of angels (Col. 2:18), called, from time to time, for a sharpening of the conceptions which the church held. An incipient Gnosticism was threatening to dispel the unique place of Christ in the relation of God to the universe. Between "heaven and earth" a host of intermediary beings as emanations of deity were being substituted for the one Christ Jesus. Had this view prevailed, in time the Lord would have become just one among many such emanations, and the Christian gospel would have thinned out into a generalized religious philosophy.

A scientific age such as ours should have no difficulty in understanding the impulse by which in the early church Jesus of Nazareth ultimately became thought of as a cosmic Christ. They had found Jesus to be the source of life in their inner being. He had overcome the hostile forces which they believed were arrayed against them—demons, powers, and principalities. Death and the grave could not hold him; he was alive and present as power and spiritual sustenance

[10] "Colossians," *The Abingdon Bible Commentary*, p. 1253. Used by permission.

in their lives. Through faith in him and his Cross forgiveness had been experienced, and righteousness before God had been bestowed upon them as they believed, by grace, from his nail-pierced hands. Such benefits as these could only be explained in terms of God and the universe itself, and the Christ through whom they had been made real must therefore have cosmic significance. As Kümmel puts it, "Paul therefore emphasises here [the Colossian passage], not only Christ's lordship over all the powers of this world, but also, with a greater clearness than we find elsewhere, his all-embracing importance in the whole universe." [11]

The thought-forms and vocabulary through and by which Paul expresses the cosmic significance of Christ are those which were immediately at hand. For instance, parallels to his statements concerning Christ as the image of God may be found in the Wisd. of Sol. (7:22-23) where Wisdom is described as "an image of his goodness." Paul had already referred to Christ as "the wisdom of God" (I Cor. 1:24), so that the transfer of the attributes of Wisdom to his Lord was logical. Wisdom was also regarded as pre-existent in Prov. 8:22: "The Lord created me [Wisdom] at the beginning of his work." This provides a background for the statement here that "He [Christ] is before all things," a reference to his pre-existence.[12]

When Paul says then "in him [Christ] all the fullness of God was pleased to dwell," he makes use of a contemporary gnostic conception of the *pleroma*; or the totality of spiritual "beings," "aeons,'" "powers," and so on, that were believed to exist as emanations of deity between God and man. This fullness or *pleroma* of the Godhead the apostle insists is to be found instead in Christ. There is no need for intermediaries. Christ is pre-eminent as the creator of the all that is, including any such aeons as might exist.

### Christ and God

Because of the high view of Christ which Paul held, the titles he ascribes to him, and the statements he makes concerning his place in the universe and in man's salvation, one is led to inquire whether the apostle believed that his Lord was actually God. In answering this

[11] *Op. cit.*, p. 140.

[12] Another possible meaning is "chief of all things," although "before all things" in the sense of priority is probably to be preferred since Christ is also referred to here as the "first-born from the dead."

question, it is easy to read back into Paul's words later theological conclusions. But to those who are familiar with the creedmaking of the church, and at the same time well versed in Pauline thought, it is clear that Paul is moving in the direction of the statement of the Godhead which finally prevailed rather than himself taking the full position of Nicaea. He prefigures this view in such a fashion that one must conclude that his writings are basic to it, although they do not state it in so many words.

In one particular statement Paul has been translated in such a way as to refer to Christ as God. The King James Version of Rom. 9:5 reads: "As concerning the flesh Christ came, who is over all, God blessed for ever. Amen." Although this reading is supported by no lesser authorities than Sanday and Headlam, another form is preferred in the Revised Standard Version: "According to the flesh, is the Christ. God who is over all be blessed for ever. Amen." This translation is favored by Westcott and Hort. Since the early Greek manuscripts were not punctuated, other factors besides grammar are decisive. The R.S.V. reading regards the final part of the statement as a doxology, and the "Amen" at its close argues for this interpretation of the text.

The decision as to whether Paul regarded Christ as God, however, does not rest upon one verse and the consideration of its punctuation. Rather it is a matter of the apostle's total view of Christ as based upon a wide reading of his epistles. On the one hand, he places Christ upon the divine side of life or being. He existed "in the form of God" prior to the Incarnation (Phil. 2:6); he is "the image of the invisible God" (Col. 1:15); "in him all things were created" (vs. 16); "He is before all things, and in him all things hold together" (vs. 17); "in him all the fullness of God was pleased to dwell" (vs. 19). Paul would not and could not have made these statements of any other person. His Lord was utterly unique in this regard.

In addition to these divine attributes, Paul refers to Christ as "the Lord of glory" (I Cor. 2:8), an expression applied to God in Enoch (25:7). He is the beloved Son of God (Col. 1:13) to whom the Kingdom belonged, a conception that in Paul moves beyond the traditional messianic view. He is also "the last Adam" who creates a new humanity, the source of the "life-giving spirit" (I Cor. 15:45), in contrast to the first Adam who was the source of the natural life in

100

his descendants.[13] And at the final judgment Christ will preside, "on that day when, according to my gospel, God judges the secrets of men by Christ Jesus" (Rom. 2:16). Again, in these references Paul assigns to Christ attributes and functions which belong to God himself.

On the other hand, there is in the apostle's conception of Christ a subordination of the Son to the Father which precludes his equating him with God, even though he regards him as divine. In Corinthians it is stated that "the head of Christ is God" (I Cor. 11:3); again, it is said that "Christ is God's" (3:23). Later, Paul indicates that Christ was subservient to God in that he "became obedient unto death." Because of this, every tongue shall confess him as Lord, but this confession shall be "to the glory of God the Father" (Phil. 2:8-11). Outstanding among Paul's passages which subordinate Christ to God is his representation of the end of the Age. At this time, "When alll things are subjected to him [Christ], then the Son himself will also be subjected to him who put all things under him, that God may be everything to every one" (I Cor. 15:28). Clearly, then, Paul thought of Christ not as God himself but as subject to him.

And yet, when all of this is pointed out, it must be said that Paul so far lifted Christ above humanity, and so far represented him as exercising the functions of God himself, that he *all but* named him God. In the trinitarian benediction, for example, "The grace of the Lord Jesus Christ and the love of God and the fellowship of the Holy Spirit be with you all" (II Cor. 13:14), the apostle moves in this direction. This is not yet the full doctrine of the Trinity, as defined later in the creeds, but it is the basis in experience for it.

What was it that kept Paul from going all the way in calling Christ, God? It may have been his background of Jewish monotheism which caused him to desist. Again, he may have held back for fear of appearing to be saying no more than the Mystery Religions were stating in their myths concerning their hero-gods. Christ was so far beyond these representations that to imply a parallelism to them would be hopelessly to mislead. Or it may be that Paul simply could not find the formula for expressing his conviction. The struggle, almost two centuries later, to arrive at the conception of unity in trinity and

---

[13] Cf. Gen. 2:7. Was Paul basing this interpretation on a midrashic interpretation of this text, which he found being used among the Christians? Cf. Burney, *The Aramaic Origin of the Fourth Gospel*, p. 46.

trinity in unity indicates how great the problem of stating this particular truth was—and is.

## The Final Consummation

We have seen how Paul's portrait of Christ represents him as having a determinative role in man's salvation. In area after area his Lord speaks the final word, performs the final act, and holds the ultimate office in man's relation to God and the universe. He stands on the divine side of life, and has the value of God himself in the experience of his followers. The apostle all but equates him with God.

Since Christ has a cosmic relation to the universe, as both to its creation and to its sustenance, it is logical to conclude that he has a cosmic office in redemption. In everything he is pre-eminent (Col. 1:18). Traditionally the Jews thought of redemption as a cosmic as well as a religious fact. Their eschatological hope included the renewal of the creation, the judgment of spiritual beings or agencies such as angels, powers, principalities, and demons, and the realization of the final destiny of man.

What might be called the doctrine of the two ages is central in this consideration. The first or present age was under the curse of sin and therefore evil. Even the material order had been corrupted by man's disobedience to God. This is not the Greek view of the evil character of materiality, but is essentially a moral conception within Hebrew thought (Gen. 3:17). The present age, however, will give way to a new one at the time of the Judgment (Enoch 91:16); creation itself will be renewed (Apocalypse of Baruch 32:6). In Isaiah (66:22) it is expressed in this fashion:

> For as the new heaven and the new earth
> which I will make
> shall remain before me, says the Lord;
> so shall your descendants and your name remain.

The prophet expected that the Lord God would bring this to pass.[14] Centuries later the seer of Patmos was also to write of a new heaven and a new earth (Rev. 21:1-2). In the meantime, the present age was thought to be under the control of agencies which had originally been created by God, but had later become wicked in their own pursuits.

[14] Cf. also Isa. 65:17. "For behold, I create new heavens and a new earth; and the former things shall not be remembered or come into mind."

Paul inherited this eschatological outlook and accepted it, by and large, as the pattern within which he did his thinking concerning the final consummation. And it was within this framework, also, that he drew his portrait of Christ in regard to the end of the Age. Passages from his epistles clearly bear evidence as to the Hebraic background of the apostle's conception at this point, even though he transmutes it by placing Christ at the center of the picture.

For instance, Paul refers to the creation as waiting "with eager longing for the revealing of the sons of God" (Rom. 8:19); even until now it had been "groaning in travail" (vs. 22). Death had spread to all men through one man's sin (5:12), and the present order of things that are seen is but temporary (II Cor. 4:18). It is not only temporary, but it is now under the control of "the spiritual hosts of wickedness in the heavenly places" (Eph. 6:12). Reference has been made already to the thralldom within which men were believed to be held by a host of demoniacal agencies.[15] Gentiles as well as Jews were subservient to these powers; in fact, a leading element in the sin of Gentiles was that they had worshiped these "weak and beggarly elemental spirits" (Gal. 4:9) as though they were God himself.

Into this cosmic situation Christ had come, and already he had, in part, brought salvation. Through the Cross the evil forces were being destroyed, principalities and powers disarmed (Col. 2:15), and triumph over the world rulers of this present darkness was being achieved (Eph. 6:12). Final victory, however, lay ahead, not that the present deliverance was unreal, or that a person who was now "in Christ" possessed only a seeming salvation—not that, but the issue would not be ultimately and eternally settled until these hostile agencies in the universe were destroyed. This included death itself, which is almost personalized by Paul.

When the end comes in this cosmic struggle, the apostle asserts that it will be Christ who shall subject these spiritual hosts of evil, put them "under his feet" and win.[16] In a significant passage from his letter to the Corinthians, Paul envisions the final consummation in this fashion:

[15] Cf. pp. 72-73.

[16] Cf. Kennedy, *St. Paul's Conception of the Last Things*, ad loc. Although this is not a new work, it has real value. A more recent volume that is helpful is H. A. Guy, *The New Testament Doctrine of Last Things*, ad loc.

Then comes the end, when he delivers the kingdom to God the Father after destroying every rule and every authority and power. For he must reign until he has put all his enemies under his feet. The last enemy to be destroyed is death. "For God has put all things in subjection under his feet." But when it says, "All things are put in subjection under him," it is plain that he is excepted who put all things under him. When all things are subjected to him, then the Son himself will also be subjected to him who put all things under him, that God may be everything to every one. (I Cor. 15:24-28.)

The all-inclusiveness of this victory is phenomenal. Redemption here has a cosmic character in which the supremacy of God is ultimately realized.

It is at Christ's return from heaven that the finality of salvation will be realized. At this time "God's righteous judgment will be revealed" (Rom. 2:5). But it shall be made known through Christ "who will bring to light the things now hidden in darkness and will disclose the purposes of the heart" (I Cor. 4:5). Paul believed that all must appear "before the judgment seat of Christ, so that each one may receive good or evil, according to what he has done in the body" (II Cor. 5:10). In this way Christ is Lord "both of the dead and of the living" (Rom. 14:9).

Paul's conception of cosmic salvation through Christ was so far reaching that it even included the redemption of the body itself. Toward the end of his ministry he wrote to the Philippians of the need to eschew those who were enemies of Christ, and who lived for the things of the belly with their minds set on earthly pleasures. Not so with the Christian, the apostle urged; his commonwealth was to be in heaven, from which he awaited the coming of a Savior, the Lord Jesus Christ. And when he comes, he "will change our lowly body to be like his glorious body, by the power which enables him even to subject all things to himself" (3:21).

In writing to the Romans, the apostle also spoke of waiting for the redemption of the body (8:23). He does not contemplate a spirit divorced from the body, as among the Greeks, nor the reconstitution of the physical body, as among the Hebrews. Instead Paul conceives of a spiritual body (I Cor. 15:42-50). At the trumpet's sound the dead will be raised imperishable, and those living will be changed, since flesh and blood cannot inherit the kingdom of God (I Cor. 15:51 ff.). This is a new conception, and what is significant here is that it has

104

its roots in Christ. Through him the transformation is to be effected, and the spiritual body is to be like his own glorious body (Rom. 8:29).

Redemption in Christ, as Paul views it, is complete when the Christian reaches the state in which he is always to be with his Lord. On one occasion the apostle contemplated whether it was better to remain on earth or to be in heaven. He concluded that the latter was preferable because it meant to be with Christ (Phil. 1:23). Some years earlier, in fact in one of his very first letters, the apostle wrote that at the return of Christ, the faithful on earth would be caught up into the air to meet the Lord and thus always to be with him (I Thess. 4:17). As the Christian on earth found his fulfillment in Christ, so in heaven he shall find his supreme joy in being with the Lord forever.

Throughout the epistles Paul does not spend much time in developing detailed pictorializations of final events, as in the Revelation to John. In the Thessalonian correspondence, however, he briefly presents such a portrayal in the interest of helping those who were concerned over the fate of Christians who had already died before the return of Christ. It was feared that they would lose out in the glory that was to be revealed. The apostle assures them that this is not the case. In fact, "the dead in Christ will rise first" (I Thess. 4:13-18) to meet the Lord when he comes.

An additional representation of events related to the return of Christ is found in II Thess. 2:1-12. It too was called into being in order to help those in the church who were upset over the question of the Lord's coming again. From a practical standpoint the passage counsels them to the effect that they should be on guard and patient. The Day of the Lord had not yet come. A restraining power was preventing the lawless one from revealing himself, and therefore the end of the Age was not yet upon them. A great apostasy must precede this event.

### A Note on Paul's Missionary Preaching in Acts

The Pauline epistles were written in the midst of a strenuous missionary activity. In analyzing their ideas, this is sometimes forgotten. Even during the times of imprisonment, whether in Caesarea, Ephesus, or Rome, there was a constant missionary outreach. In view of this it is of interest to inquire what Paul said when present on the field. A logical assumption is that he spoke in their presence along the very same lines that he wrote when absent from them. His writings consistently imply this. An author who dictated so much of his work, pacing the floor (as I think) in the very act, must have spoken to an audience much as he did when dictating. It is not difficult to assume, when one reads the literary results, that he actually brought the people to whom he wrote before him in mind as he did so. To this degree the epistles are missionary preaching.

In addition to this, we have in the Acts of the Apostles a record of some of Paul's messages to the people. The same background considerations to which attention was called in connection with the material and speeches for the primitive church, as reported in Acts, would apply here also. There is this difference, however; it is likely that the presence of Luke, the author, on some of these later occasions provides us with a more immediate source to undergird the material. If the passages in which the author uses "we," the first person instead of the third, imply that he was a part of the narrative he tells, then Luke was on hand during much of Paul's second and third missionary journeys.[17] Actually there is some reason to conclude that he was with Paul, even when the "we" passages are not a part of the record.

It is thoughtful in this connection to inquire whether the reported words of Paul in Acts are in line with his teachings in the epistles. Differences between Acts and Paul's writings in regard to chronology and other matters are well known, although probably more has been made of them in assessing the value of Acts than is warranted, when practical considerations have been allowed. Certainly they are not fatal to the significance of Acts as a whole.[18]

A lengthy and detailed study of Paul's teaching in Acts concerning Christ as compared with that of the epistles is not possible at this point. It does not modify the portrait already drawn in these chapters, particularly since the letters are primary sources for Paul's thinking and the Acts is a secondary source. A few general statements of comparison will, however, be of value.

Many of the recurrent themes of the epistles are found in the statements ascribed to Paul in Acts. Jesus is recognized as having a Davidic ancestry and is the very one promised to the fathers (13:23). It is pointed out that he was crucified by the rulers of the Jews and that he rose from the dead (13:27-32; 17:31). Forgiveness of sins is offered

[17] The "we" sections include Acts 16:10-17; 20:5-15; 21:1-18; 27:1-28:16.
[18] For an incisive study of these considerations cf. John Knox, *Chapters in a Life of Paul*, pp. 13-43, 61-73.

through Jesus (13:38), as well as a deliverance which the Law could not bring (vs. 39). This is made real through faith (13:39; 16:31). There is to be a day of judgment in which righteousness is central, and this judgment will be through Christ (17:31). The Gentiles as well as the Jews have had a revelation from God through nature (14:16-17; 17:24-28).

Such teachings as these can be paralleled in Paul's writings. They belong to the Pauline family of ideas. On the other hand, in Acts they lack the substance with which the apostle himself clothes them. As such they are reminiscent of Peter's and Stephen's preaching in the primitive church. The developed Christology of the epistles is missing. Jesus is Savior, to be sure, but the deeper implications of his person are not drawn. And we miss such themes as justification in its more robust form. Surely, if all we could know about the content of Paul's preaching depended upon Acts alone, we would be poor indeed.

What can be said concerning this lack in Luke's account? It should not be concluded that Luke seriously misrepresented Paul by introducing numerous extraneous doctrines which the apostle did not hold. On the other hand, his lack of fullness, and in some cases depth, in presenting Paul's message can partially be explained by the nature of the task which confronted him. At best he could attempt only a sketchy representation in an ongoing narrative. In addition, the character of the situations to which the apostle was speaking did not warrant the depth of analysis which is found in the epistles. And finally there is an appropriateness between the words that Luke reports Paul as speaking and the occasions on which he says them.

# EIGHT

# In the Synoptic Gospels: Their Situational Character

IN APPROACHING THE SYNOPTIC PORTRAIT OF JESUS, IT SHOULD NOT BE forgotten that the Gospels look back upon the "days of his flesh" through the eyes of a mature faith that had been developing during several decades of Christian experience. Their theme had been warmed by the fires of a personal loyalty to Christ as Lord. Each author compiled, edited, and wrote as a person who was committed to him.

Probably all the letters of Paul had been written prior to the composition of Mark's Gospel in its circulated form. How widely these documents had been read by this time is a matter of conjecture. Possibly not so much attention had been paid to them as they were later to receive when they were, presumably, brought together in a separate collection.[1] But it should not be seriously doubted that they were considerably known when the gospel writers were at work. And this means that the high view of Jesus as the exalted Christ who held a unique place in relation to God and the universe was current in the church by the time the Synoptic Gospels were written.

### Portraiture, Not Biography

What we find in the Synoptic Gospels is portraiture rather than biography. There are wide gaps in the narrative, gaps which we might wish had been filled, and which later the apocryphal Gospels sought to bridge.[2] Only one brief account is given of an event in the boyhood of Jesus when he was twelve years old and visited Jerusalem with his parents (Luke 2:41-51). With this exception, after meeting him at his birth and as a small infant (Matt. 1–2; Luke 1:5–2:38), we are given no further information concerning him until as a man of about thirty years (Luke 3:23) he presents himself to John the Baptist for

[1] Cf. Goodspeed, An Introduction to the New Testament, ch. xiii.
[2] Cf. The Gospel According to the Egyptians, The Gospel According to the Hebrews, The Gospel of Peter, and The Gospel of Thomas.

baptism. And yet these years are the time of decision for growing persons. During this period they select their professions, choose their mates, and build a pattern of thinking and living which usually holds throughout adulthood.

Furthermore, within the narrative of his ministry there are many background details that belong to the writing of biography which are missing. Notations of time and place are exceptionally brief. The sequential relation of event to event is often left undefined. It is difficult to determine whether Jesus' ministry lasted less than a year, a year and then some, or three years, as is traditionally held on the basis of the mention in John's Gospel of three visits to Jerusalem for the Passover Feast. Reference to the seasons of the year are scant, and it is only by implication that we are sometimes able to place an event.

All of this undergirds the conclusion that what we have in the Synoptic Gospels is portraiture rather than biography. They might be called psychographs in which the mind, message, and work of Jesus are presented, with some interpretation as to their significance for faith. The facts told a story, and the story had a meaning—a divine meaning involving God, salvation, history, immortality, and the end of the Age. This totality constituted the Christian message itself, and with this message the Gospels are finally concerned.

### Origins of the Gospel Portrait

The gospel portrait of Jesus began to take shape and form earlier than the writing and compilation of the Synoptic Gospels. During the days of the primitive church, to which reference has already been made,[3] Jesus was known and remembered within the context of a growing community that owed its life to him, and centered in his living presence as exalted Lord. We are particularly indebted to an approach to the study of the New Testament documents known as "form criticism" (formgeschichte) for the insights concerned in the pragmatic factors which motivated the gathering and formulation of the gospel tradition. Although it is primarily a study of the literary forms,[4] which the gospel material assumed in its earlier stages before

---

[3] Cf. pp. 38-52.

[4] Different writers in this field, while agreeing in principle and approach, attach different names to the several literary forms indicated. E. F. Scott classifies them as: "(1) miracle stories; (2) 'paradigms' or 'pronouncement stories'; (3) aphorisms; (4) tales; (5) legends; (6) controversies; (7) apocalyptic utterances." Cf. The Validity of the Gospel Record, p. 119.

its inclusion in the Gospels themselves, great emphasis is placed upon the life situation or setting (*Sitz im Leben*) out of which the tradition came and to which it was related.

Scholars majoring here include Bultmann, Dibelius, Schmidt, Taylor, Scott, Redlich, and Grant. In the view of some of these writers the life situation involved in the formulation of the tradition looms so large that it all but obliterates the historical reality of the portrait of Jesus. Bultmann, for instance, contends that an accurate picture of his personality is impossible.[5] What we have is a community interpretation of Jesus rather than a historical representation. Not all would agree fully with this negative conclusion. While recognizing the place of the Christian community in the compiling of the tradition, they do not regard it as completely fatal to historical knowledge.[6]

It seems to me that it is a distinct gain rather than a loss to recognize the place of the Christian community in the formulation of the gospel portrait of Jesus. From one standpoint, because the early church cared, he counted, and through its care, his character and nature are revealed. The lines of the portrait came into focus, not in a vacuum, but within a historical context in which both fact and meaning are merged.

For instance, most form critics agree that the account of Jesus' last days in Jerusalem was among the first of the traditions to take form. There was a reason for this. It was not simply that the Cross was the most dramatic event in the Lord's life; this it surely was, but a deeper reason must be sought. Among the Jewish Christians in the very beginning, the Cross remained a stumbling block.[7] The Law had branded a crucified one as accursed, and yet they had experienced new life at the hands of a living Lord who had been crucified. How should this seeming contradiction be resolved? The answer to this question was sought and found in Jesus' own understanding of the mission of the Cross, as the tradition concerning it was gathered and studied.[8] This analysis does not imply that the Christian community

[5] "A New Approach to the Synoptic Problem," *Journal of Religion*, 1926, p. 359.

[6] Cf. Vincent Taylor, *Formation of the Gospel Tradition*, ad loc.; Dibelius, *Gospel Criticism and Christology*, ad loc.

[7] Reference has already been made to this issue and its relation to the gospel tradition. Cf. p. 59.

[8] Some would suggest that the "understanding" here was the church's rather than Jesus'. This is largely a matter of opinion and depends somewhat, though not altogether, upon the total viewpoint concerning gospel origins of the person holding it.

freely composed the story of the Cross in order to solve a problem. Rather, it holds that as they faced the data before them in the light of their dilemma, they discovered the needed answer. Accordingly the account of the last days in Jerusalem came into being. A certain slant may have been given to it because of the motive behind the compiling of the record, but this need not mark it as basically unhistorical.

A further illustration of this procedure may be found in the issue which faced the early Christians concerning their relation to official Jewish practices. Now that they had become followers of Christ, what should they do in regard to keeping the Sabbath, fasting, and other such matters? Was there an answer in the tradition which they possessed concerning Jesus? Perhaps they might find in this data, oral or written, a record of what he said and did in his personal contact with the scribes and Pharisees which would provide needed guidance in their own case. To this end, a search was made, and situations involving this issue were discovered. I suggest that some such process as this accounts for the collection of stories found in Mark 2:1–3:6, each of which has to do with Jesus' relation with official Judaism. Here were precedents for such a stand as they must take. And once again we are able to see how the gospel portrait of Jesus came into existence in connection with actual situations which the early church faced.

### The Gospels Are Situational

Not only are the separate units of the tradition related to the life of the Christian community as it sought to define its own faith in the face of the immediate situation, but also the Gospels themselves should be regarded as situational. They too were composed and edited in relation to the demands of the environment which confronted the church. There was a reason for their appearance at a specific time and place, as well as for their character. This, in part, accounts for their vitality. They are alive at the point of personal and community needs, and they present the account of Jesus the Christ as the specific for meeting them. Here portraiture emerges.

### The Gospel of Mark

Without developing in detail the background for our conclusions concerning authorship, date and place of composition of the Synop-

tics, data which may be found in the commentaries and introductions to the New Testament, a brief analysis of the situation
underlying each will be helpful. The Gospel of Mark, for instance,
should be regarded as Roman in origin, written shortly after the
Neronian persecutions and just prior to the Jewish wars. It was a
time of controversy, rejection, and martyrdom. Both Peter and Paul
had recently lost their lives for the Faith.[9] Other nameless Christians
had been persecuted unto death, and there was the prospect of cross-
bearing in the immediate future. It was a heroic hour calling for
testimony through deeds and direct action.

To meet such a situation as this, John Mark, companion of Peter
himself, prepared the Gospel which bears his name.[10] He offered to
his readers Jesus Christ, the Son of God, as the answer to the dilemma
they faced. Here was one whose divine power was equal to their needs.
Had he not cast out demons (1:23-27; 3:11-12; 7:25-30) and overcome even the death which political authorities had meted out to
him (16:1-8)? Was he not powerful in controversy (2:1–3:6), and
did he not predict that his followers must face suffering courageously
(8:34-38)? Just as there was a divine purpose and mission in his
own life, although it was partially veiled, so there was meaning and
significance in theirs as they providentially met the challenge of the
situation which was facing them. All of this, and more, Mark brought
to the fore as he wrote the Gospel which bears his name. That he
does not specifically identify the contemporary issues which he has
in mind is due largely to the fact that he employed the gospel form
in writing rather than that of the epistles which Paul had used.[11]
Besides, the times were such that it was wiser to write in this fashion,
even as a generation later John the Seer employed apocalyptic symbols
by which to convey his message to the church.

## The Gospel of Matthew

The Gospel of Matthew also has a situational background as a
whole which gave it special significance in its own day, and which is
enlightening as we attempt to interpret it in ours. Although it has

[9] Irenaeus *Against Heresies* III. 1. 1.

[10] Cf. Papias of Hierapolis in Eusebius *Church History* III. 39. 15.

[11] Cf. the related statement of James M. Robinson in his *Problem of History in
Mark*, p. 13. "Since the Church sees its history founded in Jesus' history, it can
witness to and explain its religious experience better by writing the history of Jesus as
the Messiah than by describing its own religious life."

been traditionally associated with Matthew the apostle,[12] its author remains unknown. Whether he was a Hellenistic Jew or a Gentile is also uncertain; suggestive reasons may be adduced for either view. Its place of origin may be reasonably held to be Antioch in Syria. The writings of Ignatius and the Didache, which use Matthew exclusively, support this conclusion.

Syrian Antioch, the probable site of the composition of Matthew, was the second great center of Christianity to develop in the ancient world, Jerusalem being the first. It was here that Christian ethics was originally applied on a large scale within a population of mixed racial lines. Jews and Gentiles co-existed in this sizable community where the streams of commerce and communication from East and West met and mingled. And Antioch also was the base from which the Pauline missionary endeavor moved out into the Greco-Roman world. To it the great apostle reported regularly.

The church in Antioch in the last quarter of the first century (circa A.D. 85) was faced with needs such as its own character and the tension of the times would foster. The need for extended missionary activity remained, particularly in the face of Jewish opposition. Some exposition was required to define the Faith in its relation to Judaism so that both its individuality and dependency would be made clear. A teaching task was called for, one that would provide guidance in the ordering of daily life even as the Law had done for the Jews. The church was becoming more conscious of itself as an institutional unit, and the implications of this fact had to be considered. And finally there had developed a resurgence of the apocalyptic interest which the primitive church had known, as a result of the fall of Jerusalem in A.D. 70. Was not this tragic event a portent of the coming end of the Age?

When we turn to the Gospel of Matthew, we discover that these interests are well represented in the tradition that it contains, as well as in the editorial arrangement and emphasis of the writer. Although, like Mark, he uses the gospel form, he is concerned with the living church and its needs. In presenting his portrait of Jesus, he takes pains to set him forth in such a way that he utters an authoritative word in the very areas in which the Christians of Antioch were finding difficulties. Whether the author distorted the picture in directing it toward these problems, or whether the situation called forth in the representa-

[12] Eusebius op. cit. III. 39. 16.

113

tion lines that were already there as such, waiting to be highlighted, is a matter of difference of opinion among biblical scholars. In my own judgment the answer lies somewhere between these two points of view. Matthew's personal touch, the church's need, and the historical data remain interlocked in the document. By comparing it with Mark and Luke, this is clearly evident.

In meeting the issues that were present in the background situation, Matthew makes it clear that the expansion of the church through missionary effort must continue. The Great Commission (28:18-20) and other injunctions to such activity (24:14) leave no doubt at this point. The Faith that is proclaimed is new, and yet it does not deny its roots in Judaism; instead it fulfills them (5:17-48). The teachings of the Lord contain guidance for daily living even as did the Law (6:1-7:27). And the church must continue to develop a consciousness of itself as an authoritative body with a true foundation (16:18-19) and regulatory rules (18:15-20). Finally, it behooves Christians to be ready for the near advent of Jesus. There are signs to be discerned, and the end is at hand, although the exact day only God knows (24:3-51).

### The Gospel of Luke

When the Gospel of Luke was written (circa A.D. 85), somewhere in the Hellenistic world (Ephesus? Corinth? Rome?) certain political issues were facing the people known as Christians which called for guidance and sound judgment. It was necessary for governmental authorities, into whose hands this writing would most surely fall, to gain a perspective toward the movement which would help them in classifying it more specifically.

Rome customarily recognized different religions as permitted (religio licita) and thus gave them legal standing. Among these was Judaism. At first, Christianity was regarded by the Romans as a development within Judaism. They thought of it as a kind of Jewish sect. But the Jews resented this identification and through concerted persecution made it clear that the Christians were definitely outsiders, as far as they were concerned. The book of Acts reflects this rejection in passage after passage (13:45, 50; 14:19; 17:5-7; 18:6). More than this, they insisted that Jesus had been crucified by the state as a political criminal. Domitian was the emperor at the time of the composition of the Gospel (A.D. 81-96), he who was soon to persecute the church, which act called forth the writing of the Revelation to John. This fact points to the seriousness of the situation.

Into this picture stepped Luke, a close friend and fellow traveler of Paul's (Col. 4:14; Philem. 24; II Tim. 4:11; and the "we sections" in the Acts of the Apostles formerly referred to[13]), to write the Third Gospel and its companion volume, Acts. Only the first of these will concern us here. Lucan authorship has been traditionally held for these writings, and there is little reason to question this view on literary or other grounds.[14] His Gospel becomes an apology, perhaps the first for the Faith, particularly in regard to its emphasis upon the non-insurrectionist character of the movement.[15] And the author makes his point within the framework of a portrait of Jesus, the founder of the new religion.

Most dramatically when Jesus, accused of advocating treasonable acts, stood before Pilate, the Roman procurator, this ruler upon examining him distinctly declared: "I find no crime in this man" (23:4). Later, when Jesus was arraigned before King Herod, he was returned to Pilate without judgment being passed upon him (vss. 6-12). Again Pilate said: "You [the Jewish authorities] brought me this man as one who was perverting the people; and after examining him before you, behold, I did not find this man guilty of any of your charges against him" (vs. 14). And yet once more Pilate asserted that he found no crime in him deserving death (vs. 22). Finally, in Jesus' hour of demise the Roman centurion in charge of the Crucifixion declared, "Certainly this man was innocent!" (vs. 47). The recording of these repeated pronouncements of innocence on the part of officials of state could hardly be accidental. They are included deliberately because they clear Jesus of the charge of treason, and through him the Christian church in Luke's day.

In yet another attempt to place the Christians in an advantageous political light, Luke sought to make it clear that they were not unrelated to Judaism. In fact, they were the new Israel, and should thus be granted the same political standing which the old had already been given. As a good Jew, Jesus charged his followers to respect the Temple and make the customary offerings for cleansing (5:14; 17:14).

[13] Cf. p. 106.
[14] Eusebius op. cit. III. 4. 6. But cf. A. E. Barnett, The New Testament: Its Making and Meaning, pp. 167-68, for a listing of arguments against this conclusion.
[15] Cf. B. H. Streeter, The Four Gospels, p. 539.

He himself taught daily in its sacred precincts during his final week in the Holy City (21:37).

But more than this, Jesus and his followers were loyal to the Roman government. On one occasion a centurion had openly expressed faith in him, so much so that he had healed his son. As a result, Jesus commended the soldier for his great belief (7:1-10). Officials of state such as tax collectors did not find Jesus unpatriotic; instead they were drawn to him (15:1; 19:1-10). And finally, when asked whether it were right to pay taxes to Caesar, Jesus had replied affirmatively, suggesting that there was an area in life within which government had a right to exact a return for services rendered (20:21-25). These references are particularly impressive when viewed from the standpoint of the political problem which the church faced at the time the Gospel was written. If we were to add to this brief accounting the statements in Acts which further reveal the position of the Christian community and its missionaries in respect to the Roman government, the conclusion that Luke, in his writings, had this problem in mind is inescapable.

The Third Gospel is also situational in other respects beside its relation to the political aspects of the problem which the church faced. Although many had written of the ministry of Jesus and the things which had been "accomplished among us," Luke felt that there was need for a more comprehensive treatment of the subject. Accordingly he conceived of the gigantic undertaking of recording the story of the Christian movement from its humble beginnings at a manger-crib in an obscure village to its ultimate arrival at Rome, the capital of the world, at the hands of the apostle Paul, greatest of the missionaries. This would give both structure and stature to the church at a time when it was sorely needed. It would present the complete picture of Jesus, both in the flesh and as the exalted Lord Christ, resurrected and ascended, who was still leading his followers. Thus the Greek official Theophilus and others who were showing an interest in the new movement would be more readily convinced of its truth (1:3-4).

It would be unsound to infer from all the special interests of Luke as they appear in his Gospel that there was a corresponding need in the church at the time that he wrote. And yet some of them do suggest background concerns which fit the times as we know them. For instance, the author's preoccupation with Jesus' interest in outcasts

116

and Samaritans[16] reflects the continuous need to define the missionary movement in its broadest aspect. The church was to go not only to the lost sheep of Israel, but also to the children of God everywhere. Luke reports both the sending out of the twelve (9:1-6) and the dispatching of the seventy (10:1-12) for purposes of evangelizing. According to the view of the times there were seventy nations in the world, and it is difficult not to conclude that Luke was symbolizing the universality of the Kingdom in the latter case. This would undergird the missionary interests of his day, even as Matthew sought to do.[17]

Perhaps Luke's preoccupation with the prayer life of Jesus, the status of women in the Savior's service, as well as his concern for the poor whose plight and piety made them God's particular charges, should be put down as special interests of the author as he selected the tradition which he would include in his Gospel. In any case, they appear in his writing to an extent not found in Matthew and Mark.

### The Synoptic Gospels and the Historical Jesus

At the outset in this chapter it was indicated that the Synoptic Gospels, all three of them, regard Jesus as both exalted Lord and Christ. This should not be taken to mean that they were disinterested in the facts of his earthly life. If this were the case, why write a Gospel at all, unless we are to make the unlikely assumption that the gospel form is no more than a literary device by which to define and spread the Faith. A more considerate conclusion is that because Jesus had come to mean so much to them, even to the point of possessing the value of God in their experience, they were eager to delineate the portrait of their Lord as he was known in Galilee and Judea, when his full glory was only partially evident and the final meaning of his person but faintly grasped. Here is where it all began and the full story must be told.

We have but one chronology of events for the life and ministry of Jesus in the Synoptics. It is that which Mark gives in his Gospel. Both Matthew and Luke follow it in the main. When they have special data or material of their own to present, they may interrupt Mark's narrative, but they return to it later and continue where they left off. At best, this chronology is sketchy and incomplete. Individual

[16] 10:29-37; 14:21-24; 17:17-19.
[17] Cf. previous reference, pp. 113-14.

stories and teaching units are loosely related in the sequence which is given to them. The movements of Jesus are not always clearly accounted for as the narrative proceeds.

For this reason, as well as for others, it has been suggested that Mark's order of events is an artificial construct, intended to point up an idea rather than to describe a succession of happenings. This idea was thought by William Wrede and others to be the messianic secret.[18] Jesus, it was said, did not call himself the Messiah during his ministry, but the disciples were convinced that he was such by the Resurrection. To explain their Lord's silence on this subject, they concluded that he kept it a secret; only the demons and demon-possessed had grasped it. The story of Jesus' ministry, then, becomes the story of the messianic secret, and a genuine chronology gives way to this idea.

One does not need to follow this line of thought to realize the problems in Mark's order of events for Jesus' ministry. On the whole, however, it is quite adequate as a background for presenting his portrait. Its general character keeps us from insisting upon the exact location of an incident in any given sequence, and yet, it does possess a psychology of events which is satisfying. It is possible that the broad lines of chronology which Mark gives came from the preaching of Peter. Papias of Hierapolis (circa A.D. 140) claimed that Mark was the interpreter of Peter and that he wrote what he remembered the apostle as stating concerning the Lord's sayings or doings.[19]

Mark's Gospel opens with a record of what he calls "the beginning of the gospel of Jesus Christ, the Son of God." This section (1:1-13) includes a reference to the activities of John the baptizer and a brief account of the baptism and temptations of Jesus. Following this is a major unit presenting Jesus' ministry in and about Galilee (1:14–9: 50). Included here are miracle stories, encounters between Jesus and the religious leaders of the Jews, the call of the twelve, parables, the beheading of John, Peter's confession, and the Transfiguration. A third grouping of the tradition is concerned with Jesus' activities in Judea and Jerusalem (10:1–16:8). This centers in the issues raised in connection with the closing days of our Lord's ministry and his death on the cross. Major considerations here are the predictions of his passion, the Triumphal Entry, the cleansing of the Temple, final

[18] Cf. *The Messianic Secret in the Gospels*.
[19] Eusebius *op. cit.* III. 39. 15.

teachings, an apocalyptic discourse, the Last Supper, Gethsemane, the betrayal, the arrest, trial, Crucifixion, and finally the Resurrection. The passage which now stands at the close of the Gospel (16:9-20) was a later addition. Its original ending, which was probably quite brief, has been lost.

In this discussion we have seen that the Gospels were related to the life stream of the early church. The motive behind their composition was in no sense dilettante or academic; instead it was functional. Genuine needs are being met in a realistic fashion. This is particularly evident, we have noted, when each Gospel is viewed separately in relation to its immediate environment. This partly accounts for their individuality along with the availability of the tradition and the personal traits of the authors themselves.

We are discovering as we follow this study that the drawing of the portrait of Christ is directly related to the background of the New Testament documents, such background as we have been considering in this chapter. That he is truly Lord of the ages does not deny the historical fact that his lordship was first *known* within a particular setting, which changed from time to time as the New Testament era continued.

# NINE

# In the Synoptic Gospels:
# Gospel Writers as Interpreters

IN THE PREVIOUS CHAPTER WE HAVE INDICATED THAT THE SYNOPTIC Gospels contain both interpretation and fact in their portrait of Jesus. This was inevitable since the reason the data was recorded was that it had come to have a divine meaning, and the one to whom it referred had also come to be regarded as more than human in his person. It is therefore not always possible to separate history from the framework of significance within which it is reported in writings such as these. They rightly belong together. In the discussion which follows, we shall look first of all at the *meanings* which the gospel authors, and the church before them, found in the events of Jesus' life.

### The Birth Narratives

The Gospel of Mark does not contain birth narratives. For this author the significance of Jesus began with his baptism and introduction to public life. This may be taken to mean that Mark was unfamiliar with these stories.[1] On the other hand it may denote only that his attention lay primarily in the active ministry of his Lord, and that he did not choose to push further back in the account he was relating. The character of the advent records as found in Matthew and Luke suggest an early date for the traditions underlying them. It would seem that Mark could have referred to these had it suited his purpose. This conclusion assumes that the tradition circulated within his reach, and this, in my judgment, is a likely conjecture.[2]

That there was more than a single tradition concerning the birth of Jesus is evident from the differences in the accounts of Matthew and Luke. For instance, Matthew alone tells of the visit of the Magi,

---

[1] Cf. Mark 3:21.

[2] A Palestinian source of the tradition would not mean that Mark was unacquainted with it, even though his Gospel was quite likely written in Rome. Connections with the homeland for him were well established.

the guiding star, the slaughter of the infants, and the flight to Egypt (2:1-21). He also assumes that Bethlehem was the home town of Joseph and Mary (vss. 1, 22-23). On the other hand, Luke does not seem to have a knowledge of these traditions. He regards Nazareth as the site of the home residence (2:1-7), and relates how the angels appeared to the shepherds, how the heavenly host sang "Glory to God in the highest," how the babe was found in the manger, and how Joseph and Mary took the infant to the Temple where Anna and Simeon blessed him, giving thanks to God (vss. 8-38). In spite of this great variety in the tradition, however, it is clear that Matthew and Luke are referring to the same event.

The teaching or message of the birth stories is of greater importance than the historicity of its details. Harmonies have been attempted by which the variations in Matthew and Luke have been pressed into a unity. The results are forced and unconvincing. Such procedure does violence to the nature of the material itself, since it is essentially devotional and poetical in its emphasis. This does not argue against the fact of Jesus' birth or necessarily imply the inaccuracy of the method of his conception as reported. But it does suggest that the emphasis should be placed upon the significance of his coming rather than upon its manner.

What is it that Matthew and Luke are attempting to say in their statements about Jesus' birth, since it is evident that their interest lay beyond the reporting of vital statistics? Primarily, they are concerned to show that the ultimate origin of Jesus is God. This was not out of character for the ancient world which frequently sought to attribute heavenly sources to its leading figures, including the Pharaohs of Egypt, who were said to be the offspring of a god. Divinity itself was ascribed to Alexander the Great, Julius Caesar, and Augustus. And in the latter half of the first century, divine honors were paid to both Nero and Domitian. In addition, virgin births were claimed in the legends of Perseus and Attis. All of this would psychologically predispose the first readers of the Gospels to give credence to the birth stories. They would learn of them within an atmosphere of acceptability.

But this is not to say that the accounts of the birth of Jesus are on the same level as these. There is a moral and spiritual tone to them unlike that found in the above. God is at work to save his people, and the birth of this Savior is heralded as the beginning of a

New Age. This is particularly true in the messages of the angels (Luke 1:32-33; 2:14) and in the songs of Mary and Zechariah (Luke 1:46-55, 67-79). To Mary the angel Gabriel announces that he who is to be born will be called the Son of the Most High, and that to him will be given the throne of his father David. In the Magnificat which follows, Mary sings of God, who has done mighty things, showing mercy to the humble and judging the proud who oppress them. Zechariah is even more specific, praising God as the one who has visited his people redemptively, and exhibited his tender mercy in the new day which is about to dawn.[3]

The author of the Fourth Gospel was later to give a metaphysical expression to these convictions. Not only was he convinced that the final accounting of his Lord must be in terms of God's activity; he also went beyond this and rooted the origin of Jesus within the very being of God himself. Before coming to earth in the flesh he was the Logos (divine reason), who existed from all eternity as the Word who was God (1:1).

The genealogies, likewise, have their message concerning Jesus. In Matthew (1:1-16), he is called the son of David, the son of Abraham. This says something about his person. In that time the Messiah was thought of as the son of David, and Abraham had long since been regarded as the recipient of God's promises. The statement found in Luke (3:23-38) traces the lineage to Adam and thence to God, both David and Abraham appearing in the list also. As the descendant of Adam, Jesus has a relationship to the entire human race, and this implies that his vocation has a meaning for all humanity.

There are still other elements of portraiture in the birth stories. Matthew, for instance, reports the word of the angel, spoken to Joseph in a dream, which said that Mary's son shall be called Jesus, "for he will save his people from their sins" (1:21). And this is interpreted as a fulfillment of the Immanuel prophecy of Isaiah (7:14). Thus Jesus' mission is seen to be related to the Old Testament prophetic movement which the Hebrews regarded, together with the Law, as the sign and seal of God's activity on their behalf. The visit of the wise men who followed the star in the East, which Matthew

[3] The origin of these songs, whether original with those who are said to speak them or the composition of the authors who record them, does not affect the message they contain. Their reflections of the Old Testament mark them as genuinely within the Hebrew-Christian tradition.

also relates, carries overtones of meaning that provide a framework within which to appraise the person and work of Jesus. In their coming, there is signalized the homage which royalty and wisdom pay to Jesus as one worthy of such a tribute.

Luke has a counterpart for such recognition in his account of the visit of the shepherds to the manger. They had been informed of the birth of this "Savior, who is Christ the Lord," by none other than an angelic chorus. The angels of heaven already regard the babe as Lord, and the humble shepherds who know both the privilege and burden of toil are to follow their example (2:8-20). Later, when the babe was presented in the Temple, the aged Simeon discovered in him both the revelation to the Gentiles and the glory of Israel (vss. 29-32). In addition, Anna the prophetess, when she saw the infant Jesus "gave thanks to God, and spoke of him to all who were looking for the redemption of Jerusalem" (vs. 38).

If one approaches the synoptic portrait of Jesus through the birth stories, he finds that certain conclusions concerning his person and work are already providing the framework of interpretation for what is to follow. This is what Jesus means to the church; this is the significance his followers have discovered in his life and ministry. And this judgment is reflected and confirmed in the tradition of his advent.

### The Baptism

Our concern in this section is to take note of the significance which the Synoptic Gospels attribute to the events in Jesus' life. Much of this *meaning* undoubtedly came from Jesus himself as he revealed his mind to his followers, particularly to the disciples, in the course of his ministry. Some of the interpretation came directly from the experience of the church following the Resurrection and Pentecost. There was a perspective here for evaluating Jesus' career that revealed implications not immediately evident at the time.

As the baptism of Jesus is presented in the Synoptics, therefore, it is not simply a recital of what happened. Whatever it meant to Jesus himself, the church viewed his baptism in the Jordan River as a messianic event. In the first place, John the prophet was placing his approval upon Jesus. He regarded him as one mightier than himself, whose sandals he was not worthy to carry (Matt. 3:11), or to stoop and untie (Mark 1:7; Luke 3:16). In his recognition of this one the

123

prophetic movement of Israel was also singling him out as he who was to come.

But, more important, it was God himself in the voice from heaven (*Bath Qol*) who pointed out Jesus as the Messiah. Mark and Luke suggest that the declaration was made to our Lord himself. In Matthew, however, it was addressed to those who were standing by at the time. It is probable that Matthew really has in mind the living church of his own day in this form of the announcement. God speaks to them through the voice to the Jordan company, bearing witness to the fact that Jesus is the Son.

The words "Thou art my beloved Son; with thee I am well pleased" (Luke 3:22) are usually interpreted as resting upon two Old Testament passages: Ps. 2:7, which reads, "You are my son, today I have begotten you"; and Isa. 42:1, which states, "My chosen, in whom my soul delights; I have put my spirit upon him, he will bring forth justice to the nations." Among the Jews the expression "my beloved son" was not messianic, but the Christians did understand and use it in this fashion.[4] As employed here, it was a designation of Jesus' vocation.[5] Manson wisely suggests that it also carries a recognition of the filial relation that existed between Jesus and God. Love is at the heart of it, love and the fatherhood of God.[6]

The gospel writers further see God's proclamation that Jesus was the Messiah in the coming of the Spirit upon him at this time. Even as special servants of old were filled with the Spirit for a special vocation, so Jesus was set apart and empowered by the divine anointing. The Servant of Isaiah (61:1 ff.) was pictured in this same way as receiving the Spirit, and there may well be a reflection of this representation in the evangelists' minds as they record the baptismal experience of Jesus.

It should not be forgotten that in the early church, converts customarily received the Spirit at the time of their baptism, or shortly afterward. Pentecost and all that it meant [7] had already occurred before the tradition concerning Jesus' baptism was put into form. This means that the first writers and readers of the Gospels wrote and

---

[4] Cf. William Manson, *Jesus, the Messiah*, pp. 149-50.

[5] According to the reading of the western text concerning the utterance of the voice from heaven, it was at his baptism that Jesus first entered upon or was given the role of Messiah. This is in line with the Christology of the primitive church.

[6] Cf. Manson, *The Gospel of Luke*, p. 30.

[7] Cf. pp. 28-32; 40-41.

read the account within the framework of meaning which this ecstatic event held for them. He who had sent the Spirit upon them at Pentecost had himself received the Spirit at his baptism. There was therefore an eschatological content to the occasion.[8] It was an event in which God had parted heaven's veil and shown both himself and the Son in their true light. From "beyond time" the divine purpose had been revealed "in time." [9]

### The Temptations

Jesus was tempted throughout his lifetime. At the Last Supper he said with deep and moving affection to his disciples: "You are those who have continued with me in my trials [peirasmos]" (Luke 22:28). The Gospels present a picture of him as one who was engaged in a life-and-death struggle with Satan and the powers of evil. Here was a kingdom to be overthrown. Not until the final victory in the Resurrection was the battle ended. It was a cosmic drama which was taking place on earth, as the Son cast out demons and resisted suggestions from the Tempter to act contrary to the will of the heavenly Father.

The significance of the Temptations during this special forty-day period at the very outset of his messianic ministry, as the gospel writers view it, is that in the opening scenes of the drama of redemption Jesus met and conquered Satan. From the perspective of our interest in his individual experience, and the psychological inevitability of a period of decision following close upon the heels of a call to messiahship, the appropriateness of this time of thinking and praying is clear. But Matthew, Mark, and Luke are not so much concerned with psychology and Jesus' need for personal devotions in this case, as they are with the issue between the Messiah and Satan in which the destiny of the human race itself was at stake, which to them the Temptations represented. At this time "he was with the wild beasts; and the angels ministered to him" (Mark 1:13).

Vincent Taylor suggests that the Temptations "tested" the quality of Jesus' sonship.[10] This is true, not in the sense that the quality of his character was being determined, but rather that his power over

---

[8] The preaching of John the baptizer with its message of the immanence of the Judgment provided an appropriate setting for the baptism interpreted as an eschatological event.

[9] Cf. B. Harvie Branscomb, *The Gospel of Mark*, p. 16, for a related development of this idea.

[10] *The Life and Ministry of Jesus*, p. 62.

Satan and his kingdom was at stake. Mark implies this when he notes that immediately following Jesus' baptism the Spirit drove him into the wilderness. Again, this seems to say to us that his retreat was a psychological and personal necessity, but that is not what the writer wishes his readers to see. Instead, he is concerned to show that the newly anointed Messiah is engaged in a life-and-death conflict with Satan. And he emerged the victor from the encounter. Although the battle is not finally concluded, since Satan departed from Jesus only for a season, or until a more opportune time, the Lord was now ready to embark upon his messianic career.

We shall refer to the several elements involved in the three separate temptations when we raise the question as to what they meant to Jesus personally. For the present we are concerned to show the significance of these days as the gospel writers viewed them. They did not create the tradition, but they interpreted it in the light of the full meaning of Jesus' life and ministry, set forth within the framework of the thinking of the early church

### The Ministry of Healing

The Synoptics abound in references to the healing activities of Jesus. Early in his writing Mark carries an important record of these in connection with the first day's ministry in Capernaum. Chronology is not so significant here as the presentation at the very outset of a portrait of Jesus as one who had power over the evils that plagued men. Just as he gives us a series of clashes between Jesus and the religious leaders in the opening chapters (2:1–3:6) in which Jesus routed his critics. Mark also provides at the beginning of his Gospel a demonstration of his Lord's day-by-day victory over the kingdom of Satan through the healing of men's bodies and minds (1:21-34).

After telling of the exorcising of the demons from the man in the synogogue and of the healing of Simon's mother-in-law who lay sick with a fever, the evangelist presents a general statement which says: "And he [Jesus] healed many who were sick with various diseases, and cast out many demons; and he would not permit the demons to speak, because they knew him" (1:34). There is more or less of a continuous reference to these mighty acts throughout the Gospels, although in the latter sections they are mentioned with less frequency. This may suggest that Jesus curtailed this side of his ministry toward

126

the close of his life, either because it was interfering with his preaching of the Kingdom or because his concern with the Cross was all but completely filling his mind and soul. In any case, the types of wonder-works which Rawlinson calls "the Messianic signs" [11] which are mentioned include such conditions as the healing of curvature of the spine (Luke 13:11-17), epilepsy (Mark 9:14-29), leprosy (Mark 1:40-45; Luke 17:11-19), paralysis (Mark 2:3-12), blindness (Mark 10:46-52; 8:22-26), deafness and dumbness (Mark 7:31-37), atrophy of a bodily member (Mark 3:1-5), dropsy (Luke 14:1-6), fever (Mark 1:29-31), flux (Mark 5:25-34), and a severed bodily part (Luke 22:50-51). In addition to these, there are two instances of restoration from death in the Synoptics (Mark 5:21-24, 35-43; Luke 7:11-17) and one in the Fourth Gospel (ch. 11).[12]

The issues which the modern mind faces in regard to such wonder-deeds, because of the scientific framework within which it does its thinking, were completely foreign to the first century. Both Jews and Gentiles expected healing and mighty acts at the hands of "holy men" who had power with the gods or in the unseen world.

In considering Paul's portrait of Christ, reference was made to the world view of the day, particularly among the Jews, concerning the powers and principalities of the spirit order.[13] This same background must be brought to bear upon the portrayal of Jesus as one who cast out demons, healed, and performed other miracles. Satan was being cast out by the finger of God (Luke 11:20) as Jesus worked among men. Along with the humanitarian blessedness of this ministry, the gospel writers are concerned to show us the triumph of Jesus the Messiah over evil forces in the universe.[14] Unless the Gospels are read in this light, we shall miss the impact they carried for their first readers.

This would most assuredly be the case for those first readers who were Jewish Christians. The prophets had long since laid the foundation for expecting miraculous acts of God in the coming Day of the Lord. As we have seen already, the early church interpreted Pentecost

[11] Cf. *Christ in the Gospels*, pp. 33-40.

[12] Cf. S. V. McCasland, *By the Finger of God* and Alan Richardson, *The Miracle-Stories of the Gospels.*

[13] Cf. pp. 72-73.

[14] Cf. Gustaf Aulèn, *Christus Victor*, for a framework within which to interpret these events.

in this light. And it was perfectly natural for those acquainted with such statements as the following to do likewise:

> In that day the deaf shall hear
>   the words of a book,
> and out of their gloom and darkness
>   the eyes of the blind shall see. (Isa. 29:18.)

The Day of the Lord represented the final triumph of Jehovah over all elements, political and otherwise, which opposed him. And in Jesus' manifest power over sickness and evil the expected New Age was already beginning to appear.

### Jesus and Judaism

That official Judaism had rejected Jesus the Messiah was a matter of concern to the early church. Basic to this situation was the fact that the new religion was born within the matrix of the old, nourished its life upon its traditional piety, and interpreted its message in relation to the revelation it contained. Yet the Jewish leaders had treated it as a foundling and pushed it out of its crib. This was not only a blow to its pride; it likewise constituted a problem for faith since the God of Israel was also regarded as the God of the Christian Fellowship.

The apostle Paul grappled with this same problem in a major section of the Epistle to the Romans.[15] He concluded that the rejection was only partial, that its purpose was to make it possible for Gentiles to enter the fold, and that it was to be temporary since finally the Jews would "be grafted in" again. Readers of these chapters in Romans should not be misled by the formal character of the writing. Beneath what may appear to be purely academic argumentation is a serious consideration of an issue that was a stumbling block to belief, especially for Jewish Christians. At its close, however, after probing the question, Paul literally breaks forth in a paeon of praise, lauding "the depth of the riches and wisdom and knowledge of God" (11:33-36).

In presenting the story of Jesus, the gospel writers were faced with this same question of faith. And in putting the account together, they were concerned to meet and interpret it in its true light, as they saw it and as they believed Jesus himself viewed it. That their con-

[15] Rom. 9–11.

128

sideration is indirect rather than straightforward, as in the Epistle to the Romans, is due to the fact that it is presented within the framework of the gospel form.

It should not be forgotten that at the time of the composition of the Gospels, especially of Matthew and Luke, Jewish persecution of Christians, particularly at the hands of the Pharisees, was quite active. This highlighted the issue we have been discussing and also aroused the feelings of the church. Consequently the accounts of the conflict between Jesus and the Jewish officials reflect this tension. This may explain what has sometimes been called the anti-Semitism of the Gospels. A measure of exaggeration in presenting Jesus' denunciation of the Pharisees was to be expected, and the succession of "woes" directed against them (Matt. 23:13-36; Luke 11:42-52) may sound more virulent than they actually were when originally spoken. On the other hand, that there were deep-seated differences between Jesus and the Pharisees is hardly open to question, and that these flared into open debate on occasion would be inevitable.

The Synoptics interpret the rejection of Jesus by official Judaism and the problem of faith which this precipitated by presenting the differences in viewpoint which existed between them. These appear in personal encounters involving Sabbath observances, fasting, associating with sinners, and other matters related to the keeping of the Law. In addition, there is a reporting of the open statements of criticism, already mentioned, which Jesus made against them. There had always been false shepherds of the sheep in Israel. The prophets had cried out against such in the past because they had misled the people.[16] And this is what Jesus was doing in opposing the religious leaders. He was taking a prophetic offensive against them. As the Synoptic Gospels view it, their rejection of him, therefore, instead of discrediting him as the Christ had actually elevated him as one who was in the prophetic succession.

Matthew presents an additional tradition which he uses to interpret the rejection of Jesus by the Jews. It is a recorded word of Jesus, explaining his reason for speaking in parables (13:13-15). The exact meaning of the original statement is obscured by the purpose to which Matthew puts it. He holds that Jesus deliberately employed parables to confuse, in order to fulfill a statement of Isaiah (6:9-10) which he regards as having implications for the refusal of the nation to accept

[16] Cf. Ezek. 34:1-19; Jer. 23:1-4.

her Messiah. John and Paul both offer similar arguments (John 12: 37-41; Rom. 9:6-33). The parables presumably were intended to harden their hearts, stop their ears, and close their eyes to the truth: With them indeed is fulfilled the prophecy of Isaiah which says:

> "You shall indeed hear but never understand,
> and you shall indeed see but never perceive.
> For this people's heart has grown dull,
> and their ears are heavy of hearing,
> and their eyes they have closed,
> lest they should perceive with their eyes,
> and hear with their ears,
> and understand with their heart,
> and turn for me to heal them." (Matt. 13:14-15.)

It is unlikely that Jesus interpreted these words as did Matthew, but the evangelist found in the tradition an incentive to faith. To him the Jewish opposition to Jesus had seemingly been prophesied in this word of Isaiah.

### Jesus the Messiah

We have been considering the meanings which the church and the authors of the Synoptic Gospels find in the events of Jesus' life, together with something of the framework within which they are recorded. And as has previously been noted, these were viewed in the light of later discoveries concerning the Lord, growing out of the Resurrection and Pentecost. Insights and realizations which had been missed because of a traditional and limited outlook, with the passing of time became increasingly clear, and these are reflected in the gospel writings themselves. Their authors write as though they understand and accept the message of their own compositions, even when they record a failure of the disciples to do so.[17] Furthermore, they believe that they are interpreting the mind of Jesus correctly and that they are writing history rather than fiction or myth.

It has been seen already that the church interpreted Jesus' ministry as messianic in character. His birth signaled the beginning of a New Age; at his baptism he was invested with the role of the Messiah; in his Temptations he proved himself as the designated Christ to be victor over Satan; and by his mighty deeds of healing he dramatically

[17] Cf. Luke 9:43b-45.

overthrew the kingdom of evil spirit-forces. There are still further instances of messianic interpretation in the Gospels. In the village synagogue at Nazareth, it was noted that Jesus had applied one of the servant passages of Isaiah to himself with messianic implications (Luke 4:16-21). Peter declared him to be the Christ at Caesarea Philippi (Mark 8:27-30), and at the Transfiguration the voice from heaven again proclaimed him to be the beloved Son (9:2-8). On one occasion it was recorded that Jesus himself defended his lordship as being superior to Davidic sonship, which was the traditional messianic conception (12:35-37). From first to the last the Gospels are united in the belief that Jesus lived as the Messiah.

They are also in agreement concerning the conviction that the Lord had died as the Messiah. Immediately following Peter's declaration at Caesarea Philippi that Jesus was the Christ, we are given the tradition predicting his passion as an interpretation of the messiahship (Mark 8:31-33; Matt. 16:21-23; Luke 9:21-22). Likewise the Triumphal Entry which brings Jesus into Jerusalem for the Cross that awaits him in the Holy City is viewed by the gospel writers as messianic (Mark 11:9-10; Matt. 21:9; Luke 19:38), in spite of the variations in the wording of the ovation accorded Jesus by the populace.[18] And at the Last Supper the Eucharist is seen to possess a special messianic significance. His blood was to be poured out for many in the establishment of a New Covenant, in contrast to that of Moses at Sinai (Mark 14:23-25).

The trial and Crucifixion as presented in the Synoptics continue to undergird the conclusion that Jesus in his death is considered to be the Messiah. When brought before Pilate, he was asked the question, "Are you the King of the Jews?" and replied, "You have said so" (Mark 15:2; Matt. 27:11; Luke 23:3). This is best interpreted as an affirmative answer; although it placed the onus of decision upon Pilate, it was in no way a denial of Jesus' messianic status. The title "King of the Jews" is used several other times during these final hours. Twice Pilate inquired of the Jews whether they wanted him to release their King (Mark 15:9, 12), and before the soldiers prepared him for crucifixion, they dressed him in a purple cloak, crowned him with

---

[18] "The incident undoubtedly has a messianic character, but it is not so much an attempt to claim messiahship as a last endeavor on the part of Jesus to correct the messianic expectations of his followers and to bring home to them the nature of messiahship as he himself understood it." Vincent Taylor, The Life and Ministry of Jesus, p. 187.

a circle of thorns, and saluted him, saying, "Hail, King of the Jews" (vs. 18). Finally, even the inscription of the charge against him read "the King of the Jews" (vs. 26), and the chief priests mockingly cried, "Let the Christ, the King of Israel, come down now from the cross" (vs. 32).

As the account of the death of Jesus the Messiah is told in the Gospels, there are repeated references to the belief that these events have a place in the purpose of God. A divine drama of salvation is being enacted; only it is not play acting, it is the real thing. Contributing to this impression are the references to the fulfillment of the Scriptures which occur from time to time. The Cross did not take God by surprise; it was in his plan from the beginning.

In this connection Mark records that in the Garden of Gethsemane Jesus does not resist arrest. Instead he said, "Let the scriptures be fulfilled" (14:49). Earlier that same evening in the Upper Room he had stated that "the son of man goes *as it is written of him* (vs. 21).[19] When Peter had impulsively struck the slave of the high priest with his sword, Jesus bade him to sheath it again, saying, "Do you think that I cannot appeal to my Father, and he will at once send more than twelve legions of angels? But how then should the scriptures be fulfilled, that it must be so?" (Matt. 26:53-54), and a moment later he added, "All this has taken place, that the scriptures of the prophets might be fulfilled" (vs. 56).[20] These references to the fulfillment of Scripture, while not minimizing the suffering of the Cross, bring into the picture a sense of eternal purpose and introduce a divine meaning into what otherwise would have been stark tragedy.

### The Resurrection

Much has been said already in this volume concerning the centrality of the Resurrection for the experience and thought of the early church.[21] The lines of interpretation of this transcendent event which are found in the Synoptics were laid down already in the church of the primitive period. Mark's account as we have it contains little more than a brief record of the happening, which is cut off prematurely, probably because the full ending of his Gospel has been lost. We can

[19] Italics mine.

[20] In this connection Rawlinson makes much also of the parallelisms between the Crucifixion and the twenty-second psalm, certain words of which Jesus repeats from the cross. Cf. *Christ in the Gospels,* p. 71.

[21] Cf. pp. 13-17 *et al.*

probably see in Matthew's statement of these things, in general, the kind of treatment Mark had given, since it presents a Galilean tradition, and the First Evangelist had included the word to Peter that he should go to Galilee to meet his risen Lord (16:7).

Mark's narrative carries a sense of the astounding impact of the Resurrection upon the women who came to the tomb. Although Jesus was not there, a young man, sitting on the right side and clothed in a white robe, addressed them. They were told not to be amazed, since things had turned out as Jesus had prophesied (16:7). A higher power was in control, turning tragedy into triumph. Even so, the women were not reassured; trembling and astonishment had laid hold of them.

Matthew is more explicit than Mark in detailing the event. The stone was rolled away by an angel of the Lord from heaven, whose coming was preceded by an earthquake. This is, no doubt, intended to represent the "young man" in Mark's narrative, but his description is more ecstatic; lightning and raiment white as snow characterized the heavenly visitor. And as the women ran to tell the disciples, Jesus himself met them with the victorious greeting "Hail," causing them to worship him. As the resurrected one there was a new quality to his person, calling for adoration.

There was also a power and an authority in Jesus' being which encompassed both heaven and earth: "All authority in heaven and on earth has been given to me," he said to his disciples on the Galilean mountain where he met them (Matt. 28:18). As a result they were commissioned to evangelize all nations, and to baptize the new converts "in the name of the Father and of the Son and of the Holy Spirit" (28:19). Although this threefold reference is not yet the full trinitarian doctrine, it represents an evaluation and interpretation of Jesus as the Son which ultimately led to it. And to climax this exalted view, his unseen presence is promised to them until the end of the Age. Thus an eschatological framework for the Resurrection is found in the account of Matthew. Dwight M. Beck writes to the point when he states: "The final words of the risen One constitute a great summary of the message of Christianity." [22]

Luke views the Resurrection much like Mark and Matthew. The same high perspective as far as the person of Jesus is concerned is found in his account. Although there are specific emphases which

[22] *Through the Gospels to Jesus*, p. 325.

the third evangelist makes, Jesus is presented similarly as resurrected Lord. He had foretold his rising again in some detail, and the events had borne out his prediction (24:6-7). More than this, the prophets before Jesus had likewise proclaimed that "the Christ should suffer these things and enter into his glory" (vss. 25-27). And his presence warmed the hearts of the Emmaus travelers as they discovered in him the authoritative interpreter of the Scriptures which he himself had fulfilled (vs. 32). The disciples were told by the risen Lord that repentance and remission of sins should be preached in his name to all nations (vs. 47). But before undertaking this world mission of evangelism, they were to tarry in the city until they were clothed with power from on high (vs. 49).

Thus we see that in the Synoptics the resurrection fact is an interpreted fact. It is not just resuscitation from death. The eternal purpose of God shines through it, and the glory of heaven surrounds the event. It is related to God's revelation of his will in Moses, the psalms, and the prophets; even as it is the fulfillment of Jesus' own prophecy regarding himself. Because of it a new future is possible involving world evangelism and the omnipresence of the risen Lord. History itself has been set on another course because God brought forth Jesus from death. Great things are in the offing as men make ready for the end of the Age.

All in all, the writers of the Synoptic Gospels regard the events in Jesus' life as possessing a more than personal significance. God is seen to be at work in the advent, baptism, temptations, healing ministry, conflict with Judaism, death and resurrection of their Lord. The redemption promised through centuries past has come upon the living present, and the beginning of a New Age is at hand.

# TEN

# In the Synoptic Gospels: The Historical Jesus

IN THE PRECEDING CHAPTER IT WAS POINTED OUT THAT THE SYNOPTIC
Gospels tell the story of Jesus within a framework of interpretation
by which its significance for faith is made explicit. He had come to
mean certain things in the life of the church, and the account of
his sojourn on earth was inevitably written from this perspective.
Consequently later discoveries concerning his person were read back
into the earlier period when he ministered to men. The soundness
of this procedure from the standpoint of objective (abstract) history
may be questioned, but its necessity in terms of a final evaluation
of the person of Jesus should not be denied.

But this is not to say that the gospel writers were not writing
history, and that their portrait of Jesus is religious myth. Not at all!
They were concerned with *facts* and *meanings*, at both one and the
same time as they wrote. And if the facts were removed from the
picture, the meanings they supported would soon vanish. What we
have, then, to use an expression of James M. Robinson, is theologically
understood history.[1] Some modern historians, including Arnold
Toynbee, may also be said, in their own way, to be viewing history
within a theological framework, just as earlier in the century several
of our leading physicists, among them Arthur S. Eddington and
James Jeans, considered physical science in relation to its philosophical
implications.

In the gospel records the meaning of the events in Jesus' life is
so closely intertwined with the facts themselves that it is often quite
difficult with the tools of historical science at our disposal to separate
them. A comparison of earlier and later manuscripts, as in the case of
Mark with Matthew and Luke, may seem to be of some help since
differences can be found.[2] But when all of this has been accounted

---

[1] *Op. cit.*, pp. 12 ff.
[2] Cf. "Peter answered him, 'You are the Christ' " (Mark 8:29), "Peter answered,
'The Christ of God' " (Luke 9:20) and "Simon Peter replied, 'You are the Christ,
the Son of the living God' " (Matt. 16:16).

for and faced, we discover that the essential faith of the church concerning Jesus which the later documents reveal is likewise found in the earlier ones.

This may lead to a historical skepticism which concludes that it is all but impossible to know the Jesus of history through the Gospels.[3] Such a conclusion, however, is unwarranted. The imprint that he made upon his immediate followers was indelible, and their discovery of new life at his hands, both during his lifetime and later in the Christian Fellowship, makes them the best possible sources for our information. To be sure, they were not scientific historians as we use the term, but their concern for truth shines forth in their writings, and their basic good sense is likewise evident. The Gospels remain great historical works in their own right, and show evidence of gifted and sensitive authorship.

### A Real Person Emerges

Altogether apart from the message of the Synoptics, the writings give the impression that they are concerned with a real person when they tell of Jesus of Nazareth. His humanity as a historical individual is assumed on every hand. He was born, grew up, matured into manhood; felt a mission to fulfill, faced the alternatives involved, ventured forth to do the will of his heavenly Father; gathered about him some close friends for the undertaking, taught, healed, and helped the needy; met opposition with intelligent directness, faced the crises that developed by faith and in prayer; moved toward the tragic outcome at Jerusalem with deliberate tread, made his witness to the people as he entered the Holy City for the last time; counseled his disciples as he took leave of them, shrank from the pain of the cross but pursued his course to the end, stood unafraid before the religious and civil courts which tried him, accepted crucifixion at their hands and died, committing his soul to God.

This story is told with a simplicity and forthrightness that constitute an invitation to take it at its face value as an accurate accounting of the events it describes. There is not the slightest suggestion that its authors or compilers regard it as allegory or myth. On the contrary, they expected it to be read as it stands, as "a narrative of the things which have been accomplished" among them (Luke 1:1). And

[3] Cf. R. H. Lightfoot, *History and Interpretation in the Gospels*, ad loc.

in Luke's case eyewitnesses are claimed as the source of the material, in addition to a careful processing of the tradition on his own part.

## A Real Physical Life

A recognition of the reality of Jesus' physical life which the Synoptics contain has bearing upon two issues in the history of the Church. The first was the gnostic controversy which began even before the close of the first century. A full discussion of this movement, if such it might be called, is not pertinent to this consideration; only its teaching that Jesus' life in the flesh was unreal concerns us here. This view is known as Docetism. It should be said, in passing, that probably all Docetists were Gnostics, but not all Gnostics were Docetists. This teaching was particularly alive when the Gospel of John was written and may account for the author's insistence that the Word became flesh and dwelt among men (1:14). But even earlier than the writing of the Fourth Gospel the gnostic controversy was incipiently present, and the portrait of Jesus in Matthew, Mark, and Luke as a person of physical vigor provided a foil to the developing heresy.[4]

The second issue upon which the synoptic portrait of Jesus as a real physical person has bearing is the question of his actual historical existence. This matter is not discussed prominently today since it is widely recognized that adequate evidence for his historicity exists, but earlier in this century it was raised loudly by such writers as William B. Smith, James M. Robertson, Arthur Drews, and M. Paul-Louis Couchoud. Obviously, the fact that the Synoptics everywhere assume the reality of Jesus' fleshly existence does not settle the historical question, but it does prejudice the case against viewing the Gospels as pure myth.[5]

The physical life of Jesus has been romanticized in the interest of spirituality, on the one hand, and on behalf of a concern for his manliness, on the other. Some artists and writers have pictured him as almost feminine in form to suggest tenderness and meekness, while others have portrayed him as strong of back and a leader of men. Altogether apart from piety and other similar motives, the Gospels indicate that Jesus was vigorous in body, even as he was in spirit.

[4] Cf. references to Gnosticism in the discussion of the background of the Pauline letters, Colossians in particular, p. 98.
[5] Cf. Chester C. McCown, *The Search for the Real Jesus*, pp. 69 ff.

He was a carpenter by trade and, as such, had to handle heavy timbers. His knowledge of nature was considerable, suggesting frequent contact with the outdoors. During his ministry he lived mostly afoot, preaching from seashore, plain, and hillside, and tramping the dusty roads from morning till nightfall. He probably slept on the fragrant earth under the stars more frequently than in a Palestinian house. The ass which he rode into Jerusalem on what we call Palm Sunday may not yet have been broken to ride (Mark 11:2), and may have required both manual dexterity and strength to handle. All in all, these factors suggest a physical life of vitality and impressiveness.

## A Real Mental Life

Just as the Gospels give us an account that makes it clear that Jesus' physical life was real, they likewise picture him as possessing an active mind. It may seem to some that it is presumptuous even to suggest that Jesus did any serious thinking; they assume that his knowledge was completely immediate and intuitive. Without denying in the least that there was a directness and immediacy to Jesus' insights, it remains true that as he is represented in the Synoptics, more so than in the Fourth Gospel, he was given to deep concentration on the meaning of his ministry, as well as concerning the way to express it.

For instance, Jesus' use of parables called for a quality of mind that was penetrating and lively. From a literary standpoint alone, to say nothing of the truths they teach, they are creative and imaginative. With a brevity of words that is striking, the characters they portray are delineated with cameolike sharpness. For instance, there is the judge who "neither feared God nor regarded man" (Luke 18:2), and the rich fool who said to himself, "Soul, you have ample goods laid up for many years; take your ease, eat, drink, be merry" (12:19). Of this one Jesus said that he had laid up treasure for himself but was not rich toward God.

On occasion his parables bring together in startling contrast two opposites, suggesting on Jesus' part a flair for the dramatic that characterizes a fertile mind. This is the case in the parable of the Pharisee and the publican (Luke 18:9-14). Two more different persons could hardly be imagined as, side by side, they prayed. The Pharisee was clothed in both his official garments and his self-righteousness, while the publican was robed in his repentance and humility. With a decisive and revealing stroke, Jesus said that the Pharisee "stood and prayed *with himself.*" Here was the problem in a single phrase. Those whose business it is to work with words know that such literary effectiveness does not just happen. It is the result of deliberate thought.

The use of parables itself calls for both keen observation and deep thinking, since it involves probing beneath outward appearances and relationships. On the basis of passing events, eternal meanings are deduced. All visible life is made to speak of unseen truths; the material world cries aloud of spiritual values, and each growing thing becomes a "burning bush." Jesus spoke in parables because he first thought in parables. Everything his mind touched was to him a word of God.

To the parables should be added the metaphors and figurative sayings of Jesus, since these, too, indicate a verdant intellectual life. He called the hypocrisy of the Pharisees leaven (Luke 12:1), referred to the disciplines of the soul as the entering of a narrow gate (Matt. 7:13), compared false prophets to ravenous wolves who were dressed in sheep's clothing (Matt. 7:15), and suggested that efforts spent upon those whose minds were closed was like casting pearls before swine or giving to dogs what was holy (Matt. 7:6).

Sometimes Jesus used hyperbole in order to be certain that his message was heard. The shock of overstatement would alert the hearer to its truth. For instance, he said that cutting off one's right hand or plucking out one's eye was not too great a price to pay in order to enter the Kingdom (Matt. 5:29-30). And to be certain one was on the giving side of life, God's side, he counseled, "Give to every one who begs from you; and of him who takes away your goods, do not ask them again" (Luke 6:30). We are not to think that Jesus expected these words to be carried out literally. To do so would be contrary to the truths they were intended to teach. But he did intend that they should be taken seriously.

Not only did Jesus possess a creative mind himself; he also assumed that others were capable of thoughtful response to his teaching and frequently addressed himself to them accordingly. He sometimes asked a question of his hearers which would put the burden of understanding upon them and their ability to think. "What man of you, having a hundred sheep . . . ?" or "What woman, having ten silver coins . . . ?" Again, "Which of you who has a friend . . . ?" and "What father among you . . . ?" Question follows question in his teaching relationships, and these constitute an appeal to reason itself.

### A Real Social Life

In yet another respect the Synoptics portray the reality of Jesus' personal life. Altogether apart from theological considerations, he is depicted within their pages as one who had wholesome social contacts with his fellows. Whether it was on the public highways, in the market place, by the side of the sea, on the hillside, in the home, at a wedding, or in the synagogue, Jesus enjoyed human companionship. And in all of this he was not one who merely lent his presence to the passing scene; instead he entered the circle as a happy participant.

Frequently he was a guest for dinner, both in the homes of those who opposed him (Luke 7:36-50; 11:37-41), as well as in those of his friends and followers (Luke 10:38-42). Sometimes the other guests would not have been acceptable to the religious leaders, and they complained that Jesus was eating with tax collectors and sinners (Luke 5:30-32; 19:7). Because of this they dubbed him "a glutton and a drunkard, a friend of tax collectors and sinners" (Luke 7:34).

Apart from the social factors involved in such fraternization, there were also specific religious implications in this practice. Jesus was not an ascetic; neither was he an Essene. He would not have fitted easily into the order of the Dead Sea community. Its Manual of Discipline would have been a burden to him.

And John the baptizer's particular form of religious discipline was also not congenial to Jesus. Our Lord distinguished himself from his forerunner on one occasion by saying, "For John the Baptist has come eating no bread and drinking no wine; . . . The Son of man has come eating and drinking." (Luke 7:33-34). In spite of this, however, Jesus held John in the highest possible regard and paid him a greater compliment than he gave to any other person. He said to his disciples on the occasion when John, now in prison, had dispatched some of his followers to inquire whether he was the Christ, "I tell you, among those born of women none is greater than John" (Luke 7:28).

### His Relation to Contemporary Issues Was Real

In this chapter we are considering the reality of the personal life of Jesus as it is made known in the Synoptic Gospels. These docu-

140

ments combine, as we have seen, both fact and interpretation, but the latter does not finally obscure the portrait. John Knox's statement of this truth bears strongly upon this conclusion when he writes: "Athough the Gospels do not succeed fully in revealing him [Jesus], they are utterly unable to conceal him, and no critical reader, unless he be entirely devoid of imagination, can miss the mighty and distinctive force of the personality which moves through their pages." [6] This is particularly evident at the points of his relation to specific issues and groups in his own time.

For instance, the Synoptics delineate Jesus' relationship to official Judaism with considerable detail. Although it is not possible to chart the course of this contact from its beginning, through the conflict, and to the denouement which followed, because of the way the material is presented, the strong lines of the issues which developed may be clearly traced. The tension between Jesus and the religious leaders centered in actual practices relating to such issues as the Sabbath (Mark 1:21-28; 2:23-28; 3:1-6), fasting (2:18-22), ceremonial cleansing (7:1-8), tithing (Matt. 23:23), the forgiveness of sins (Luke 5:21), the free association with sinners (Luke 5:29-32), and the observances at the Temple (Mark 11:15-17).

In most of these areas Jesus was critical of the legalism of the Pharisees which prevailed in the interpretation of the Law. And yet, in spite of this, as Klausner says, he "remained steadfast to the old Torah." [7] He did not seek to overthrow it (Matt. 5:17), but was concerned to liberalize its application to persons so that men would not be enslaved by its proscriptions, but would be lifted up into that freedom which was their divine heritage as children of the heavenly Father. For this reason he was angered at a callous insistence upon keeping the letter of the Law by refusing to allow the application of healing arts on the Sabbath, impatient with the practice of tithing as an end in itself, and indignant at the administration of a religious system which outlawed a redemptive association with sinners and outcasts because they were ceremonially unclean.

Pharisaism is not adequately presented in the Synoptics because the emphasis is placed largely upon the areas of conflict between Jesus and their leaders. This was inevitable since the authors were not preparing a treatise upon contemporary Judaism but were

[6] *The Man Christ Jesus*, p. 24.
[7] *Jesus of Nazareth*, p. 275.

telling the story of Jesus, and a recording of the opposition to him from the Pharisees and his criticism of them could not be omitted. Actually, there were many high-minded and devoutly sincere persons within this group. It is unfortunate that only the negative aspects of the movement are considered in the Gospels. And yet, the fact remains that the Pharisees regarded Jesus as a dangerous opponent, and that he was incisively critical of the weaknesses in their practices. On one occasion it is reported that he said, "For I tell you, unless your righteousness exceeds that of the scribes and Pharisees, you will never enter the kingdom of heaven" (Matt. 5:20). Here was an actual situation in which it is made clear that Jesus' relations to contemporary issues as depicted in the Gospels were real.

Although the Sadducees do not appear in the Synoptics as prominently or as frequently as the Pharisees, they are nevertheless a part of the situation which Jesus is depicted as facing. They are seen confronting him during the final days in Jerusalem in an attempt to discredit his teaching, embarrass his person, and finally to put him out of the way permanently. It sometimes happened, though not always, that the high priests were Sadducees, and the Temple rather than the synagogues gave them their main theater of operation. It was at this point that Jesus was most critical of them for insisting upon observances that interfered with true spiritual worship (Mark 11:15-18). He also took issue with them concerning their disbelief in life after death (Luke 20:27-40).

The Roman state was much in evidence across its far-flung empire at the time of Jesus' ministry. Through its representatives—Antipas, Philip (sons of Herod the Great), and Pontius Pilate (procurator) —it kept a strong hand upon Palestine, although it knew how both to give and to take in public administration. There was the ever-present burden of taxes which were levied upon the people, only some of which supported the local government. Publicans, or tax collectors, were familiar personages and the Jews particularly resented them as the servants of a pagan power. The presence of foreign armies quartered upon the soil of "the promise land" was a continuous irritation to this people for whom religion and politics were all but synonymous issues.[8] Resistance movements during the

---

[8] Palestine had been conquered by Rome under Pompey in 63 B.C.

thirty years (67-37 B.C.) before the reign of Herod the Great had taken an estimated toll of more than 100,000 lives alone.[9] All of this together made Roman rule a contemporary issue for the Jews.

Jesus' personal relationship to this issue is not stressed directly in the gospel narratives. It would seem, however, that his words as reported in John's Gospel correctly represent the position he took. In replying to an inquiry from Pilate at the hearing (trial) where he was sentenced to be crucified, he said, "My kingship is not of this world; if my kingship were of this world, my servants would fight, that I might not be handed over to the Jews; but my kingship is not from the world" (18:36). Even though in the Synpotics Jesus did not interpret for Pilate the expression "king of the Jews" in this spiritual sense, his daily practices support this view. This suggests that Jesus did not regard the political question as a major issue in his ministry. His apocalyptic expectation of the coming end of the Age, no doubt, contributed to this position, as well as his own understanding of the nature of the messiahship he was called upon to express.

On the other hand, he appeared to support the cause of good government, as such, when he said to the Herodians who asked him outright if it were lawful to pay taxes to Caesar, "Render to Caesar the things that are Caesar's, and to God the things that are God's" (Mark 12:13-17). Caesar had a right to a proper return for services rendered, even as did God for his gifts of life and daily watch-care. In all probability the Herodians anticipated that he would reply as a patriotic zealot, for Mark says that they were seeking to entrap him in his talk. But they were mistaken.[10]

Jesus evidently had a particular appeal to servants of the Roman state as evidenced by the tax collectors (Mark 2:13-17; Luke 19: 1-10) who turned to him, and the friendly interest of the centurions who are mentioned in the Gospels (Luke 7:1-10; 23:47)—and this in spite of the nonpolitical character of his teaching. In any case, there is the accent of reality in the synoptic portrayal of him in his relation to government, brief as it is.

[9] Klausner, *Jesus of Nazareth*, p. 144.

[10] The fact that the coin which the Herodians showed him on this occasion at his request carried an inscription in Latin, reading "Tiberius Caesar, August Son of Divine Augustus," clearly a claim that the emperor was divine, gave added verve to Jesus' insistence that certain loyalties belonged to God alone. There was a rebuke here under the circumstances for those who were giving to Caesar what belonged only to God.

## His Personal Religion Was Real

The Synoptic Gospels, from first to last, portray Jesus as one whose personal religion was real. Even though the authors had already taken a theological position concerning him, they were so impressed with the reality of his individual experience that they included references to his prayer life, his deep struggle with temptation, and the impact of developing circumstances upon his own faith. All of these factors are structurally a part of the narrative itself, growing out of the life our Lord actually lived, rather than imposed upon the narrative for theological ends. At times, however, they lead to problems of interpretation, as when Jesus, the sinless one, presented himself to John the Baptist for what the preacher had been announcing as a baptism of repentance for the remission of sins. But, in spite of this, the reality overflows the problem and the story is told, sometimes with an attempted explanation.[11]

### In Prayer

In relation to Jesus' personal religious experience, his prayer life in particular should be considered. He is shown in the Synoptics as a person to whom prayer was tremendously real. It was to his soul what breathing was to his body. In moments of crisis when significant decisions had to be made, decisions involving his own destiny and that of his mission as well, Jesus turned to his heavenly Father in prayer for illumination of mind and strength to do God's will. The author of Hebrews caught the meaning of such communion when he wrote, "In the days of his flesh, Jesus offered up prayers and supplications, with loud cries and tears, to him who was able to save him from death, and he was heard for his godly fear. Although he was a Son, he learned obedience through what he suffered." (5:7-8.)

A listing of some of the occasions when the gospel writers take note of the fact that Jesus prayed indicates that these were hours when the direction of his life was being shaped. At such times prayer was the very movement of his spirit. Although each of the Synoptics carries such references, Luke in particular takes special pains to include them. Jesus prayed at his baptism (Luke 3:21-22),

[11] This is probably the reason for the dialogue between Jesus and John in which the baptizer desisted, but was assured by Jesus that he must be baptized "to fulfil all righteousness" (Matt. 3:13-15).

at the close of the first day's ministry at Capernaum (Mark 1: 35-38), when he healed the leper (Luke 5:12-16), prior to selecting his disciples (Luke 6:12-16), after feeding the five thousand (Mark 6:45-46), at Caesarea Philippi when Peter confessed him to be the Christ (Luke 9:18-22), when praying about his coming death at the Transfiguration (Luke 9:28-29), at the time of giving the Lord's Prayer (Luke 11:1-4), in the agony of Gethsemane (Mark 14:32-42), and from the cross itself (Mark 15:34).

Prayer at such times made a difference in the inner life of our Lord. Vision, poise, and a renewal of heart resulted from his communion with God. Although they do not say it in so many words, the gospel writers are united in giving the impression that Jesus prayed out of a deep personal necessity; he was not just setting an example but expressing his very being through prayer. He offered prayers of *inquiry* (Mark 15:34), prayers of *petition* (Mark 14:36), prayers of *intercession* (Luke 22:32), prayers of *thanksgiving* (Luke 10:21-22), and prayers of *committal* (Luke 23:46). Usually they were brief; great faith had made them so. Bultmann points out that the "Prayer of Eighteen Petitions," which was a repetitious "overloaded" type of Jewish praying, should be contrasted with Jesus' simple form of address.[12] Because God is near, hears, loves his children, and understands, lengthy and self-conscious praying is unnecessary.

The Lord's Prayer is a significant example of the prayers of Jesus (Luke 11:2-4; Matt. 6:9-13). It has a liturgical, almost melodic bearing, and yet it is intensely personal. One can readily see why it has become the prayer of the Christian community through the years. Its use of the words "our," "us," and "we" makes it impossible to pray it in an ingrown, individualistic manner. The differences in Matthew's and Luke's forms of the prayer are well known. Sometimes it is concluded that Luke's reading was the original because it is the shorter; in this case Matthew's additional phrases might be regarded as interpretative.[13]

[12] Op. cit., I, 23-24. Used by permission.

[13] "Our" before Father; "Thy will be done, on earth as it is in heaven" following "Thy kingdom come." "But deliver us from evil" after "lead us not into temptation." "For thine is the kingdom and the power and the glory, forever, Amen" constitutes a special case on manuscript grounds. There is always the further possibility that the differences in the two versions are due to separate traditions coming from different sections of the church.

145

On the other hand, Ernest F. Scott has developed at some length the hypothesis that Matthew's longer version might be the earlier one, suggesting that Luke may have sought to divest the new ideas in the prayer of their Jewish associations and for this reason shortened it. His argument is worthy of serious consideration.[14] In any case, this prayer may be said in minute or capsule form to contain the religion of Jesus, and the fact that it was his prayer places him at the center of it, making it a proper consideration for the religion about Jesus, if one is drawing a distinction between the two.

### In His Messiahship

In the preceding chapter it was indicated that the writers of the Synoptic Gospels interpreted Jesus' ministry as messianic.[15] The baptism, temptations, deeds of healing, his relation to official Judaism, as well as his death and resurrection are all presented in this light. The question here for the biblical interpreter, in connection with a discussion of the reality of Jesus' personal life, is whether or not Jesus took this same view of himself.

Let us suppose that it were possible to delete from the account of Jesus' ministry the messianic framework within which the story is told. This is exceedingly difficult to do because it is structurally a part of the narrative itself. And yet, an attempt in this direction, however inconclusive it might be, is rewarding, for it reveals a person with a profound sense of mission, one who believed that he held a unique place within the will of God as that will determines the destiny of men and nations.

For instance, Jesus is seen thus in the Gospels as one who felt himself summoned by God to a significant calling (cf. the baptism[16]); who spent many days in the wilderness facing the alternatives for fulfilling this call (cf. the temptations; through bread-giving? miracles? military force? [17]); who announced to his home-town associates that he had a task to perform of which the Scriptures had spoken (cf. the Nazareth visit [18]); who regarded his preaching and healing as an overthrowing of the kingdom of

---

[14] The Lord's Prayer, pp. 27-30.
[15] Cf. pp. 130-32.
[16] Mark 1:9-11.
[17] Matt. 4:1-11.
[18] Luke 4:16-30.

Satan (cf. Satan fallen as lightning [19]); who accepted and interpreted the title ascribed to him by Peter in terms of one who suffers (cf. Caesarea Philippi pronouncement [20] and the Transfiguration [21]); who entered Jerusalem in humble dignity without rejecting the plaudits of the multitudes (cf. the Triumphal Entry[22]); who established a sacred meal centering in his death (the Last Supper[23]); who stood before the Jews and Pilate as knowing full well what he was about (cf. the trials[24]); and who died with deliberate purpose on the cross (the Crucifixion[25]).

Such an experience for a devout Jew would most likely be interpreted either within the prophetic conception and heritage of the nation or within its messianic hope and expectation. The prophets felt called to special missions by God, to be sure, but there was more in the experience of Jesus as it developed than the prophetic outlook could contain. A more adequate basis of interpretation was to be found in the messianic hope. Whether it be the royal ruler of Isaiah (7:13-17; 9:7; 11:1-9), the servant of Deutero-Isaiah (52:13–53:12. Cf. also 42:1-7; 49:1-6; 61:1-3; 62:1, 6-7) or the Son of man, the new Israel, ideal and glorified, coming down from the heavens (Dan. 7:13-14)—whether it be any one, a combination, or a reinterpretation of these, the messianic outlook provided the likeliest framework for Jesus himself in assessing his experience with God and the nation. It is interesting to note, in this connection, that Charles A. Guignebert [26] and Maurice Goguel [27] combine both the prophetic and messianic in their portrayal of Jesus. They suggest that at the baptism Jesus received a prophetic sense of mission which later developed into a messianic consciousness.

As might be expected, scholars hold a variety of conclusions in this regard. This is understandable since it is largely a matter of interpretation as one seeks to pierce beneath the records to the facts themselves. As far back as 1901 Wrede presented his con-clusion that it was the church that ascribed messiahship to Jesus as

[19] Luke 10:17-20.
[20] Mark 8:27-38.
[21] Luke 9:28-36.
[22] Mark 11:1-10.
[23] Mark 14:22-25.
[24] Mark 14:53–15:15.
[25] Mark 15:21-39.
[26] Jesus, p. 295.
[27] The Life of Jesus, pp. 577-78.

a result of Peter's experience of the resurrected Christ.[28] Wrede's position is treated at length, and sympathetically in English by Lightfoot.[29] In this same vein, but with his own approach, Bultmann concludes that "the synoptic tradition leaves no doubt about it that *Jesus' life and work measured by traditional messianic ideas was not messianic.*"[30] This view is all but inevitable if, as Bultmann does, one considers the account of Jesus' baptism, the temptation story, the narrative of his entry into Jerusalem, and the passion record either as legend or as heavily overlaid with legendary material.

Typical of another view is the position taken by Clarence Tucker Craig.[31] He concludes that although our Lord regarded himself as the Messiah, he did not present any messianic claims. It was a question of waiting for God's intervention before he could exercise his messianic rule fully. In the meantime it was his mission to call men to repentance. As the Messiah, Craig believes that Jesus identified himself with the apocalyptic figure of the Son of man found in the Similitudes of Enoch.[32] Here he is pictured as an ecstatic and dramatic individual from heaven who would pass upon men and nations at the Judgment. In this view Craig follows the lead, although in his own way, given by Albert Schweitzer in his *Quest of the Historical Jesus*, where the idea is developed that Jesus identified himself with the heavenly Son of man and dedicated himself to carrying out his program. This called for him to take the last messianic woes upon himself and go to Jerusalem to die so that he might return in glory.[33]

A further refinement of Jesus' relation to the Son-of-man conception is found in Branscomb's commentary on the Gospel of Mark.[34] It is his conclusion that not Jesus but the early church identified our Lord with this heavenly figure, following the Resurrection. The title was used largely in referring to his return, and the thinking of the church was dominated by this expectation.

In matters such as this where terms that were current in an earlier environment are involved, one must not too easily apply or accept a

---

[28] *Das Messiasgeheimnis in den Evangelien.*

[29] *History and Interpretation of the Gospels,* pp. 16 ff.

[30] *Op. cit.,* I, 27.

[31] "The Proclamation of the Kingdom," *The Interpreter's Bible,* VII, 145-54.

[32] I Enoch 46:3-4. The title "Son of man" appears also in Ezekiel (2:1, etc.) where it is a designation of the prophet, and in Daniel (7:13-14), where it relates to the messianic reign of Israel. In Aramaic the term simply means "man" in general.

[33] Jesus fits his life into an external apocalyptic pattern.

[34] *Op. cit.,* pp. 146-49.

rigid interpretation which does not allow for the individuality and originality of the persons who use them, or to whom they refer. Biblical scholarship sometimes becomes artificial because other factors besides language and terminology are omitted. In the issue at hand, instead of taking at face value the term "Son of man" as found in Enoch, Daniel, and Ezekiel, Jesus may well have applied it to himself in his own way, to suggest a significance for his person and mission which he felt to be unique. It carried the ideas of both humility and exaltation that enabled him to keep from seeming to suggest an earthly royal ruler (Davidic), and yet made it possible to assert that there was a special significance to his person and work.

There is a further sense in which the title "Son of man" had a particular meaning for Jesus. Although, in my judgment, he did not think of the coming of the Kingdom, God's reign on earth, *solely* in apocalyptic terms,[35] he did hold that ultimately it was God's to give and looked forward to the hour of its final coming. On the very eve of his death, he was so sure of its arrival that he said to those gathered about the table at the Last Supper, "I tell you that from now on I shall not drink of the fruit of the vine until the kingdom of God comes" (Luke 22:18). Since the Son of man in Enoch is expected to act as judge at the final judgment, and serve as one who shall "raise up the kings and the mighty from their seats" (cf. I Enoch 46:3-4), Jesus' application of the expression to himself suggests further his conviction that he will return at the end of the Age, and in all probability that it will be in the not too distant future.[36]

It is my personal conclusion that Jesus did regard himself as the Messiah. This does not mean that he fitted himself automatically into any one of the historic or contemporary messianic patterns. Neither was it a matter of holding a specific title, as George S. Duncan has so ably reminded us.[37] Instead, it was the reality of the relation he felt to God and men in the Kingdom that constituted for him a special function, and gave an unprecedented meaning to his life and death. He chose to do the will of his heavenly Father, and God chose

[35] Cf. Jesus' statements which suggest a gradual growth of the Kingdom: Luke 13:20-21; Mark 4:26-29. In Luke 17:20-21 he indicated that in one sense he believed that the Kingdom was already present. Cf. my *Life and Teachings of Jesus*, ch. xiv, "Preaching the Kingdom of God."

[36] Cf. Grant, *op. cit.*, p. 11; Rudolf Otto, *The Kingdom of God and the Son of Man*, pp. 47-48, 59 ff.

[37] *Jesus, Son of Man*, p. 274.

to make him both Lord and Christ. In him all history found and will yet find its destiny. This was a part of his personal consciousness, even as it became, and is, the Faith of the church.

Our study of the portrait of Jesus in the Synoptic Gospels has shown that they present him as the living Lord of the early church. The final significance of his life is to be found, not in a mere recital of the details of his career, real as these were for Jesus himself, but in an evaluation of these events by faith and for faith. When this is done, God is seen to be at work through his Son for the redemption of the world. A New Age has dawned, and the consummation of history in the near future is bright with promise for those who believe.

ELEVEN

# In the Johannine Writings: Background

THE DRAWING OF THE LINES IN THE PORTRAIT OF JESUS BECOMES A
fine art in the Gospel of John.[1] We have seen already how portraiture
emerges, indirectly for the most part, in the Acts of the Apostles and
in the epistles of Paul. In addition we have considered the conception
of Jesus as it is found directly in the Synoptic Gospels. But the
authors here were also interested somewhat in a course of events.
They had a story to tell as well as a person to present. In John's
Gospel, however, story and events are secondary, while the portrait
of Jesus is primary.

### The Portrait and Chronology

This emphasis upon the portrait of Jesus to the neglect of the
background narrative is, in part, the explanation for John's apparent
disinterest in chronology,[2] at least in the chronology of the Synoptic
Gospels.[3] Whereas Matthew and Luke are deliberate in preserving
Mark's order of events, even when they temporarily interrupt it to
introduce material of their own, John takes a different course. He
presents his portrait against a backdrop of the great feasts of the Jews,
Passover (2:13; 6:4; 11:55), Pentecost (5:1),[4] and Tabernacles (7:2).

[1] In this discussion the Johannine writings are accepted as including The Gospel of
John and the three epistles I, II, and III John. The Revelation to John is considered
separately as non-Johannine in origin. Reasons for this conclusion and procedure may
be found in the chapter dealing with the portrait of Christ in the Revelation to John.
Cf. p. 195. Chronologically the Letter to the Hebrews precedes the Johannine writings,
but the latter are examined first because of the Fourth Gospel's classification as a Gospel.
[2] But, see Wilbert F. Howard, "Chronology and Topography," The Interpreter's
Bible, VIII, 447, for a discussion in favor of John's interest in chronology. He finds it
shown not in the details, but in the "narrative as a whole."
[3] This should not be taken to mean that John regards history lightly. It was important to him that the Word actually became flesh. What it does suggest is that it was
the meaning of events as these contributed to the portrait of Jesus as the Christ, the
Son of God, which concerned him most.
[4] If the events in ch. 6 should precede those in ch. 5, then the reference to "a feast
of the Jews" in 5:1 should probably be taken to mean Pentecost, following the Passover of 6:4.

151

In this way Jesus acts and speaks as a symbol of the new revelation in contrast to the old. This provides a Johannine counterpart for the same theme as given by Matthew in his version of the Sermon on the Mount (chs. 5–7).

The chronology of the Fourth Gospel further stresses the superiority of the new word in Jesus as over against the old in Judaism by placing the cleansing of the Temple at the opening of Jesus' ministry, rather than at its close as in the Synoptics. Some modern scholars maintain that the occurrence took place twice,[5] but more conclude that such an event would hardly have happened more than once, and that its location at the beginning of Jesus' last week's ministry in Jerusalem is to be preferred, on both psychological and historical grounds.[6] In the Synoptic Gospels it is the cleansing of the Temple which precipitated the final crisis that led to Jesus' death. Having placed it at the beginning, for dogmatic purposes involving portraiture, John must find the denouement which provided the motive for Jesus' final arrest elsewhere. He does so in the raising of Lazarus. Here the council of the Jews argues, "What are we to do? For this man performs many signs. If we let him go on thus, every one will believe in him, and the Romans will come and destroy both our holy place and our nation" (11:47-48). They then concluded, at the urging of Caiaphas, that Jesus should be killed, since it was expedient that one should die, rather than that the whole nation should perish (vss. 49-50).

### Portraiture and Purpose

That portraiture is central in the Gospel of John may further be seen in the statement of the purpose of the author. After commenting on the fact that he had not recorded all the signs of Jesus, he added, "But these are written that you may believe that Jesus is the Christ, the Son of God, and that by believing you may have life in his name" (20:31). Here it is clearly stated that it is necessary to take the high view of Jesus as the Christ, the Son of God, if one is to believe unto

---

[5] Cf. Alfred E. Garvie: "More probable is it that there were two cleansings; the first here recorded an outburst of enthusiasm . . . ; the second a more definite assertion of authority as the Messiah." "John," *The Abingdon Bible Commentary*, p. 1069.

[6] Cf. G. H. C. Macgregor: "That there were actually two 'cleansings' will hardly be maintained, and though it may be argued in favour of the Johannine placing that a protest against the desecration of the Temple would be called for on Christ's first public appearance, such an act whenever performed must inevitably have provoked arrest, and the balance of probability is against our Gospel." *The Gospel of John* (New York: Harper & Bros., 1929), p. xv. Used by permission.

life. To be sure, the final goal is *life*, but this can come, in the judgment of this author, only by a certain view of the person of Christ which will call forth belief. And thus it is that in the Fourth Gospel, a portrait of Jesus is regarded as the specific for this world's darkness.

In this statement of purpose two aspects of the portrait are stressed. Jesus is first of all the Christ or Messiah; then he is the Son of God. Historically these have not always been synonymous identifications. The distinction between the two is well stated by Strachan when he writes, " 'Son of God' is not an alternative for 'Messiah.' Sonship is likeness to God. Jesus is a Divine Being." [7] But the Synoptic Gospels unite the two when interpreting the baptism of Jesus,[8] and throughout the Fourth Gospel a messianic and a filial consciousness are joined together. There are repeated references to the fact that Jesus is the Christ (1:41; 4:25, 26; 7:25-31; 9:35; [9] 11:27; 18:33-38a) and the divine Son of the Father (3:16; 5:19-23; 6:46; 8:36; 10:34-38; 11:27; 13:3; 14:12-14; 17:1). As elsewhere in the New Testament, the identification of messiahship with divine sonship to God moves beyond the traditional conceptions of the Old Testament.[10]

In presenting his portrait of Jesus as the Messiah and Son of God, the author lifts out from the tradition within his reach sayings, incidents, interviews, discussions, and miracle stories which are best suited to accomplish his purpose. A comparison of the Fourth Gospel with the Synoptics will show that the process behind the composition of the writing was highly selective. Whether he was acquainted with Matthew, Mark, and Luke, familiar with the same body of tradition upon which they based their compositions, or whether he had his own special and particular sources has been a much-debated question.[11] For the moment this is not the issue. On the basis of his

[7] *The Fourth Gospel*, p. 39.

[8] Cf. pp. 123-25.

[9] "Son of man" is to be taken to mean "Messiah" as John uses it here.

[10] The "son" of Ps. 2:7-8 was not taken in its original context to refer to a divine being in the New Testament understanding of the term. For a further consideration of this point cf. George S. Duncan, *Jesus, Son of Man*, pp. 106-18. Manson suggests that in the Old Testament the Son-of-God conception carried a *messianic potential* and that the Christian usage was *higher* in meaning. Cf. *Jesus the Messiah*, pp. 146 ff.

[11] G. H. C. Macgregor suggests that John is primarily dependent upon Mark. Cf. *op cit.*, p. xx. Cf. also Charnwood, *According to St. John, ad loc.*

Streeter accepts Mark and possibly Luke, but not Matthew. Cf. *op. cit.*, pp. 393-426.

P. Gardner-Smith favors sources, either written or oral, but separate from the Synoptics. Cf. *Saint John and the Synoptic Gospels.* Dodd leans in this direction also when he writes, "Definite evidence pointing to documentary relations between John and the Synoptics is seen to be singularly sparse when once the presumption in favour of

own statement (20:30-31) he chose his materials from a larger body of available resources. And having done this, he put them together in such a way that they delineate the portrait and point up his thesis with marked effectiveness.[12]

A dramatic illustration of the deliberate and selective method which the author used is to be seen in the miracle stories which he presents as indications (revelations) of the fact that Jesus is the Christ, the Son of God. Instead of the considerably greater number to be found in the Synoptics, John gives us but seven, no more and no less.[13] Since this figure had an esoteric significance for the Jews, symbolizing completeness, it may be concluded that the author was concerned to give a full witness to Jesus as Christ and Son.

Quite suggestively, these miracles are called "signs" (sēmeion) by the author of the Fourth Gospel. This means that it is not the event itself, but its inner meaning and significance which is important. The final question to ask in these miracle stories is not what happened but what is the *meaning* of what occurred. For this reason the author frequently gives a sermonic interpretation of the miracle immediately following his presentation of it.[14] And even in the telling of the miracle itself there will be interpretive touches to make certain that its meaning is not missed.[15] Thus it becomes a sign of the glory of Christ (2:11) which leads to belief.

### The Fourth Gospel Is Situational

Although the statement of purpose which we have been considering is central in the Gospel of John, there are subsidiary purposes as well. These are not seen as competing with the main intention of the author; instead they undergird it by relating the book closely to

---

such relations is abandoned." Cf. *The Fourth Gospel* (New York: Cambridge University Press, 1953), p. 449. Used by permission.

[12] This can be clearly seen in spite of the probability of textual disarrangement in our canonical version. Cf. Macgregor, *op. cit.*, pp. xxxix ff.

[13] (1) Changing water into wine (2:1-11); (2) healing the nobleman's son (4: 46-54); (3) healing the lame man at the pool (5:2-18); (4) feeding the five thousand (6:1-14); (5) walking on the water (6:16-21); (6) healing the man born blind (9: 1-41); (7) raising Lazarus (11:1-53).

[14] For instance, following the miracle of the healing of the lame man at the pool, and growing out of it, is a sermonic discourse on Jesus the source of life. And the feeding of the five thousand is followed by a discourse on Jesus as the bread of life which came down from heaven.

[15] This may be seen quite easily in the account of the raising of Lazarus when the situation is presented so that it leads inevitably to the declaration of Jesus that he is "the resurrection and the life" (11:25).

154

its immediate environment. In this way they contribute further in the presentation of Jesus as the Christ, the Son of God, to the very first readers of the Gospel.

One of these interests would seem to have been the desire to meet the cynicism and disillusionment which were likely to have come upon the church when the promises of the Revelation to John were not literally fulfilled. Its members had been led to expect the immediate judgment and destruction of Rome, and the return of Christ, the King of kings and Lord of lords. They also were encouraged by this significant writing to anticipate the overthrow of Satan. When these events did not occur, it may well have been a shock to the faith of the church which had undergone suffering and persecution at the hands of Domitian (A.D. 81-96), and had been encouraged to persevere until the glory of Christ would be revealed in a cosmic event that would mark the end of the Age. What better way would there be to cushion this shock and to redeem such a situation than to present a nonapocalyptic portrait of Christ, and an interpretation of the faith in universal terms? This is exactly what is done in the Gospel of John.[16]

This analysis presupposes a date for the Gospel at about the turn of the century (circa A.D. 100-110), which is now regarded as most likely by a majority of scholars.[17] It also is based upon the widely held assumption of an Ephesian background for the writing. From time to time other places of origin have been suggested, but these have not met with broad acceptance.[18]

The question of authorship is not finally determinative in this consideration of the conception of Christ in the Fourth Gospel, because we are interpreting the portrait as it appears in the writing itself. This remains as it is, regardless of the identity of the author. It should be said, however, that he is at present unidentified. John, the disciple of Jesus, has traditionally been considered as the writer of the Gospel, but differences between it and the Synoptics make this view difficult, if not impossible, to hold. John the Elder is a more likely candidate

[16] Cf. my unpublished thesis for the doctorate, "The Fourth Gospel—A Reply to the Apocalypse of John," library of Boston University School of Theology.

[17] Consult the commentaries and introductions to the New Testament for a detailed discussion of date and authorship.

[18] Alexandria in Egypt has been proposed, largely because of the philosophical tradition which was associated with this city. Similarity of thought and expression between the letters of Ignatius, bishop of Antioch, and the Fourth Gospel has led also to the suggestion of Antioch as the site of its origin.

as we meet him in a quotation from Papias,[19] but this too is conjectural. In this chapter we shall sometimes refer to him simply as John.

Similarities of terminology, and to some extent, of conceptions between the Gospel of John and the Dead Sea Scrolls have led to a discussion as to whether the Gospel should be dated as late as is customarily done. Might it not even be the first of the Gospels to be written, since the scrolls should probably be dated within the first two centuries B.C.? Basic to this consideration is the question as to whether what we find in the Fourth Gospel calls for the background of Gnosticism as it existed in the Hellenistic world at the close of the first century, or whether the emphases upon "knowledge," "light," and "darkness" in the scrolls is sufficient to account for the stress upon these ideas in John. In my judgment it is too soon to draw final conclusions in this discussion.[20] But the so-called Gnosticism of the scrolls hardly seems sufficiently thoroughgoing to explain what we find in the Gospel.[21]

To return to the question of some secondary or subsidiary purposes which the author of the Fourth Gospel may have had in mind, mention should be made of his desire to combat the Gnostic denial of the reality of Jesus' life in the flesh, his concern to meet the movement in the interest of the supremacy of John the Baptist over Jesus, his interest in replying to objections of the Jews in his own day to the messiahship of Jesus, and to his purpose in interpreting the Gospel in the light of Hellenistic outlook and practice.[22] And in each instance

[19] Cf. Eusebius, op. cit., III, 39.

[20] Cf. a bibliography on this discussion:

Theodore H. Gaster, The Dead Sea Scriptures, pp. 13-15.

Millar Burrows, The Dead Sea Scrolls, ch. xii.

L. Mowry, "The Dead Sea Scrolls and the Gospel of John" in Biblical Archaeologist, 1954, pp. 20-28.

J. L. Teicher, "Jesus' Sayings in the Dead Sea Scrolls," in the Journal of Jewish Studies, 1954, p. 38.

Duncan Howlett, The Essenes and Christianity (New York: Harper & Bros., 1957), pp. 166-68.

Frank Moore Cross, Jr., The Ancient Library of Qumrân and Modern Biblical Studies (New York: Doubleday & Co., 1958), ad loc.

[21] Cf. Burrows: "On the whole, however, it seems unnecessary and only confusing to apply the term Gnosticism to the form in which such ideas appear in the Dead Sea Scrolls." Op. cit., p. 259. Used by permission.

[22] For a detailed discussion of these issues cf. Ernest C. Colwell, John Defends the Gospel, ad loc. and Wilbert F. Howard, "Apologetic Interests in the Fourth Gospel," The Interpreter's Bible, VIII, 449 ff.

it is his portrait of Jesus Christ, the Son of God, which he offers as a specific for the situation at hand.

### The Historical Question

Because the drawing of a portrait which will lead to such belief, as results in life, is the author's main concern, it should not be concluded that John was disinterested in history. This interest, however, was not wholly that of an objective reporter; instead it was akin to that of the artist or dramatist who highlights his characters so that their significance as well as their likeness will be shown. Even as the Synoptists, the author of the Fourth Gospel is an interpreter as well as a chronicler. In some respects he is more creative in presenting his material than they, but at no time, in my opinion, is he conscious of basically misrepresenting the real Jesus of history.

Whether or not John turned to the Synoptic Gospels and/or to other special sources, written or oral, for the data he uses in delineating his portrait, is not necessarily determinative in deciding the historical question. The issue does not rest wholly upon the identity of the sources but upon their trustworthiness, as well as upon the way in which the author employs them. And in the final analysis there is an opportunity to check any single telling of the story of Jesus in the New Testament with other representations in the same scriptures. The validity of John's general outline in such a comparison is evident. In the words of C. H. Dodd:

> In the first place, he can be shown to have followed the broad general outline of the ministry, death, and resurrection of Jesus Christ which is presupposed in the Synoptic Gospels, reproduced in the Apostolic preaching in Acts, and attested up to a point in the Pauline epistles. This outline we have good reason to believe primitive, and by his fidelity to it, the evangelist gives proof of his intention to expound the meaning of *facts*, and not to invent a dramatic plot.[23]

The fact that within this general outline there are divergencies between John and the Synoptics does not mean that the author is erratic and misleading. We have already noted that these appear in relation to chronology, when the cleansing of the Temple is placed in the Fourth Gospel at the beginning of Jesus' ministry instead of its close, as in Matthew, Mark, and Luke. Here we concluded that

[23] *The Fourth Gospel*, p. 447. Used by permission.

the synoptic date was preferable.[24] There are differences also between them in the dating of the Last Supper. In John it is a memorial meal on the evening before the Passover supper (evening of Thursday, Nisan 13), while in the Synoptics it is the Passover meal itself (evening of Thursday, Nisan 14) which Jesus eats with his disciples.

In this case there are reasons for preferring John's date.[25] It is questionable whether some of the activities described in the passion narrative would have been permitted by Jewish law on the first day of the feast, which the Synoptic placing would require. These include the bearing of arms on a feast day, the making of purchases (spices for embalming Jesus' body), the trial, and the crucifixion itself. Also, it is reasonable to assume that Jesus would have had a more extensive Judean and Jerusalem ministry than the Synoptics report, where there is recorded but a single visit to the Holy City. John, on the other hand, chronicles such. The point in this recital of divergencies in chronology is that the fact of differences between John and the Synoptics, and between the Synoptics and John, should not lead one to conclude that either or all are essentially untrustworthy as historical representations. Varying sources for the tradition, particular purposes behind the writings, and individualities of temperament and style of the authors go far in accounting for them.

### Creative Artist

It has already been indicated that the expressed purpose of the author gives him certain freedoms in handling his materials.[26] Eric L. Titus is speaking to this conclusion when he says, "With regard to history, the evangelist's interest was in the *event*, not in the events. It was important for him that the Incarnation had occurred in history." [27]

This assertion serves to emphasize the centrality of the author's intention in interpreting his writing. He is concerned, however, not only with the incarnation as a bare fact, but also with *the glory* that men beheld in the Word that was made flesh. It was "glory as of the

---

[24] Cf. p. 152.

[25] Cf. a suggestive discussion of this issue in Henry Major, et al., *The Mission and Message of Jesus*, pp. 866 ff. There is also no Lord's Supper at the Last Supper in John. It is treated instead in the sermon on Jesus as the Bread of life (6:25-59).

[26] Cf. pp. 152-54.

[27] *The Message of the Fourth Gospel*, p. 17.

only son from the Father" (1:14). This constitutes the ultimate in portraiture.

As a creative artist, John makes sure that the glory will not be missed in this account. He achieves this by the selection and arrangement of his materials. In addition, he further accomplishes this by showing concern for detail that is unlike anything found in the Synoptics. Such expressions occur as "Now six stone jars were standing there, . . . each holding twenty or thirty gallons" (2:6); "It was about the sixth hour" (4:6); "for you have had five husbands" (vs. 18); "So the woman left her water jar" (vs. 28); "A pool . . . which has five porticoes" (5:2); ". . . who has five barley loaves" (6:9); " . . . his feet bound with bandages, and his face wrapped with a cloth" (11:44); ". . . and at once there came out blood and water" (19:34); ". . . myrrh and aloes, about a hundred pounds weight" (vs. 39); ". . . and hauled the net ashore, full of large fish, a hundred and fifty-three of them" (21:11).[28]

These details are sometimes regarded as eyewitness touches, suggesting that closely behind the Gospel is one who was present when the events described took place. This one, it is thought, might be the witness mentioned in 19:35, "He who saw it has borne witness—his testimony is true, and he knows that he tells the truth—that you also may believe." In certain instances the possibility of such a witness is evident.[29] On the other hand, sometimes the event described in detail happened with apparently no witnesses present. The conversation with the Samaritan woman is one such case. Here the details, on this basis, would have to have been shared later by Jesus, as in the Temptations which the Synoptics record. Yet, again, they may be regarded as due to the dramatic touch of the author in presenting his material.[30] This conclusion seems to me to be a likely one, not only where the events described took place in private, but elsewhere in the Gospel as well.

In my judgment, the historical question is not basically affected by the view held in regard to these details, no more than it is in the Synoptics where sometimes, although not so frequently, such refer-

[28] Even though ch. 21 is an appendix to the Gospel and quite likely a later addition, the reference is included here because it is of the same sort as the others listed. The italics in this enumeration are mine.

[29] For a suggestive discussion of "the witness" see Garvie, The Beloved Disciple, ad loc.

[30] Cf. Strachan, The Fourth Evangelist: Dramatist or Historian? ad loc.

ences occur. They belong to the narrative as the author has presented it. In most cases they are natural to the situation described. They make for good drama, and do not create bad history. Sometimes they have been made to carry more history than they should be expected to bear, and again they have been made to support more dogma than is reasonable under the circumstances.[31] But that they make vivid the portrait of Christ, the Messiah and Son, and contribute to the message of the author should be clear to any thoughtful reader of the Fourth Gospel.

### The Author-Mystic

As far back as Clement of Alexandria (*circa* A.D. 150-220) the spiritual character of John's Gospel was recognized. This church father and theologian of the Greek world is quoted in Eusebius as saying, "Last of all John, perceiving that the bodily facts had been set forth in the other Gospels, at the instance of his disciples and with the inspiration of the Spirit composed a spiritual Gospel." [32] This statement has almost become a dictum; it has been recognized and accepted by biblical scholars from that day to this, not because a church father said it, but because it has commended itself to the minds and the hearts of those who have studied the Fourth Gospel deeply.

One of the reasons for this conclusion is that the author stresses inner spiritual fellowship between the Father, Jesus, and his followers more than external relationships. Such statements as this from the Upper Room discourses (chs. 14-17) are typical of this emphasis, "If a man loves me, he will keep my word, and my Father will love him, and we will come to him and make our home with him" (14:23). Or take another, from the priestly prayer of Jesus, "I have made known to them thy name, and I will make it known, that the love with which thou hast loved me may be in them, and I in them" (17:26). Such words as these constitute the heart of what is often referred to as Johannine mysticism.

In this connection a unique characteristic of the Gospel emerges. It is often difficult to tell where the author leaves off speaking and

[31] As when the "five husbands" of the Samaritan woman are allegorized into the the five gods whom the Samaritans worshiped (II Kings 17:30-34), or the five books of the Law. Jesus, before whom she is standing, is superior to these. The 153 fish of John 21:11 have been also said to have its point in the fact that, according to Jerome, in that day there were 153 varieties of fish. The number, therefore, is said to symbolize the universality of inclusion of the Gospel. It is intended for all.

[32] *Op. cit.* VI, 14.

Jesus begins in a given passage (cf. John 3:6-15). And in the discourses particularly Jesus speaks in the same words that the author customarily uses; the vocabulary and style are all but indistinguishable. The explanation for this interesting phenomenon, in my judgment, is that John is a mystic. As he wrote, he was conscious in the Spirit of the presence of the risen Christ. What came to him in this state or relationship, he regarded as a word of Jesus, just as truly as any statement he found in the tradition before him. Therefore he does not always distinguish between what Jesus said and what the living Christ is now saying. He would not be sympathetic with the view that he, John, is doing the talking rather than Jesus in these instances. Even though the vocabulary seems to be his own, he would contend that the sentiments were truly those of his Lord.

What saves the author of the Fourth Gospel from the excesses often characteristic of those who speak or write "in the Spirit" is that he has before him the tradition concerning the historical Jesus. At the outset, he had stated in the prologue to his Gospel that "the Word became flesh and dwelt among us" (1:14), and for all the individualities of his presentation, he does not forget this fact. He will not, therefore, substitute ecstasy for the life Jesus lived in the flesh.

In this chapter we have seen that portraiture is a fine art for the author of the Fourth Gospel, whatever his name might be. His purpose was to present Jesus as the Christ, the Son of God, so that belief and life-giving commitment to him might result. Although he universalizes and eternalizes the portrait, so that his Lord is seen as the Savior of all and for all time, he is not unmindful of the needs of his own generation as he writes. Because his concern is spiritualized portraiture, John takes some liberties with the tradition of the church concerning Jesus, but he is not unmindful of the importance of the Jesus of history. That the Word became flesh is a major consideration in his Gospel.

# TWELVE

## In the Johannine Writings: Delineation

WE HAVE BEEN CONSIDERING THE PORTRAIT OF JESUS IN THE GOSPEL of John as it is related to the purpose, sources, style, and personality of the author, as well as to its significance for the day in which it was drawn. If this seems a rather complex procedure, it should not be forgotten that because the Gospels came forth out of the life stream of the early church, these factors are necessarily involved. Furthermore, it is because of them that the Gospels are creative documents rather than abstract chronicles of past events.

### The Divine Logos

But what of the portrait itself; what is the author's conception of Jesus? It is to this question that we shall now turn. Perhaps it is best to begin where John himself opens his Gospel. At the very outset in the Prologue (1:1-18)[1] he writes, "In the beginning was the Word, and the Word was with God, and the Word was God" (vs. 1). Later in this section he adds, "And the Word became flesh and dwelt among us, full of grace and truth; we have beheld his glory, glory as of the only Son from the Father" (vs. 14). In the first of these words, John is saying that Jesus pre-existed as the divine Logos (Word) in the closest possible relation to God. This relationship was active, involving the most intimate fellowship.

In connection with the virgin-birth accounts, it was stated that their message basically was that the ultimate explanation of Jesus is God. This Gospel is now saying that Jesus actually lived as the Logos with God before his advent.[2] Thus his origin is traced beyond con-

---

[1] The question of the literary source of the Prologue is not essentially pertinent to this study, since it has been a part of the Gospel from the first, and we are concerned with the conception of Jesus in this writing as it stands. It should be noted, however, that some have held it to be an adaptation of a hymn honoring Wisdom, John replacing Sophia with Logos (Rendel Harris). In any case, the Prologue as we have it is saturated with John's own mind.

[2] Cf. the previous discussion of the pre-existence of Jesus in Paul's letter to the Colossians, pp. 95-99.

ception through the Holy Spirit to the heavenly realm itself. But he did not remain in the heavens; instead "the Word became flesh" and dwelt among men on earth. There is no indication here in the prologue as to how this occurred.[3] The Incarnation as a fact is the author's concern.

Why did John think of the origin of Jesus in terms of the Logos (Word), and of the Incarnation as the Logos made flesh? It would not seem to have been because of an interest in philosophical speculation as such. More probably his purpose was to interpret the significance of Jesus as the Christ and Son of God in terms of the highest thought-forms of his own day. Having said this, it is difficult to specify the exact sense in which the term "Logos" is used. Is John thinking of the creative word (Memra) in the Old Testament which God uttered in creation, a word that carried the power to call its object into existence (cf. "And God said, 'Let there be light'; and there was light." Gen. 1:3)?[4] Does he have in mind the Wisdom which Jewish writers sometimes referred to as the thought of God actively creating in the universe (cf. Prov. 8:22-31),[5] or is he identifying Jesus with the Logos of Hellenistic-Jewish thought as exemplified in the Stoics and adapted in Philo where the Word stands for the reason or rational principle through which, as a divine hypostasis, God created the universe?[6]

Up to a certain point each of these possibilities is pertinent to John's use of the expression "Logos." And it may well be that this is the reason he selected the term. Here was a concept that was rich in its implications of ultimate significance for his readers, Hebrew and Greek alike. When used in relation to Jesus, it provided a philosophical setting and explanation for the high position given to him throughout the Gospel. Before John wrote, both Paul and the author of Hebrews had begun to think somewhat along these lines (Col.

---

[3] Titus argues for the position that, in the Fourth Gospel, this took place through the coming of the Spirit upon Jesus at the time of John's baptism: "The divine Spirit merges with the man from Nazareth at the time of its descent; this is the point of the Incarnation" (op. cit., pp. 51-54). In the immediate context of the references to the descent of the Spirit upon Jesus, however, the purpose is to point out Jesus to John the Baptist as the Christ.

[4] Cf. Strachan, The Fourth Gospel, ch. vii.

[5] Cf. T. Rendel Harris, The Origin of the Prologue to St. John's Gospel, ad loc.

[6] Cf. Dodd, The Fourth Gospel, p. 277: "It is the meaning, plan or purpose of the universe, conceived as transcendent as well as immanent, as the thought of God formed within the eternal Mind and projected into objectivity." Used by permission.

1:15 ff.; Heb. 1:2-3a). But the author of the Fourth Gospel, in the Prologue at least, is more fulsome in his references than they.[7]

It was stated previously that John's interest in the Logos conception was not motivated by speculative ends. He employs it to convey values already seen in the historical Jesus, as though faith was turning to reason to explain what it had previously discovered.[8] Although he actually believes that Jesus' origin is the Logos, his concern in the Gospel is with the Word made flesh. One reason for this may have been to combat current Docetic teachings on the unreality of Jesus' fleshly life.[9] Even though this may be true, the Incarnation itself for the sake of its own message is also, in my judgment, of prime importance to John. As he says at the close of the Prologue, "No one has ever seen God; the only Son, who is in the bosom of the Father [as Logos], he has made him known" (1:18). There is an awesome sense of the wonder and glory of the revelation in these words.

As we look, therefore, to the Fourth Gospel for its portrait of Jesus, we shall discover that this high view of him as the eternal Logos made flesh is basic throughout. Although the flesh may veil his true identity, and the term "Logos" does not appear except in the Prologue, it is the underlying reality beneath his words and deeds. And it also undergirds John's claim that Jesus is the Christ, the Son of God.

### Portraiture and the New Birth

Titles in the Fourth Gospel are more than ascriptions of identity; they signify life-giving relationships as well. For instance, as the Christ, the eternal Son, Jesus brings to men the experience of new birth. This is first recognized in the Prologue where it states that "to all who received him, who believed in his name, he gave power to become children of God; who were born, not of blood nor of the will of the flesh nor the will of man, but of God" (1:12-13). The

[7] It is sometimes said (Harnack, et al.) that apart from the Prologue, John does not refer to Jesus as the Logos throughout his writing. Dodd argues against this view, holding that John's use of "Son of Man" is equivalent to the Idea of Man, which in Philo is identified with the Logos. (Ibid., p. 279.) Cf. also Macgregor: "The thought of Jesus as the revelation of the Logos in history is the key-note which vibrates throughout the entire Gospel" (op. cit., pp. XXXVII-XXXVIII). Used by permission.

[8] Cf. E. F. Scott, The Fourth Gospel, p. 163.

[9] Docetism was the first Christian heresy. It was not a philosophical system as such, or a specific sect. Instead it was a view taken concerning Jesus' life in the flesh. Some regarded our Lord's entire physical life as unreal; others would include only certain aspects of it, such as his birth and death. Some of the Gnostics were Docetists, but not all.

reference here is to a supernatural birth which comes to those who believe in Jesus as the Christ who is God's Son. This supernatural birth should not be confused with the experience of being "initiated" through the mystery religions. Although the language used in referring to the latter is sometimes similar to John's, the centrality of Christ and the moral elements in the Johannine new birth make it a completely different thing.[10] It is faith or active belief which transports men into this newness of life as the children of God.[11] Sometimes it is asserted that John teaches that men come into newness of life through knowledge (gnōsis) rather than faith.[12] Certainly this teaching is present, but that it dominates the Gospel to the exclusion of other emphases may be questioned. When John speaks of believing, there is more than the gnostic stress on knowledge. Moral commitment such as is found in faith is at the heart of such an act of believing.

The new birth is further defined in the account of the interview between Jesus and Nicodemus (3:1 ff.) Here our Lord expressly tells the distinguished Pharisee that he must be born from above (again or anew) if he is to see (enter) the kingdom of God.[13] And by way of defining what he means, Jesus distinguishes between physical birth and spiritual regeneration. The flesh gives birth to what is physical, but the Spirit creates a spiritual life after its own kind. It is not that the flesh is inherently sinful, else how could it contain the Logos? Instead, the flesh is physical and thus can only lead to a physical harvest.

We have already noted that the Prologue suggests that the new birth comes from believing on or in Jesus' name as the Christ. When Nicodemus inquires "How can this be?" he is upbraided for not understanding this experience which takes place on earth, even though its source is in heaven. As a teacher in Israel (along with the Jews of

[10] Cf. Strachan, *Fourth Gospel*, pp. 70 ff. Cf. also previous discussion of the Mysteries in this book, pp. 92-94.

[11] For a suggestive analysis of the Johannine meaning of faith its relation to the word and person of Jesus, and its eschatological character, cf. Bultmann, *op. cit.*, II, 70-92.

[12] Grant: "For him [John], 'knowledge' means the warm intimate personal knowledge of God as revealed in Christ (17:3b), not information about a body of metaphysical speculation." *The Gospel of John*, I, 12. The latter was characteristic of the salvation by knowledge as taught by the Gnostics.

[13] In the Fourth Gospel the expression "eternal life" is most often used as a counterpart for the Synoptic "kingdom of God." This has the effect of universalizing and spiritualizing what among the Jews traditionally was local and political.

John's day) he should have been familiar with these things. Like the wind whose origin and destiny are unknown to the senses, but whose force they can feel, so is the new birth. Even though it is a mystery, it can be experienced. And Jesus has now revealed its source and purpose in the Spirit.[14]

If in the interview between Jesus and Nicodemus the new birth is presented and defined, in his dialogue with the Samaritan woman it is further interpreted, if not actually illustrated (4:1-42).[15] Jesus here invites this world-weary woman to come to him for the living water (vss. 10, 13-14). He is the source of the new life she needs. As they converse, such matters as the confusion between literal and spiritual water, the woman's marital and extramarital situation, and the proper place for worship are touched upon. Out of it all emerges an announcement of Jesus that he is the Messiah[16] and his acceptance by the woman as such (vss. 29, 42). She came to "see" the kingdom of God.

Undoubtedly there are other strains of thought in this dialogue, such as the relation of Judaism, Christianity, and the religion of the Samaritans to one another, but the woman's progress in faith as she comes to belief and the new birth would seem to be central. Although her story is as suddenly dropped as it is begun, which is typical of the presentation of witnesses in this Gospel, it serves to point out the relation of new birth to Jesus himself. There is no contradiction here between the Spirit as the source of the new birth (ch. 3) and Jesus as the one who gives the living water, since in this Gospel it is Jesus who sends the Spirit (15:26; 16:7).

The healing of the man born blind (9:1-41) also presents an account of growth in faith that leads to the realization and acceptance of the fact that Jesus is the Messiah, a belief which may be said to

[14] There is no contradiction in John's insistence that one needed to be born of water, as well as of the Spirit (vs. 5). Baptism and the coming of the Spirit frequently came together in the New Testament. The emphasis here would not be upon baptism as an outward act, but in true Johannine fashion, upon the spiritual aspects of repentance and commitment which attended the sacred rite.

[15] Theories of partition usually include ch. 4 as a section in which a redactor has been at work. These vary from scholar to scholar as they employ a type of literary criticism which of necessity involves subjective elements. For the most part, however, they do not affect the position taken here. Cf. Macgregor, op. cit., pp. lxvi-lxvii, 93-117; Howard, The Interpreter's Bible, viii, 459-60.

[16] This declaration of messiahship by Jesus to another, coming as it does presumably so early in the ministry of Jesus, may be compared with the much later self-revelation in the Synoptics. If it is questionable history, it is, nevertheless, sound homiletics from John's point of view. He is presenting a thesis primarily.

result in his new birth. In both this narrative and that of the Samaritan woman, Jesus is the source of the new life into which these witnesses are introduced. Both, therefore, constitute portraiture where Jesus is concerned. He is such a one that those who believe in him receive life in his name.

### Portraiture and Spiritual Sustenance

Not only does John present Jesus as the Christ and Son of God who brings those who believe in him into an experience of new birth; he also sees him as their source of spiritual sustenance. This theme is repeated over and over again in the Gospel. It is dramatically asserted in the great "I ams" which appears as a symphonic theme in chapter after chapter. There are seven such statements which, like the seven signs or miracles, give their complete witness:[17]

"I am the bread of life." (6:35.)
"I am the light of the world." (8:12.)
"I am the door of the sheep." (10:7.)
"I am the good shepherd." (10:14.)
"I am the resurrection and the life." (11:25.)
"I am the way, and the truth, and the life." (14:6.)
"I am the true vine." (15:1.)

There is nothing like these as stated in the Synoptic Gospels, either in the sense of the constant assertions of his own significance or in the extensive use of metaphor, although on occasion there are comparable expressions of authority and attitude on the part of Jesus (Matt. 11:27). But this, again, in the Fourth Gospel must be taken as an example of the writer's special touch as an artist-author.

Behind these seven "I ams" lie three generations of Christian experience at the hands of the living Lord, Jesus Christ. They are true because they have been found to be so in the personal lives of his followers. Through toil, persecution, and travail, their Lord had actually been proved to be the sustaining vitality of their lives. This is not theorizing; instead it is witnessing in the true Johannine sense.

When these statements are examined closely, it will be seen that each is an assertion of necessity in the area or relationship involved. Bread and light are basic to the continuance of life. Doors are neces-

[17] Actually there are eight, if by implication Jesus' reference to himself as the giver of living water in 4:14 be regarded as such a statement.

sary for entrance; sheep could not exist in a Palestinian environment without the guidance and protection of shepherds; death calls for resurrection if life is to continue; men will be lost without a way to follow, a truth to embrace, and a life to sustain them; and branches will shrivel and die apart from their attachment to the vine. The point of each of these metaphors, therefore, is that Jesus is a basic necessity to life. Apart from him it does not truly exist. This fact constitutes a major stroke in John's portrait of Jesus.

## The Eucharist

Special consideration should be given to John's interpretation of the Eucharist in relation to Jesus as the source of spiritual sustenance. As has been noted previously, there is no Lord's Supper at the Last Supper in the Fourth Gospel.[18] Instead, it is dealt with in the discourse on Jesus as the bread of life which follows the account of the feeding of the five thousand in ch. 6. And the heart of this interpretation is found in the words:

Truly, truly, I say to you, unless you eat the flesh of the Son of man and drink his blood, you have no life in you; he who eats my flesh and drinks my blood has eternal life, and I will raise him up at the last day. For my flesh is food indeed, and my blood is drink indeed. He who eats my flesh and drinks my blood abides in me, and I in him. As the living Father sent me, and I live because of the Father, so he who eats me will live because of me. (Vss. 53-57.)

In these significant sentences certain claims are made concerning Jesus as the source of true spiritual sustenance which are penetrating and incisive. It is stated that in the Lord's Supper men eat his flesh and drink his blood. As a result they have eternal life and will live at the final judgment. But more than this, partaking of the elements in the Eucharist brings one into mystical union with Christ. It is basic to the relationship which John elsewhere compares to that which exists between the vine and the branches (15:1-11).

It is not likely that John goes as far here as to assert that the elements of bread and wine are not necessary, just because he does not mention the passing of the bread and cup.[19] That the emphasis, however, is upon the spiritual realities which are in and attend the partaking of

[18] Cf. p. 158.
[19] Cf. Titus, op. cit., p. 124.

the Lord's Supper seems clear. When his words had caused offense to those with a Jewish background, to whom the drinking of blood was forbidden (Deut. 12:23), Jesus replied, "It is the spirit that gives life, the flesh is of no avail; the words that I have spoken to you are spirit and life" (6:63). In this light, it should not be concluded that the Fourth Gospel takes a *strictly* sacramentalist view of the Eucharist, even as Paul did not.[20] And it is equally unlikely that John's view rests upon the Hellenistic sacramental meals, although he may have had them in mind.[21] He is closer to Paul and the Synoptics than to the Greeks in this regard.

In the passage on the Eucharist which we are considering, we find the expression "the Son of man" (6:53). This reflects the use of this phrase by Jesus as a title for himself in the Synoptics. The idea of pre-existence which it carries is characteristic of the Fourth Gospel, particularly in the Prologue where our Lord is identified with the pre-existent Logos (cf. also John 8:58). Also, the exalted character of the Son of man in Enoch [22] is fully in harmony with John's portrait of one who possesses such glory as is found in God (1:14). For these reasons the title was congenial to John's thought of Jesus.

But its apocalyptic connotations, by and large, are left behind, even though in this Gospel a reference is made to the last day.[23] Spiritually Jesus, the Christ, has already returned in the coming of the Spirit (14:16-18). And even the Judgment is no longer wholly future in the Fourth Gospel. It is happening in the present as men receive or reject Christ, the light of the world (3:17-18; 9:39-40). In this teaching John is moving along the lines of thought already laid down by Paul, except that he carries them further than the great apostle.

### Portraiture and the Spirit

It was stated above that for John, Christ had already returned in the coming of the Spirit. In this interpretation the Fourth Gospel brings to full maturity the experience and thought of the church concerning the Spirit from Pentecost on through to the end of the first century.

[20] Cf. pp. 88-91. Cf. Major, *et al.*, *op. cit.*, pp. 775-76.

[21] Cf. Macgregor, *op. cit.*, pp. 161-62. Rawlinson, *New Testament Doctrine of Christ*, pp. 270-84.

[22] Cf. previous discussion, pp. 148 ff.

[23] John 12:48. In connection with this reference there is no detailed apocalyptic program. It probably reflects, in passing, a current eschatological outlook, but is not characteristic of John's portrait of Jesus.

169

A term John uses frequently in referring to the Spirit is "counselor" or "paraclete" (*paraklētos*). This Greek expression when employed thus usually refers to one who takes his place beside another as an advocate, and argues his cause. On behalf of another he pleads a case. John's choice of the word is related to his understanding of the function of the Spirit.

The reason John's references to the Spirit are related to his portrait of Jesus, the Christ, is that he sees the Counselor as an alter ego of Jesus himself. The work he is represented as undertaking is the very ministry of Christ. He will dwell with them and be in them even as Christ (14:17-18). In this same sense, he will teach them and recall to their minds the words of Jesus (14:26). The things our Lord would have said to his followers while yet on earth, but could not because of their immaturity, the Counselor will reveal to them in the future (16:12-13). In doing so, he will not speak for himself, but on behalf of Christ. Thus he will glorify the Son, and declare things to come.

As in Peter's sermon at Pentecost the exalted Christ is regarded as the one who "poured out" the Spirit (Acts 2:33), so in the Fourth Gospel it is the Son who sends the Counselor (16:7). This is further reason for considering the Spirit in delineating the portrait of Jesus, the Christ. But he proceeds also from the Father in order to bear witness to the Son (15:26; cf. also 14:16).[24] This cannot occur, however, until Christ returns to the Father and, therefore, it is to the advantage of the disciples that he "go away" (16:7).

Another name for the Spirit in the Fourth Gospel is "the Spirit of truth." The truth here probably refers to the truth concerning God, his relation to the universe, and to the Logos made flesh. It is within the context of the message of the Gospel itself that the meaning is to be sought. When John tells of Jesus' trial before Pilate, he records that Jesus said, "I have come into the world, to bear witness to the truth" (18:37). And in the Prologue it was stated that "grace and truth came through Jesus Christ" (1:17). As the alter ego of Christ, the Spirit continues the work of revealing the truth.

Yet another activity of the Spirit should be mentioned, the Spirit whom Christ sends and who is, therefore, involved in his portrait. He will "convince the world of sin and of righteousness and of judgment" (16:8). In this immediate setting, the Spirit as Counselor is con-

---

[24] John's focus here is not on the inner structure of the being of God, but upon what the Father and the Son are doing.

cerned with Christ's death and with the attitude men take toward him. Through the Spirit the true meaning of that death will be revealed, and the sin of powers, both earthly and invisible, who crucified him made plain. Christ will be seen to have been accused falsely (16: 9-11). Those who refused (and refuse) to believe will be pointed out through the Spirit as guilty.

### The Son and the Father

The relationship of the Son to the Father and of the Father to the Son is of final significance in the portrait of Jesus as Messiah and Son in the Fourth Gospel. As a theme this relationship is dealt with by John from the beginning to the end of his writing. It is introduced in the situations as presented with a deliberateness that is unmistakable. Sometimes where one does not expect it, a phrase or clause will be inserted which makes a claim concerning the relation between Jesus and God. It is a continuous and superb obsession of the author.

Apart from the Prologue, where Jesus' relationship to the Logos and the Logos' relationship to God is stated, the consideration of this theme is not overtly metaphysical but essentially religious. A formal theology is not drawn; instead a spiritual union is described. And yet, this union goes beyond that of the prophet and priest in their association with God, so much so that metaphysical overtones inevitably come to mind. As in the epistles of Paul, Jesus possesses the religious value of God, so in John's Gospel, our Lord is given a place in the experience of men which belongs, or should belong, only to God himself.

We have already considered John's identification of Jesus with the Logos in the Prologue.[25] This rooted his existence in the very being of God. Later in this introductory statement Jesus is referred to as the "only" or "only begotten" (monogenēs) Son (1:14). The same expression occurs in 1:18 and also in John's statement concerning God who so loved the world that he gave his only Son so that he might bestow life upon all who believed in him (3:16). It is difficult to tell whether "only" refers to the being of the Son as one in essence with God, or to the uniqueness of his ethical union with the Father. John would not have hesitated to assert the former, but whether he is doing so here is the real question. Since, however, in Philo the

[25] Cf. pp. 162-64.

Logos comes from out God's nature, it is probably more correct to regard John's meaning in the context of the Prologue as referring to a metaphysical rather than an ethical relationship.[26] Jesus' divine nature is thus asserted in his relation to the being of God when he is referred to as the "only" Son.

In considering the relation which exists between Jesus and God in the Gospel of John, reference must be made to the well-known statement, "I and the Father are one" (10:30). Here again the question arises as to whether the claim is being made that Jesus and God are a single metaphysical entity. These words lend themselves so aptly to a theological defense of this position that they are often taken to be an open assertion on its behalf.[27] Within the context in which they occur, however, they seem to refer to the spiritual and ethical union which exists between Jesus and the heavenly Father.[28] As the Messiah, Jesus does both the will and the work of God (10:25). So much is this true that if men will only "believe the works," they will come to realize that the Father is in the Son and that the Son is in the Father (10:38). One might choose to raise the question as to whether such complete spiritual and ethical unity does not carry certain metaphysical implications, but this is another thing from asserting that John's thought moves along this line in this particular reference.

The pragmatic result of the unity which exists between Jesus and God is that the Father may be seen and known in the Son. When the Prologue states that no one has ever seen God, and adds that the only Son who is in the bosom of the Father has made him known (1:18), it is saying just this. The same theme is repeated later in the Upper Room discourses (chs. 14–17), particularly in the statements, "If you had known me, you would have known my Father also; henceforth you know him and have seen him" (14:7), and "He who has seen me has seen the Father" (14:9). In their own experience the disciples have and may confirm this fact.

[26] "There is a mystical overtone, as in the Hermetica and elsewhere, implying the derivation of the Logos from the depths of the divine nature." F. C. Grant, The Gospel of John, I, 21. For a contrary view stressing ethical oneness, cf. Macgregor, op. cit, p. 18.

[27] Of these words Augustine said, "Mark both these words, one and are, and thou wilt be delivered from Scylla and Charybdis. In that He says one, the Arian, in we are the Sabellian is answered." Cf. C. J. Wright's discussion in The Mission and Message of Jesus, pp. 829 ff.

[28] In the Intercessory Prayer (ch. 17), Jesus prays that the unity which exists between the Father and the Son, might also exist among his followers. This further suggests that the passage (10:30) is not concerned with metaphysics.

But even though the Fourth Gospel stresses this unity which leads to such a sublime vision and knowledge, it does not hesitate to assert that the Son is subordinate to the Father. The Father is greater than the Son (14:28), and gives all things to him (3:35). The Son did not come in his own name, but in the name of the Father (5:43); he follows the course of action which he sees the Father performing (vs. 30), and shares the truths which he heard from him (8:40). It is the Father's own word which the Son keeps (8:55), and it is his teaching which he proclaims (7:16). Finally, in all of this and because of it, the Father glorifies the Son (8:54). John's Gospel comes nearer to the Synoptic portrait of Jesus in this emphasis than at any other point, for there the representation of Jesus as doing the will of his heavenly Father as he sought to fulfill his messiahship is basic throughout (cf. Mark 14:36, et al.).

### The Death of Jesus

A consideration of the portrait of Jesus, the Christ and Son of God, as it is drawn in the Fourth Gospel would not be complete without some reference to the author's presentation of his death.[29] As elsewhere in the New Testament this event is not only recorded but is also interpreted. References to the "hour" (of his death) appear early in this writing and continue to do so periodically throughout (2:4; 7:30; 8:20; 12:23, 27; 13:1; 17:1). Sometimes they occur in John's comments, and again they are found on the lips of Jesus himself. An accent of determinism rests upon them. The heavenly Father is controlling what is happening, and the death of the Son will not take place until he wills it to be so. On the other hand, Jesus is seen to embrace fully his Father's will and shows little hesitancy to accept the Cross.[30] Instead he prays, "Father, glorify thy name" (12:28), and boldly declares in the Intercessory Prayer that "the hour has come; glorify thy Son that the Son may glorify thee" (17:1).

The use of the word "glorify" in the references just quoted introduces us to another aspect of John's interpretation of Jesus' death. It is not his shame but his glorification. As Strachan writes:

[29] Some consideration of our Lord's passion has already been given in connection with the discussion of the Eucharist in terms of what it meant to eat his flesh and drink his blood. Cf. pp. 168-69.

[30] There seems to be a momentary indecision when Jesus is visited by the Greeks (12:20-33), but it does not last long and lacks the anguish of Gethsemane in the Synoptics.

The "glorifying" of Jesus always means his dying (13:31). It is God who thus glorifys him, and in his dying God himself is glorified. The cross is the complete manifestation of God's glory, revealing his goodness or love to the utmost, yet not complete unless that love is accepted or reproduced in men's lives.[31]

This is somewhat reminiscent, although it is not a complete parallel, to Paul's assertion that because Jesus humbled himself to accept the Cross, God had highly exalted him (Phil. 2:9-11).

One of the reasons that the Cross is the glorification of Jesus is to be found in the tremendous results which grow out of it. In being thus "lifted up," he will draw all men to himself (12:32). And in that very hour they will realize not only that he is the Christ, but also that he acts and speaks within and by the will and authority of God (8:28). More than this, by his exaltation on the cross, he will bring eternal life to all who respond in belief to him as crucified, and thus revealed in his glory (3:14-15).

It is not to be wondered that such results will come from the Cross when the proper response is made. There is involved here the very principle of sacrifice by which new life can only grow out of death. As it is expressed in 12:24, "Truly, truly, I say to you, unless a grain of wheat falls into the earth and dies, it remains alone; but if it dies, it bears much fruit." [32] This principle also underlay Jesus' words in the Synoptics when he told his disciples that they too must bear crosses, "for whoever would save his life will lose it; and whoever loses his life for my sake and the gospel's will save it" (Mark 8:34-35).

There is yet another aspect to John's interpretation of Jesus' death. It appears twice quite early in the Gospel and is found on the lips of John the Baptist in both instances. The forerunner of Christ points him out first to his followers and then to two of his disciples, saying, "Behold the Lamb of God" (1:29, 36). In the first instance he adds "who takes away the sin of the world." This represents two Old Testament conceptions, that of the Paschal Lamb (Exodus 12:21-27) whose blood marked those who belonged to Jehovah, establishing a protective and mystical relationship between them, and also that of

---

[31] *Fourth Gospel*, p. 106.

[32] "It is only by Jesus' physical death that his spiritual powers can be released into the world and multiplied beyond measure." Macgregor, *op. cit.*, p. 265. Used by permission.

the suffering servant (Isa. 53:12) who, in death, "bore the sin of many, and made intercession for transgressors." [33]

That John the evangelist has the Paschal Lamb in mind in these words of the Baptizer may be further seen in the fact that, according to his dating of the Last Supper,[34] Jesus is being crucified at the very time that the Jews would be killing their lamb for the Passover meal. In these references the Fourth Gospel is in harmony with a line of interpretation already established in the early church. He does not pursue it, however, to the depths which the apostle Paul develops. Although he sees in Jesus' death the judgment of the world and the overpowering of Satan (12:31), his main concern is with the glory that is revealed in the Crucifixion, which draws all men unto the Son and, upon belief, results in eternal life. This is the life-centered approach to the atonement that is found in the Gospel of John.

### The Johannine Epistles

The first, second, and third epistles of John also belong in the Johannine corpus, although their exact relationship to the Gospel of John is still a question of debate. The differences in view among the scholars bears not so much upon the association of these with the Gospel as upon identical authorship with it. Some hold that there is a high probability that the same person wrote all four;[35] others favor a view that the epistles were written by a pupil of the author of the Fourth Gospel,[36] or by someone from the same circle,[37] which would account for the similarity of ideas among them. From the standpoint of the concern of this study, they are treated as Johannine, without arguing the question of authorship. Although I lean personally toward the second view expressed by Dodd, namely, that the author was a pupil of the person writing the Fourth Gospel, the decision here is not finally germane to a discussion of the portrait of Jesus in the Johannine epistles.

[33] "We are moving in a realm of ideas derived from Isaiah 53, and the central thought is not expiation or propitiation, or the cancelling of guilt, but the actual removal of sins." Grant, Gospel of John, I, 22-23. Cf. a fuller consideration of the servant passages in Sigmund Mowinckel, He That Cometh (Nashville: Abingdon Press, 1954), ch. vii.

[34] Cf. previous discussion of this point, p. 158.

[35] R. H. Charles, The Revelation of St. John, pp. xxxiv ff.; Garvie, The Abingdon Bible Commentary, p. 1065; Easton, The Abingdon Bible Commentary, p. 1352; Macgregor, op. cit., p. li.

[36] Dodd, The Johannine Epistles, p. lvi.

[37] Grant, The Gospel of John, Vol. II, and The Epistles of John, p. 41.

The general situation behind the writing of the First Epistle of John, as it appears in the book, is not unlike that which undergirds the Fourth Gospel. It may vary in intensity, but the issue is relatively the same. The beginnings of a gnostic emphasis upon "knowledge" and "light," and the urging of a docetic view of the flesh of Jesus, which appeared to compromise if not to deny the reality of the Incarnation, threatened the Faith. It would seem that certain teachers had left the church in the interest of following or actually promulgating these ideas (I John 2:19). This, along with other factors, would most likely date the epistle at about the same time as the Fourth Gospel (circa A.D. 100-110), probably shortly after, since it appears to take for granted the teachings of the larger work and build upon them. The second and third epistles may be similarly dated, although they are concerned mostly with matters of pastoral administration and personal interests, and have limited bearing upon our consideration in the study.

### Specific Teachings

The portrait of Jesus in the Johannine epistles, as in the Fourth Gospel, is essentially the portrait of the Christ, the Son of God. The author holds that a denial of this truth is the lie of the antichrist (I John 2:22); to confess it, however, is to possess the Father (vs. 23). Indeed, we are commanded by God to believe "in the name of his Son Jesus Christ" (3:23). Furthermore, it is the Spirit of God who inspires the recognition that Jesus is the Son, and that he has come in the flesh (4:2). And such a confession is, therefore, the mark of being a child of God (5:1). Even in the words of a benediction we find the statement, "Grace, mercy, and peace will be with us, from God the Father and from *Jesus Christ the Father's Son*[38] in truth and love" (II John 3).

Of particular concern to the author of the epistles is the fact that Jesus the Christ came in the flesh. In the opening verses of the first letter he goes out of his way, even as the author of John's Gospel in his prologue (1:14), to make an unmistakable assertion of this fact. Members of the earliest Christian Fellowship are claimed to have seen and touched the "word of life" which "was made manifest" (I John 1:1-2). And those who preach otherwise are called "deceivers"

[38] Italics mine.

(II John 7).[39] This obvious pressing of a point calls for an explanation. Here again, it would seem that the reality of the Incarnation itself is felt by the writer to be at stake. If docetic claims that Jesus' fleshly existence was unreal were to prevail, he is convinced that the true basis of the Fellowship itself will be sacrificed (cf. I John 4:2-3).

It is not clear as to whether the author thinks of Jesus in a metaphysical sense as the divine Logos when he uses the expression "word of life" in the opening verse (I John 1:1). He does assert that the word existed "from the beginning," and in the light of the Prologue of John's Gospel (1:1), this might seem to suggest immediately the Logos which was from all eternity with God and which was God. Another possibility is that the "word of life" refers to the gospel itself which was manifested in Christ, the Christ whom they saw and touched. It is an eternal gospel in that it is the gospel of God, no less. In the case of either interpretation, however, the reality of the Incarnation is asserted.

The epistles portray Christ, not only as the divine Son of the Father, but also as one in whom men may abide and find newness of life (I John 2:28; 3:24; 4:15; II John 9).[40] For God sent his only Son into the world that men might "live though him" (I John 4:9). In Christ they walk in the true (not the pseudo light of gnostic systems) light which is already shining and driving away the darkness (I John 1:7; 2:8). Thus it is that they may overcome the world, possess true understanding, and know eternal life (I John 5:5, 11, 20). How like the Gospel of John! [41]

The Christ of the Johannine epistles is one who hears the prayers of those who ask according to his will (I John 5:14-15). His blood cleanses from all sin (I John 1:7),[42] and he serves as an advocate with the Father when men sin, representing them before him and helping on their behalf (I John 2:1). As the expiation (*hilasmos*) for the sins of the world (including the forces of the pagan order that

---

[39] Dodd raises the question on linguistic grounds as to whether the author was referring to the second coming of Christ in this verse but decides in favor of a historic reference to his first advent. Cf. *Johannine Epistles*, p. 149.

[40] In the latter reference it speaks of abiding "in the doctrine of Christ" rather than "in Christ." The writer is thinking perhaps of those who seek a so-called more advanced point of view and turn to gnostic teachings.

[41] In a suggestive listing of parallels between the Johannine epistles and the Gospel of John, cf. Grant, *Gospel of John*, Vol. II, and *Epistles of John*, p. 42.

[42] Cf. the previous discussion of the conception of blood and its meaning in connection with the death of Christ for sin, p. 71.

are at enmity with God), Christ in his birth, life, death, resurrection, and ascension places God's forgiveness within men's reach (I John 2:2). He does this at the behest of his Father.

The portrait of Jesus in the Gospel and epistles of John brings to a mature expression the lines which had been developing in the primitive church, the Pauline age, and the synoptic period. Individuality in authorship, particular purposes, and changing backgrounds are responsible for different accents which appear throughout this development, but the relationships among them are evident. We have seen that such themes as the pre-existence and sonship of Jesus the Christ, the newness of life which comes from being in or abiding in him, the character and work of the exalted Christ through the Spirit, and the place of our Lord in the experience of forgiveness come to a fullness of conception in the Johannine writings which is monumental. Their place in interpreting the Faith of Christians has been and still is distinctive.

# THIRTEEN

# In the Letter to the Hebrews

IN THE PREVIOUS FIVE CHAPTERS WE HAVE BEEN CONSIDERING THE portrait of Jesus in the Synoptic Gospels and the Johannine writings. The Letter to the Hebrews, in a certain sense, stands midway between these two bodies of literature. Its date, somewhere around the year A.D. 90, places it there,[1] as does also its conception of Jesus. In stressing the genuineness of his humanity, it looks back to the Synoptic Gospels, and in emphasizing his eternal priesthood in the heavenly tabernacle it looks forward to the metaphysical view of his person in the Johannines.[2] But this is not to say that Hebrews does not possess uniqueness on its own. It has an individuality which gives it a particular place among New Testament documents. The fact that it was accepted late as canonical in the Western church (the Muratorian Canon, circa A.D. 200, does not list it) does not detract from its significance in the least. It was widely circulated and greatly appreciated throughout the second century.[3]

### The Situation

Although in some ways this writing is abstract in its interpretation of Scripture and in its use of allegory, the situation to which it was addressed was far from formal. Persecution by the Roman state was already beginning (10:32-34), although it was afterward to become more severe (12:4), and the temptation to turn from the Faith was very real (3:12; 10:23). There was a pressing need for these second-generation Christians (13:7, 17) to hold fast (3:6), especially since the author was convinced that it was

impossible to restore again to repentance those who have once been enlightened, who have tasted the heavenly gift, and have become partakers

[1] Cf. the commentaries for a detailed discussion of the date of the epistle. We have suggested a date for the Synoptics, A.D. 65-85, and for the Johannines, A.D. 100-10.

[2] This does not imply that the Synoptics did not hold a high view also of Jesus. Throughout he was the Christ, the Son of God.

[3] Cf. Moffatt, Epistle to the Hebrews, p. xv.

of the Holy Spirit, and have tasted the goodness of the word of God and the powers of the age to come, if they commit apostasy, since they crucify the Son of God on their own account and hold him up to contempt. (6:4-6; cf. also 10:26-31).

Although the writing as we have it is titled "The Letter to the Hebrews," it is unlikely that the author had Palestinians in mind. Frequent references to the tabernacle and the old covenant might seem to suggest, at least, that he was thinking of Aramaic-speaking Christians. And yet, the basic thought-pattern and background in terms of which these are interpreted are essentially Hellenistic.[4] There is considerable justification for the suggestion of Robinson that Hebrews was addressed to a particular group in the Hellenistic world whose situation resembles that of the Seven Churches of Asia in Revelation.[5] They need not actually to have been Jews at all to follow the argument that is presented,[6] although it seems to me that a follower of Christ who was a Hellenistic Jew would have found its appeal more congenial than an out-and-out Gentile.

Rawlinson and others suggest that the recipients may have lived in Rome.[7] The statement at the very close of the epistle, "Those who come from Italy send you greetings" (13:24), does seem to place Rome in the picture, although it is not clear whether the reference is to Roman Christians living in Rome at the time of the writing who were greeting friends elsewhere, or to Romans abroad who were sending best wishes to their brethren in the celestial city on the occasion of the penning of the epistle.

## The Author

When we come to the question of authorship, another unknown factor is introduced into the picture. In spite of the multitudinous speculation on this subject, Origen's comment which Eusebius

[4] But cf. H. T. Andrews, "Hebrews," *The Abingdon Bible Commentary*, p. 1298, who argues for a Hebraic rather than a Hellenistic group.

[5] The list includes Ephesus, Smyrna, Pergamum, Thyatira, Sardis, Philadelphia, and Laodicea (Rev. 2–3).

[6] T. H. Robinson, *The Epistle to the Hebrews*, p. xvii.

[7] "It is tempting to think rather of Rome where the Epistle is first quoted (*The Epistle of Clement of Rome*, circa A.D. 96) as the place of destination, and of Ephesus (on the somewhat conjectural ground that this writer's theology is in some respects transitional between the work of S. Paul and the point of view of the Fourth Gospel) as the place of composition." *The New Testament Doctrine of the Christ*, p. 176. Used by permission.

quotes[8] to the effect that only God knows, still stands. To the list of proferred candidates Tertullian suggested Barnabas, Luther offered Apollos, and Harnack and Rendel Harris named Priscilla. Others who have been mentioned from time to time include Silas, Philip, Luke, and Clement of Rome. In all likelihood, judging from his thought processes and his use of the Septuagint, the Greek translation of the Old Testament, he was probably a Hellenistic Jew who was familiar with the Alexandrian forms of interpretation.[9] The dualism of Plato, the Logos ideas as used by Philo, and the Wisdom conceptions of the Hebrews come readily to his mind and pen.

Brief reference should be made, perhaps, to the view traditionally held that the apostle Paul wrote Hebrews. Some of the church fathers subscribed to this position, including Pantaenus (circa A.D. 185), Clement of Alexandria (circa A.D. 215),[10] Dionysius of Alexandria (A.D. 247-64), and Eusebius (A.D. 325).[11] This ascription to the apostle, however, was not unanimous. Reference has already been made to Tertullian's support of Barnabas for the role (circa A.D. 225).[12] Modern disinclination to accept Pauline authorship for Hebrews is based largely upon differences in style, teachings, and interests between his writings and the epistle. The latter's stress upon the Hebrew sacrificial system which finds no counterpart in Paul is but one instance of this difference. His dismissal of Paul's Christ-mysticism in favor of the high priesthood of Jesus, who brings men to God, is another case in point.

Whoever the author of Hebrews might have been, he appears in his writing as an ardent Christian who was concerned with the true meaning and means of worship, on the one hand, and desperately in earnest in the practical matter of stemming the tide of defection from the Faith on the other. His is a unique combination of liturgical interest and evangelistic fervor. Although his argumentation may seem to be involved and artificial to the modern reader, who is not informed or who does not take the trouble to understand the particular

[8] Op. cit. VI. 25.

[9] The point of view of Alexandria represented a combination of the Wisdom approach of the Jews with the Hellenistic philosophical tradition. It accomplished this in large measure through the use of allegorical interpretation of the Scriptures.

[10] Written by Paul in Hebrew, but translated by Luke into Greek.

[11] Written by Paul in Hebrew but translated for Greeks by Clement of Rome.

[12] For an excellent consideration of traditions in the early church concerning Hebrews, with quotations from the original sources, cf. Alexander C. Purdy, The Interpreter's Bible, XI, 581-82.

type of approach that is made, frequently there are passages in his writing of penetrating insight that are helpful in Christian living today. And many of these occur at the very point where he is drawing his portrait of Christ.

## Jesus' True Humanity

The main interest of the author of Hebrews in his presentation of Jesus is to show how it is that his Lord is able to bring men to God. This concern is basic to what he has to say about Jesus as the eternal high priest and as the perfect sacrifice for sins, which we shall consider later. It also underlies those lines in the portrait where the true humanity of Jesus is emphasized. And it should be said at the outset that this humanity is not depicted as in conflict with his divinity. Instead, it becomes a medium through which his work as the Son of God becomes effective. Because he was made like unto his brothers in the flesh, he can function as the divine Savior which he is.

This is made particularly explicit in the author's statement that Jesus "had to be made like his brethren in every respect, so that he might become a merciful and faithful high priest in the service of God, to make expiation for the sins of the people. For because he himself has suffered and been tempted, he is able to help those who are tempted." (2:17-18.) It is not only that Jesus has been tempted and therefore understands the stresses of men's souls; it is also that, being tempted, he overcame it without yielding: "For we have not a high priest who is unable to sypathize with our weaknesses, but one who in every respect has been tempted as we are, yet without sinning" (4:15).

What does all of this mean? It has been called "Atonement by Sympathy." [18] By experiencing in his own person the buffeting of every kind of temptation and coming off victorious, Jesus has *done something* that draws us through him to God. It has given us confidence to approach "the throne of grace, that we may receive mercy and find grace to help in time of need" (4:16). In this representation the Incarnation and the Atonement are joined together, as they truly must be in any adequate theology.

There is yet another result of Jesus' possession of our flesh and blood, according to Hebrews. It made it necessary for him to experience the death of the body, even as we must die. This he did, and in

[18] T. H. Robinson, op. cit., p. 50.

so doing he destroyed "him who has the power of death, that is, the devil" (2:14).[14] Just how Jesus destroyed the devil through his death our author does not say. Could it be that he is thinking of the victory of the Resurrection by which the devil in his final attempt to conquer Jesus was vanquished? In any case, our author is not concerned so much with the *how* as he is with the *fact*. As a result of Jesus' dying as men must die, the fear of what happens after death has been removed. What he calls a "lifelong bondage" has been broken. Men can die in confidence because Jesus has passed through the valley before them.

### The Eternal High Priest

But Jesus is more than one who bore our kind of flesh. Hebrews also sees him as the eternal high priest. This conception comes quite logically to the mind of an author whose chief concern is worship, particularly that aspect of it which brings men to God (7:25). It was a matter of experience that this had already happened through Christ, and that to an extent which the Law had not achieved (7:19). How should this fact be explained and interpreted? This was the question which faced the writer. And he answered it in terms of the tabernacle service of the Jews, seen not in its imperfect historic expression, but in the light of its perfect existence in heaven where Christ acts as an eternal high priest.

It is at this point that our author probably turns to Platonic philosophy for his conception of an ideal order in heaven of which objects on earth are an imperfect counterpart. Things below, in this system of thought, were regarded as pale copies of their perfect types above. This is true of the tabernacle in Hebrews. Below, it is imperfect; above, it is "the greater and more perfect tent" (9:11). Below the priesthood is ineffectual; "every priest stands daily at his service, offering repeatedly the same sacrifices, which can never take away sins" (10:11). Above, "Christ appeared as a high priest of the good things that have come" (9:11), entering there as a forerunner on behalf of men, he became "a high priest for ever after the order of Melchizedek" (6:20).

But what is meant by the order of Melchizedek? Melchizedek is a shadowy figure from the Old Testament (Gen. 14:17 ff.; Ps. 110:

---

[14] It was a contemporary belief, both among Jews and Christians, that the devil possessed the power of death.

183

4), a king of Salem who as priest of the Most High blessed Abraham. Since no genealogy is given for him, it was assumed that he was without beginning or ending; resembling the Son of God, he would continue a priest forever (Heb. 7:3). By comparison the author of Hebrews asserted that the Levitical priesthood on earth could not bring about perfection and that the order of Aaron was finally ineffectual. It was necessary, therefore, for God to make a New Covenant (8:8-13).

As the eternal high priest there is a further distinction to be noted between Jesus' services and those of the Levitical priesthood. Its priests needed to offer sacrifices for themselves to cover their own sins before they could effectively offer them for the people. This is because the "law appoints men in their weakness as high priests" (7:28). But not so with Jesus. He is "holy, blameless, unstained, separated from sinners, exalted above the heavens" (7:26); he is "a Son who has been made perfect for ever" (vs. 28). No sacrifice is needed for his sins.

### The Better Sacrifice

In relation to sacrifices even as in the case of the priesthood, the author presents Christ's offering as the "better" one, superseding those based on the old covenant (8:6). By developing this comparison, Hebrews might be called the first Christian dissertation in comparative religion, even as H. T. Andrews has referred to it as the "first great attempt that was made to explain Christianity in terms of Platonic philosophy." [15] The author is doing some original thinking as he interprets the Faith in the light of other thought-systems. The apostle Paul confronts competing points of view with his gospel; this writer considers differing positions by way of showing that Christianity is better. And yet there is no lack of feeling in this more analytical procedure. He is an evangelist quite as much as the apostle, and his concern for the practical results of believing in Christ is just as deep-seated as that of the missionary to the Gentiles.

There is a distinctive element in the portrait of Jesus as the eternal high priest in Hebrews in the fact that he is both the priest and the sacrifice. Instead of the blood of goats and calves, he offered his own blood; that is, he gave his very own life. By doing this, as eternal high priest he secured an eternal redemption (9:12), "for if the

[15] "Hebrews," *The Abingdon Bible Commentary*, p. 1295.

sprinkling of defiled persons with the blood of goats and bulls and with the ashes of a heifer sanctifies for the purification of the flesh, how much more shall the blood of Christ, who through the eternal Spirit offered himself without blemish to God, purify your conscience from dead works to serve the living God" (9:13-14). It should be noted here that the author, while moving within the ancient thought-forms of blood offerings which are so difficult for modern occidentals to follow, transcends this realm when he refers to the effects *in the conscience* which Christ's sacrifice brings. The moral and ethical consequences of our Lord's death, rather than its results in the sacramental cleansing of sinful flesh comes to the fore in this remarkable passage. It would be going too far to conclude that Hebrews wholly turns from the idea that blood offerings in themselves have merit. But it does begin to interpret them in spiritual terms.[16]

Perhaps one of the reasons that our author is able to see the results of Christ's sacrifice as affecting the consciences of men is that he has caught a glimpse of personal elements involved in our Lord's acceptance of the Cross. Although in one respect Christ was offered up, in a deeper sense he offered himself (9:25). At this point the personal will enters the picture, and this introduces moral and ethical factors not found in the case of a helpless animal whose blood was poured out at the altar. Christ was not a victim, but a voluntary participant. What a difference!

There is yet another distinction between the sacrifice of Christ himself and those offered by the Levitical priesthood. It was required that theirs be repeated daily (7:27), while the high priest entered the Holy Place on the Day of Atonement once every year (9:25). Not so with Christ. As the high priest he offered himself but once: "he has appeared once for all at the end of the age to put away sin by the sacrifice of himself" (vs. 26).

In the above reference the author uses the phrase "at the end of the age." [17] This introduces his belief in the return of Christ, and combines "his dominant idea of Christ as the priest who introduces us

---

[16] Cf.10:22: "Let us draw near with a true heart in full assurance of faith, with our hearts *sprinkled clean from an evil conscience* and our bodies washed with pure water." (Italics mine.)

[17] Cf. also *"in these last days"* in 1:2. (Italics mine.) For a significant discussion of the eschatology of Hebrews cf. C. K. Barrett, "The Eschatology of the Epistle to the Hebrews," *The Background of the New Testament and Its Eschatology,* ed. W. D. Davies and David Daube.

185

to the heavenly sanctuary, i.e., to the true realm of reality, with the primitive eschatology which moves in terms of a time sequence." [18] For all his individuality of presentation, the author in this regard remains within the line of succession which comes down from the earliest church. He confidently expects the return of Christ, at which time he will judge the wicked and "save those who are eagerly waiting for him" (9:28).

But to return to the portrait of Christ as the eternal high priest after the order of Melchizedek and as the perfect sacrificial offering himself, our author is convinced that, as these, our Lord is the final and absolute mediator between man and God. This, concludes E. F. Scott, "in one aspect or another must ever belong to the substance of Christianity, . . . that through Christ we have been brought near to God, . . . that men have learned through him that they are God's people, that their sins have been forgiven, that they can now come boldly before the throne of grace." [19] This gives to Christ a position no one else can fill. Salvation, if it is to be had, must come through him.

### The Son of God

In all of this, as both the eternal high priest and the perfect sacrifice, Jesus is at one and the same time uniquely the Son of God. In the author's mind there is no contradiction between these representations. They belong together. Actually, his sonship is basic to his priesthood and sacrifice. This is made clear in the opening verses of chapter one where his sonship is stated and interpreted (1:1-3a) before reference is made to the purification he made for sins (1:3b). Although he achieved the latter, the former was his by virtue of the nature of his person in relation to God.

In the opening paragraph of the writing, Jesus the Son is presented as distinct from the prophets who had preceded him in a glowing succession of inspired messengers from God (1:1). Later this theme is developed at some length, and it is shown that being the Son, he is superior to Moses and Joshua (3:1–4:13). As the one through whom the Law was given, Moses held an unprecedented position in Israel. Even so, "Jesus has been counted worthy of as much more glory than Moses as the builder of a house has more honor than the house"

[18] Purdy, op. cit., XI, 698.
[19] The Epistle to the Hebrews, p. 139.

(3:3). Moses had done his work well, but the Law had proved to be ineffectual. He was faithful as a servant, but "Christ was faithful over God's house as a son" (3:6).

And as for Joshua, after the struggle of the wilderness wanderings he had brought the people, humanly speaking, a rest, to be compared with the rest that God knew on the seventh day following the Creation. But Joshua's was not the eternal rest of God which the Father would give his own.[20] Our author calls this latter a "sabbath rest," his own expression, which in its perfect form already exists in heaven, but which is incompletely realized on earth (Platonic dualism).[21] Only through Christ the Son would this full realization be available. Thus the superiority of Jesus over Joshua is shown, even as his superiority over Aaron and the Levitical priesthood is developed by the author.[22]

As the Son, Jesus is also presented by the writer of Hebrews as superior to angels (1:4-14). No angel was ever addressed, "Thou art my Son, today I have begotten thee" (vs. 5);[23] to none of them did God say, "I will be to him a father, and he shall be to me a son" (vs. 5).[24] Instead, God bade the angels worship him as "the first-born" (vs. 6).[25] They are servants, winds, and flames of fire (vs. 7),[26] but the Son has an eternal rule and a righteous scepter (vs. 8).[27] He sits at God's right hand (vs. 13),[28] a position granted to no angel.

The author's use of these scriptures, in which he concludes that certain Old Testament passages were speaking of Christ, rather than referring to their immediate context, is characteristic of his method of argumentation. Sometimes it is known as "typology" in which Old Testament figures or events are regarded as types of foreshadowings of New Testament figures or events, so much so that ideologically they are interpreted as one.[29] His thought-patterns, like those of his

---

[20] "We have, then, the conception of a divine and archetypal rest, which belongs by nature to God, but which he would share with his creatures." T. H. Robinson, op. cit., p. 40. This conception of a rest is an aspect of the author's eschatology.

[21] Even the psalmist (said to be David) indicated that the rest had not been fully known (Heb. 4:7).

[22] Cf. pp. 183-84.

[23] Ps. 2:7.

[24] II Sam. 7:14.

[25] Deut. 32:43 (Sept.); Ps. 97:7.

[26] Ps. 104:4.

[27] Ps. 45:6-7.

[28] Ps. 110:1.

[29] For a suggestive study of typology cf. G. W. H. Lampe and K. J. Woolcombe, Essays on Typology.

readers, were such that this kind of biblical interpretation carried considerable weight. This was also reasoning after the fact, or in the face of the fact that God was supremely at work in Christ, the same God who had spoken in the past. Therefore all former intimations of greatness and blessings to come must have referred to Christ, through whom such surpassing glories had been and were being experienced.[30]

The emphasis of the author upon the superiority of Jesus, the Son, over angels in these passages is somewhat self-conscious. It has a labored quality which suggests that there might have been a particular reason in the situation facing the readers to account for it. We have already referred to Paul's admonition against the worship of angels in Colossians (2:18) as indicating that there was some pressure at this point upon the Christians at Colossae.[31] If Hebrews was addressed to this same area, which is a real possibility, the writer's argument that the Son is superior to angels takes on additional interest. There may have been a secondary and practical issue at stake in this presentation beyond the author's concern to show that Jesus is the Son and that, as such, he deserved the highest possible honor.[32] Once again we see that the drawing of portraiture in the New Testament, where Christ is concerned, is related to the genuine needs of the church. Only in a secondary sense is it speculative.

### The Son, God, and the Universe

As the unique Son, Jesus is presented as the supreme expression of God. The author asserts, "He reflects the glory of God (cf. Wisdom 7:26), and bears the very stamp of his nature" (1:3a). By these metaphors he is saying that imprinted upon the being of Christ is the image of God (cf. Col. 1:15-20), and that the glory of God also shines forth from his person. Although the writer does not actually

[30] I am reminded of identifications of Kaiser Wilhelm, Hitler, Mussolini, and Stalin with the beast in the Revelation to John which have been made in this century. Although from the standpoint of a historical reading of the Bible, they were quite incorrect, in another sense the evils that these figures represented were such that, ideologically speaking, they typified the beast, so that there was a kind of logic in the claims that were made.

[31] Cf. p. 98.

[32] But cf. Purdy: "While this (a polemic against the worship of angels) is not impossible, the evidence is against it. The verses do not sound like a polemic. Not only is there no positive intimation that angels were regarded as worthy of worship or as mediators of the divine salvation, but the writer gives them a high place in 2:2 as the beings through whom the law was delivered, and in 1:14 as ministering spirits." Op. cit., XI, 603.

identify Christ with God in these statements, there is here the assertion that the Son is a divine person, for of no other human could these things be said to be true in such absolute terms.

It is sometimes held that Hebrews may actually address the Son as God in the quotation from Ps. 45 which is applied to him.[33] The quote from Heb. 1:8 is prefaced by the words "But of the Son he says," and then continues:

> Thy throne, O God,
>     is for ever and ever,
>     the righteous scepter is the scepter
>     of thy kingdom. (From Ps. 45:6.)

This may be translated "God is thy throne" (as in R.S.V. footnote). Considering the immediate context, as well as the position of the Son in the entire work, it should probably be concluded that the author is here stressing the uniqueness of the Son in his relation to God rather than making an identification of the two.

As in Paul (Col. 1:16-17) and in John (1:3), the author of Hebrews likewise thinks of Jesus not only as uniquely related to the being of God, but also as involved in the creation and support of the universe. Although it may be difficult to ascertain whether they hold this view on identical grounds, philosophically or theologically, since in no case is it fully developed, their assertions of it are equally definite. And behind all three expressions of it there probably lies the Philonic and Wisdom patterns of thinking to which reference has already been made.[34] The theology of Alexandria undoubtedly influenced the writer of Hebrews here, as elsewhere, in his epistle. This is not to say, however, that the Logos conception dominated his thinking throughout. He seems closer to the Wisdom conceptions of the Jews.

It is intriguing to envision a line of influence from Paul to Hebrews to John, in regard to the statements of each concerning Christ's relation to the universe. And it is not impossible that such was the case. But it must not be forgotten that this need not be so in order to explain the positions they take. All three lived in a time when background conceptions which would encourage such interpretations were

---

[33] Rawlinson, op. cit., pp. 187-88. "He implies by quotations from the Old Testament (those in this section) that the Son may be addressed rightly as 'God!'" Used by permission.

[34] Cf. pp. 95, 99, 162-64.

189

a part of the intellectual climate in Hebraic, Hellenistic, and Christian centers. It should not be hastily concluded, however, that the original impulse to thinking in these directions was a borrowed one. The supremacy of Christ *already experienced* impelled the search for broader horizons of thought within which to probe the ultimate implications of the Faith. And such inquiry necessarily took place within the thought-outlook of the day. This dynamic adaptation to contemporary thinking has been the history of Christian theology through the centuries. It is a sound and inescapable procedure which must be repeated over and over again if the Faith, "once delivered to the saints," is to have point and meaning for succeeding generations, including most surely our own.

### Pioneer and Perfecter of Faith

The main thesis of Hebrews concerning Christ, the divine Son, superior to both prophets and angels, agent of creation and sustainer of the universe, who has made access to God possible by overcoming temptations, so that he became at once the eternal high priest and the perfect sacrifice—this main thesis is completed in chapter ten. What follows in the remaining sections is a practical exhortation to respond to "so great a salvation." And how does one respond? The answer to this question is that one responds through faith—faith interpreted as patient, loyal endurance with one's eyes fixed upon Jesus.

It is the human Jesus to whom men are invited to look, he who himself endured the Cross even though he despised its shame. As in overcoming temptations, just so here also as he met suffering (martyrdom) and death, Jesus held firm to his course. And he did this with joy at the prospect of the outcome. This outcome should be interpreted within the total context of the writing. It was nothing less than the bringing of men to God.

It is also the heavenly Christ to whom men were to look. For he is now to be seen as sitting "at the right hand of the throne of God" (12:2). All of the divine prerogatives which this expression had come to suggest in the early church lie behind the author's use of it. But the particular view of the Son as the eternal high priest, serving in the perfect heavenly tabernacle, is probably foremost in the writer's mind.

In connection with this high call to faith, interpreted as looking to Jesus, we find two statements concerning him which constitute additional elements of portraiture. He is called "the pioneer (archēgon) and perfecter of our faith." Once before in Hebrews (2:10) Jesus was referred to as the pioneer of salvation. As the pioneer of faith, Jesus is its author or originator. It is not that men had not shown faith prior to him. The listing of those who have exhibited it in chapter eleven of this same writing leaves no doubt at this point. But Jesus becomes the author of faith within the context of the salvation God initiated in the last days when "he has spoken to us by a Son" (1:2). In this sense there is a "betterness" to his faith even as there was a "betterness" to his priesthood and sacrifice.

Jesus not only is the author or pioneer of faith; he is its finisher and perfecter as well. In him the goal of faith reaches its fulfillment. Having endured he conquered and, as we noted previously, he became the eternal high priest and the perfect sacrifice forever.

The writer of Hebrews is at heart a pastor. His concern is not in ideas or conceptions for their own sake, although one might conclude this in view of the pains he takes to develop his thesis. Instead, it is with persons who are beginning to meet persecution and will likely be called upon to face it more fully in the future. This is quite evident in his presentation of Jesus as the pioneer and perfecter of faith, where he calls upon his readers to follow Jesus' example. The Son is an inspiration to faith as well as its object. As Andrews has so aptly said in this connection, "Hence the Christian life must be an *Imitatio Christi*." [35]

[35] H. T. Andrews, *op. cit.*, p. 1322.

# FOURTEEN

# In the Revelation to John

IN THE PREVIOUS CHAPTER WE SAW HOW THE AUTHOR OF HEBREWS presented his portrait of Jesus Christ in such terms that he might, in the main, meet the needs of the church, which was beginning to feel the pressures of persecution under the Roman ruler Domitian (A.D. 81-96). It had not yet broken out in full force, but there was sufficient indication of its coming so that defection from the Faith was a real threat, if not an actuality.

### The Situation

At the time of the writing of the Revelation to John, this storm cloud which had been on the horizon was now beginning to release its destructive forces. At least one Christian, Antipas of Pergamum, had been martyred, and the frequent references to martyrs (6:9-10; 13:15; 17:6; 19:14; 20:4) suggest possibly a larger number than this with the prospect of considerably more to come. Martyrdom is in the atmosphere from first to last in this volume, both as already present and as anticipated increasingly for the immediate future.

The cause of this death would seem to have been the enforcement of emperor worship by the ruling Caesar, Domitian, and the refusal of Christians to practice it. Other emperors before him had accepted divine honors. Among these were Augustus (27 B.C.-A.D. 14), and Vespasian (A.D. 69-79). Domitian, however, was the only one who enforced it under the severest penalties, including death. Caligula (A.D. 37-41) was about to compel his own veneration by force when he died.[1]

But with Domitian, as has been said, a pathological compulsion to be recognized as a god led him to go to great lengths in enforcing emperor worship. There is a graphic picture in the thirteenth chapter

---

[1] Nero (A.D. 54-68) also persecuted the Christians, but this was in connection with blaming them for the burning of Rome and not for a refusal to pay him divine honors.

of the Revelation depicting the priests of state as they conducted such services before the emperor's image, referred to by the writer as the image of the Beast.[2] It would seem that ventriloquism and even something resembling breath (fire?) were used, so that the image both talked and breathed (13:15).

As a means of keeping check upon those who obeyed the imperial command, whoever honored the image was said in the Revelation to have received a mark on the right hand and on the forehead. Without this sign they could neither buy nor sell. Since contemporary records do not mention this procedure in connection with emperor worship, although seals were often employed in the relationships, and since in this writing certain other marks (7:3; 14:1) are frequently symbolical in character, it may be questioned whether the author intended to be taken literally in this reference. In any case, he was using pictorial language to stress the seriousness of the situation which the Christians faced when they refused to participate in the emperor cult.

Emperor worship was, in part, a political and social instrument for achieving unity in the Roman world. It focused attention upon the ruler and developed a considerable degree of emotional attachment to him. If the Christians could have viewed it in this light only, they might have performed the prescribed rite in a perfunctory manner. But their loyalty to Christ as the supreme authority in their lives made this impossible. Besides, the emperor was presented by the author of the Revelation as the Beast or servant of Satan, as were also the priests, collectively considered, who conducted his worship. To recognize him was therefore not only to turn from allegiance to Christ, but also to embrace Satan as well. For this reason the Christians were called upon to resist unto death.

### Purpose, Date

The purpose of the Revelation to John was to meet the needs of the church, especially in Asia,[3] as it was faced with this persecution from the Roman state. Since, as we have seen, resistance was inevitable, and with it the dire consequences prescribed, what should Christians do? The answer given was that they should hold fast in faith,

---

[2] As to this identification, p. 11 note.

[3] The teachings of the book were applicable elsewhere throughout the Empire, but the fact that the volume opens with letters to seven Asian churches, together with other references, suggests Asians in particular as its recipients.

whatever happens, since martyrs would be abundantly rewarded in heaven.[4] But more than this, they were given a preview of coming events, soon to occur, which would mark the end of the Age.

In this panorama of the future they were shown the overthrow of all forces which opposed Christ and his followers; Satan, the Roman state and priesthood, pagan kings, and evil men would be judged, sentenced, and destroyed. The present earth would vanish, and in its place a new heaven and a new earth would be let down from above. Here the martyred dead, together with the saints who had died or been saved out of the final calamities, would live with Christ and God eternally.

In all of this Jesus Christ has a pre-eminent place, both as the revealer of the future and as the agent of God's judgment, destruction, and blessings. It is in connection with this activity that his portrait in the Revelation emerges with a distinctiveness that sets it apart from other New Testament representations. Before considering in some detail this portraiture, however, brief attention should be given to the date, authorship, conceptual form, and literary characteristics of the writing which contains it.

In this discussion we are accepting a date of circa A.D. 96 for the Revelation to John.[5] This represents the conclusion of most modern scholars in the New Testament field. It is based largely upon internal evidence, particularly those references to enforced emperor worship that we have been noting. These fit best into the latter part of Domitian's reign.

One other consideration should be mentioned in connection with the dating of the Revelation. It is the reflections of the Nero-redivivus myth which the book contains (13:3; 17:8, 11). This stated that Nero, whose death was shrouded in some mystery, would reappear at a later time, leading armies from the East in triumph. Toward the close of Domitian's rule this myth was widely circulated, so that its appearance in the Revelation helps to fix the date of the book.

[4] Charles holds that the author anticipated the martyrdom of the entire church on earth, op. cit., II, 113, 456. Whether his expectation went this far or not may be questioned, but he did look for increased persecution with its attendant martyrdom. Cf. Rev. 6:11.

[5] Cf. the commentaries on the Revelation to John and the several introductions to the New Testament for a detailed treatment.

## Authorship, Conceptual Form, Literary Characteristics

The identity of the author of the Revelation to John is not necessarily basic to the portrait of Christ which is found there. This means that a lengthy presentation of the maze of argumentation in favor of this or that person which has developed through the centuries need not be reviewed in these pages.[6] The book itself says that his name was John (1:1, 4, 9; 22:8),[7] that he was a servant of Christ and a Christian brother of those to whom he wrote (1:1, 9; 19:10), sharing with them "the tribulation and the kingdom, and the patient endurance." He regards himself as a prophet (1:3; 19:10; 22:7, 9, 18) and states that his prophecy came to him while he was on the island of Patmos because of the word of God and his testimony to Jesus (1:9). This was a penal colony, and we may assume that John was imprisoned there because of his refusal to indulge in emperor worship. Although he refers to the apostles, as such (18:20; 21:14), he does not include himself as belonging to their number.

The author was identified with the apostle John as early as Justin Martyr, probably in his debate with Trypho (A.D. 136). He is joined in this view by Irenaeus (circa A.D. 180), Clement of Alexandria (circa A.D. 215), Tertullian (circa A.D. 225) and Origen (A.D. 185-254). But this conclusion was opposed by Marcion, the Alogi and Dionysius of Alexandria (A.D. 247-64), while Eusebius (circa A.D. 325) attributed the writing to John the Presbyter. This is sufficient to show that during the first four centuries there was no unanimity of opinion in this matter. Nor is there today, when most scholars prefer to withhold judgment, although few would assign the book to John the apostle. It is wisest to conclude that, for all his greatness, the identity of the author remains unknown.

In delineating the portrait of Christ in the Revelation to John, it is necessary to take into consideration the conceptual and literary form involved in the type of writing which presents it. The Revelation is an apocalypse (apokalupsis), a word which means literally a revelation or unveiling, usually of hidden heavenly mysteries. It is to be distinguished from a prophecy, although prophetic elements are

---

[6] Cf. the commentaries and New Testament introductions for a review of this argumentation.

[7] Many apocalyptic writings are pseudonymous, ascribing their authorship to well-known figures of the past or present. In this case, however, the character and simplicity of the reference to "John" suggests that the author used his own name.

195

found in the work. I. T. Beckwith has expressed this difference clearly when he wrote:

While the expectations of both prophecy and apocalyptic center in a coming messianic era, that is, in a final era in which the kingdom of God will be established, the former conceives this kingdom chiefly in political and earthly aspects, the latter in those that are non political and supernatural. The main interest of the one is mundane; of the other supermundane.[8]

Apocalyptic writings customarily take the view that at the end of the Age supernatural agencies will bring into existence a new society to replace the present evil one. Universal judgment with the destruction of the wicked, both men and spiritual beings, and the rewarding of the faithful are characteristic of this outlook. The apocalyptic view is therefore eschatological because it points to the final end or summation of things.[9] Behind this climactic denouement lies a dualistic death struggle between the forces of evil and those of goodness. In this crisis the world in the present age under the temporary control of evil is delivered, renewed, or replaced by a new age with a new world of supernatural origin. This type of thinking tends to appear in times of dire distress when men feel helpless and all chance of earthly deliverance seems utterly remote.[10]

Not only does an apocalypse possess the unique conceptual form which we have just described; it also is characterized by a literary type which is highly individualistic. Intense symbols, dramatic figures of speech, and even weird visions are typical. It is not always possible to determine whether the visions are actual, in a psychological sense, or literary devices to heighten interest. And even where they seem to be genuine, the writer usually formalizes them by adding descriptive details drawn from other apocalyptic writings or based upon certain suggestive scriptural passages.[11]

The Revelation to John is the most impressive of extant apocalyptic

[8] The Apocalypse of John (New York: The Macmillan Co., 1919), p. 167.

[9] Eschatology is the science of final things. It may involve such considerations as death, resurrection, the end of the world, final judgment, and the future state.

[10] For a significant analysis of the apocalyptic outlook see the Introduction to the commentary treatment of the Revelation to John, written by Martin Rist in The Interpreter's Bible, XII, 347-51.

[11] For a discussion in general of possible sources, Jewish and Jewish-Christian, cf. H. B. Swete, The Apocalypse of St. John, p. xlvi, and James Moffatt, Introduction to the Literature of the New Testament, pp. 489-90.

documents. Others which belong to this literature include Daniel, Isa. 24–27, the threefold apocalypse in Mark 13, Luke 21 and Matt. 24, and such Pauline passages as I Thess. 4:1-18 and II Thess. 2:1-12. These are all found in the Scriptures; outside this body are materials in such works as Enoch, Baruch, II Esdras, the Apocalypse of Peter, the Apocalypse of Elijah, and the Apocalypse of Paul. Although there is a basic similarity of literary pattern and thought outlook among them all, a close comparison will reveal numbers of specific variations. To consider these in detail, however, would take us beyond the purpose of this chapter. It is sufficient to indicate that they exist.

The portrait of Christ as it is drawn in the Revelation to John must be interpreted within the context of the nature and purpose of apocalyptic conceptions. Only in this way will its unique characteristics be understood and appreciated. And only from this perspective, also, can some of its quite puzzling features be explained.

### The Son of Man

The high place given to Christ in the Revelation is evidenced by the fact that, at the very outset, the claim is made that the book is "the revelation of Jesus Christ" (1:1). God has chosen him as the one through whom to reveal his divine purposes to John the Seer. What follows, therefore, will be "the word of God and the testimony of Jesus Christ" (1:2). It shall be written down, and all who read the words of the prophecy, even reading them aloud, and who also keep them, will be blessed.

In order to undergird further the fact that the authority for the representations of coming events is none other than Christ, the seer was given a vision of "one like a son of man" who commanded him to write what he was to see in a book.[12] He was also told to send it to the seven churches, Ephesus, Smyrna, Pergamum, Thyatira, Sardis, Philadelphia, and Laodicea. Although these particular churches were probably intended to receive the Apocalypse, the fact that seven were named logically implies that it was intended for the entire church, since seven stands for completeness in Hebrew apocalyptic writings.

The Christ of this ecstatic vision (1:12-20) was seen as a heavenly

---

[12] Whether this and other visions in the work are truly visions in the psychological sense or literary constructions of the author is an open question. A combination of the two seems likely. The decision here is not basic to the conception of Christ, since it is the ideological conclusion and not the medium which concerns us. Cf. Rist, op. cit., p. 372. Martin Kiddle, The Revelation of St. John, pp. xxiv-v.

figure, calling to mind the Son of man in Enoch (I Enoch 46:2-8), to whom reference has already been made in this book.[13] Although suggesting the title used in Daniel where it stood for the saints of Israel, the phrase here, referring to an individual person, is more closely related to its meaning in Enoch. As such Christ is the exalted Messiah of heavenly origin and significance who stands in the presence of God, "the Lord of Spirits," whose pre-eminence in uprightness is forever, and who shall control the destiny of kings.

And what John "sees" confirms these implications of the title:

Then I turned to see the voice that was speaking to me and on turning I saw seven golden lampstands, and in the midst of the lampstands one like a son of man, clothed with a long robe and with a golden girdle round his breast; his head and his hair were white as white wool, white as snow; his eyes were like a flame of fire, his feet were like burnished bronze, refined as in a furnace, and his voice was like the sound of many waters; in his right hand he held seven stars, from his mouth issued a sharp two-edged sword, and his face was like the sun shining in full strength. (1:12-16.)

Here is a figure of authority, insight, power, rule, and judgment. The detailed description is representative of personality and functional characteristics of Christ as one like a Son of man. It is quite likely that the author is drawing from biblical and other sources for the details, either in the sense of being familiar with them and therefore experiencing the vision accordingly, or of consciously combining, as a literary artist, previous representations.[14]

The reaction of the seer before this vision was such as might be expected in the presence of so exalted a personage. He fell at his feet as though dead (cf. Dan. 10:8-11; Enoch 71:1-3), only to be lifted up and reassured: "Fear not, I am the first and the last, and the living one; I died, and behold I am alive for evermore, and I have the keys of Death and Hades." (Rev. 1:17b-18.) The expressions "the first and last," "the living one," "alive for evermore," and "the keys of Death and Hades" suggest an eternality, absoluteness, inclusiveness, and decisiveness in the person of Christ that were equal both to the crisis

[13] Cf. pp. 148-49.

[14] Cf. the description of the angel in Dan. 10:5-6, Apocalypse of Zephaniah 9; cf. also Dan. 7:9; I Enoch 46:1; Apocalypse of Abraham 11; Ezekiel 43:2; I Enoch 82:7-8; III Enoch 17:4-7, et al. Consult the commentaries for specific relationships between Revelation and possible sources.

hour which the church was facing and to the denouement of history which the Apocalypse was to announce.

Whence came this supernal portrait of Christ? How are we to account for its features which move beyond those of the Jesus of history? It is not sufficient simply to say that at a specified time it was revealed, although elements of revelation most surely contributed to it. Two generations of Christian experience also underlie it. The Resurrection, Ascension, and Pentecost opened the way for its coming. In addition, the missionary activities of Paul and others, accompanied by persecution and culminating in martyrdom, contributed a knowledge of Christ which moved in the direction of the figure of the Son of man in the Revelation to John. Although the form of the portrait with its scintillating symbolism may strike us as startling, its essential convictions concerning Christ had been in the making for seven decades.

### Christ Speaks to the Seven Churches

Mention has already been made of the seven churches who were to receive the revelation, after the seer had recorded it in a book (1:11). This referred to the entire contents of the Apocalypse. Chapters 2 and 3, however, contain individual letters to each of these churches.[15] They are penned with such specific notations of accomplishments, faults, and failures that one is tempted to draw a detailed picture of each. On the other hand, they are so stylized and unlike the customary epistle form that the merits and weaknesses mentioned are probably best regarded as typical of the church as a whole.

Each letter begins with a reference to the angel of the named church, probably regarded as a heavenly protector, or as a personification of the church itself. Then, an identification of the speaker whose words the seer is recording is given. This is followed by a description of the church, a warning or order to give heed to the prophecy,[16] and a promise of blessing to those who overcome in the present crisis and the life-and-death struggle soon to begin.

At one particular place in this schematic arrangement an aspect

---

[15] Whether these were ever circulated independently of the Apocalypse as a whole or, from the first, were an integral part of the work, is sometimes debated. Although I accept the latter conclusion, this does not affect our concern, for we are considering the canonical writing as it appears in the New Testament.

[16] In the letter to Thyatira (2:18-29), Sardis (3:1-6), Philadelphia (3:7-13), and Laodicea (3:14-22) the warning to heed and the promise of blessing are reversed.

of the portrait of Christ emerges in each letter. He it is who speaks the word to the churches. The identification is clear, even though it is somewhat indirect. A quality or function of his person is mentioned, letter by letter, usually in terms of the symbolic representations in the vision of one like a Son of man. (1) *Ephesus* (2:1): "The words of him who holds the seven stars in his right hand, who walks among the seven golden lampstands. (2) *Smyrna* (2:8): "The words of the first and the last, who died and came to life." (3) *Pergamum* (2:12): "The words of him who has the sharp two-edged sword." (4) *Thyatira* (2:18): "The words of the Son of God, who has eyes like a flame of fire, and whose feet are like burnished bronze." (5) *Sardis* (3:1): "The words of him who has the seven spirits of God and the seven stars." (6) *Philadelphia* (3:7): "The words of the holy one, the true one, who has the key of David, who opens and no one shall shut, who shuts and no one opens." [17] (7) *Laodicea* (3:14): "The words of the Amen, the faithful, and true witness, the beginning of God's creation."

In all of this Christ is represented as the revealer of destiny. It is he who knows the character of the church, its power and its weaknesses. It is he also who judges, corrects, and warns it. And finally, it is he who promises the victory to all who will conquer in the crucial hour. As he performs these functions, Christ is more than a prophet in the usual sense. He is involved in them and belongs to the heavenly side of reality, holding a dynamic relationship to his church which none other than God himself has the right to assume.

### The Slain Lamb

The Apocalypse to John opens with a portrait of Christ as the authority behind the revelation which is to be made (1:12-20). Then, as if to present conditions on earth where future events are to occur, it moves on to describe these in the letters to the seven churches (chs. 2–3). Here, too, Christ is the one who brings the "word." Next the writing turns to the situation in heaven from which the Judgment and deliverance are to come (chs. 4–5). And once again Christ has a prominent place in the vision. He is seen in the throne room before

---

[17] Beckwith: "The epithet given to Christ at the opening of this epistle, like that in the following epistle, v. 14, and in part also in the preceding one, v. 1, is not taken from the vision of 1:10 ff., but from a thought prominent in the author's mind and expressed elsewhere in the book; Christ is the Davidic Messiah, who will receive his own share in his kingdom, cf. 2:26; 3:21; 5:5; 19:11-16; 20:4; 22:16." Op. cit., p. 479.

the presence of God as the slain Lamb, slain, yet standing in om- nipotence (seven horns) and omniscience (seven eyes) as the only one who can unlock the secrets of the future. This constitutes portrai- ture of a high order.

The situational setting provides a dramatic background for this portrait. God, who has just been worshiped as creator (ch. 4), is depicted as seated on his throne, holding a scroll which is sealed with seven seals in his right hand. It contains the blueprint of final future events and can be opened only by one who is worthy to do so. When it seemed as though such a person could not be found, much to the grief of the seer, one of the twenty-four heavenly elders announced, "Weep not; lo, the Lion of the tribe of Judah, the Root of David, has conquered, so that he can open the scroll and its seven seals" (5:5).

But when the seer looks, he does not see a lion; instead he discovers a "Lamb standing, as though it had been slain, with seven horns and with seven eyes, . . ." This creature immediately takes the scroll from God's hand, preparatory to breaking the seals and opening it. Whereupon, the Lamb is worshiped by members of the heavenly court, even as God had been. The "new song" of praise said:

> Worthy art thou to take the scroll
>   and to open its seals,
> for thou wast slain and by thy blood
>   didst ransom men for God
> from every tribe and tongue and
>   people and nation,
> and hast made them a kingdom and
>   priests to our God,
> and they shall reign on earth. (5:9-10.)

This utterance marked the beginning of further worship as myriads of angels and created creatures throughout the universe joined antiphonally in ascribing praise to the Lamb who is worthy. Of this hymn Rawlinson says, "There could be no better summary of the Christology of the Apocalpse." [18]

The portrait of Christ in this throne-room scene is a composite of a number of conceptions found elsewhere in the Scriptures. For in- stance, as the "Root of David," he is the traditional Davidic Messiah (Isa. 11:1, 10; II Esdras 12:32), and as the Lion of the tribe of Judah,

---

[18] *The New Testament Doctrine of the Christ*, p. 194. Used by permission.

201

he is victorious in his kingly power (Gen. 49:9; II Esdras 12:31). The figure of the Lamb adds a further interpretation of Christ; he is seen here both as the triumphant Christ [19] and as the sacrifice for sins (Isa. 53:7; John 1:29, 36).

Particular attention should be paid to the portrait of Christ as the slain Lamb. In its combination of triumph, power, and humility it is almost unique in the New Testament. It has an accent that is reminiscent of Paul's passage in Philippians (2:5-11), where the humble servant-slave is exalted to an unprecedented place by God and receives universal worship. The Lamb of the Apocalypse is no weakling. He shares omnipotence and omniscience with God.

In an impressive summary Beckwith has pointed out that the title of Lamb is used of Christ

in the most august scenes. As the object of the worship offered by the hosts of heaven and earth, chapters 4-5; as the unveiler of the destinies of the ages, chapters 5-6; as one enthroned, before whom and to whom the redeemed render the praise of their salvation, 7:9 ff.; as the controller of the book of life, 13:8; as the Lord of the hosts on mount Zion, 14:1; as the victor over the hosts of Antichrist, 17:14; as the spouse of the glorified Church, 19:7; as the temple and light of the new Jerusalem, 21:22; as the sharer in the throne of God, 22:1,—Christ is called the Lamb.[20]

Usually these exalted functions and characteristics are not symbolized by a lamb, and this fact further highlights the uniqueness of the portrait in the Apocalypse. It is the author's conviction that Christ's death for sin, by which he "ransomed men for God" (5:9), was so determinative in the course of history that the symbol of the Lamb, which had traditionally been associated with sacrifice for sins, is made to stand out above all the rest. He heightened it to include other functions and qualities formerly associated with more vigorous representations, such as the lion.

One further aspect in the portrait of Christ as the Lamb which is found in the throne-room scene should be mentioned. He possessed seven eyes (cf. Zech. 4:2-10). We have already interpreted this as indicating that John attributed to Christ complete knowledge or omniscience. He also sees in this fact a relationship between Christ and the Spirit of God, or the Holy Spirit, for he says that the seven

[19] The Messiah is depicted outside of the New Testament as a victorious Lamb in the Testament of Joseph 19:8. Whether John had this passage in mind is open to question.

[20] Op. cit., p. 315. Cf. also Charles, op. cit., I, cxiv.

eyes "are the seven Spirits of God sent forth into all the earth" (5:6; cf. also 1:4). This relationship is found elsewhere in the New Testament where the Spirit of Christ, the Spirit of God, and the Holy Spirit are equated or used interchangeably.[21] In the present reference Christ is represented as at work through the Spirit of God in all the world.

### Christ, the Warrior-Messiah [22]

The opening of the seven seals (6:1–8:6) by Christ, the slain Lamb, released a series of judgments upon the earth which were continued in the blowing of the seven trumpets (8:7–11:19), and the emptying of the seven bowls of the wrath of God (15:1–16:21). These are probably not three separate sets, but a threefold representation of a single period of judgment. The opening of the seventh seal, for instance, instead of being a separate judgment marks the beginning of the trumpet series.[23] The purpose of these judgments upon the earth would seem to be that of softening up the society which was under the control of Satan for the final assize. The evil situation was too matured to expect repentance. A close reading of the Apocalypse leads to the conclusion that it was intended primarily to strengthen the faithful who were already within the fold, rather than to evangelize the wicked. They were being encouraged to hold out to the very end, and thus to conquer (nikaō), assured that God would act on their behalf in the immediate future.[24]

The final judgment toward which the events envisioned by John were leading included a struggle-to-the-death battle between the forces of evil and those of righteousness. It was to occur, he states, at "the place which is called in Hebrew Armageddon" (16:16). In Ezekiel (39:1 ff.) and Daniel (11:45) such a conflict was located among the mountains of Israel. The Word "Armageddon" in Hebrew originally meant Mount Megiddo, which should be translated "hill of victory." This calls to mind the plains of Megiddo where a battle took place involving Deborah (Judg. 5:19). Whether the seer

[21] Cf. Rom. 8:9; also our discussion of this fact in relation to Paul's portrait of Christ, pp. 76-77.

[22] As I have used it, I am indebted for this title to Beckwith, op. cit.

[23] Between the blowing of the seventh trumpet and the emptying of the first bowl are to be found a number of visions intended to explain the situation involved in the judgments. They do not carry the reader along progressively, but give him a chance to catch his breath and understand better what is taking place.

[24] This is the motivation that is urged in the letters to the seven churches: 2:7, 11, 17, 26; 3:5, 12, 21.

was designating an actual geographical location such as Rome (built on seven hills) or Jerusalem (built on Mount Zion) is open to question. Certainly he anticipated the overthrow of Rome and devoted a considerable section of his writing (ch. 18) to a dirge proclaiming the doom of the city (referred to as Babylon). It is possible, however, that in this instance he is dealing in eschatological symbols rather than actually locating an event. This does not mean that he does not expect the issue to be drawn; it does suggest that he may not be pointing literally to the site.

The portrait of Christ is involved in the issue that is to be decided at Armageddon, since he is pictured as leading an army of heavenly martyrs which oppose the Beast and his false prophet, both of whom are agents of Satan. Reference was made earlier in this chapter to the Beast, identified with the imperial rule of Rome, who was enforcing emperor worship, and to his false prophet, the Roman priesthood, who presided over the cult ritual.[25] Both are involved in the decisive final battle where they are overcome by Christ.

Our author regards the Beast as the Antichrist of Hebrew apocalyptic, an evil human figure embodying world power who sets himself against God, especially in the final crisis. Usually he is distinguished from Satan and serves as his agent in the last days (II Thess. 2:3 ff.; I John 2:18, 22; 4:3; II John 7). It is in this light that he appears in the Revelation to John.[26]

The portrait of Christ, however, rather than that of the Antichrist, concerns us in connection with Armageddon. This is contained in the following passage:

Then I saw heaven opened, and behold, a white horse! He who sat upon it is called Faithful and True, and in righteousness he judges and makes war. His eyes are like a flame of fire, and on his head are many diadems; and he has a name inscribed which no one knows but himself. He is clad in a robe dipped in blood, and the name by which he is called is "The Word of God." And the armies of heaven, arrayed in fine linen, white and pure, followed him on white horses. From his mouth issues a sharp sword with which to smite the nations, and he will rule them with a rod of iron; he will tread the wine press of the fury of the wrath of God the Almighty.

[25] Cf. p. 193.

[26] The Antichrist is referred to in II Esdras 5:6; the Sibylline Oracles III. 63 ff.; and the Apocalypse of Baruch 36 and 40. He also appears in certain early Christian writings; cf. the Teaching of the Twelve 16, and the Ascension of Isaiah 4.

On his robe and on his thigh he has a name inscribed, King of kings and Lord of lords. (19:11-16.)

Christ is seen here in his supreme power over evil forces, such forces as were actually threatening the first readers. As the conquering warrior-Messiah from heaven, he rides a white horse, followed by an army of celestial martyrs clad in linen, pure and white. With eyes like a flame of fire, his head crowned with many crowns, and his robe dipped in the blood of his enemies, he is an awesome figure. Out of his mouth extends a sharp sword with which to smite the nations (cf. 1:16).

In addition, Christ, the warrior-Messiah, is represented in this vision as possessing several names; three are known, and one is a secret. All the significance attributed to names in Hebrew apocalyptic is brought to bear upon his designation. He is called Faithful and True, the Word of God, King of kings and Lord of lords. Whatever their derivation,[27] they signify his character as the Messiah. He is true to his mission, imbued with the power of creation, and supreme over all earthly rulers. The secret name known only to himself adds a further element of power to Christ's person. It was currently believed that a secret held miraculous potentialities, especially an unknown name (cf. 2:17; 3:12). And the warrior-Messiah has a secret name! [28]

Not only does Christ as this warrior-Messiah have a specific kind of character and significant names, both known and unknown; he also has a mission to fulfill. Even as the messianic figure of Isaiah (11:3-5), he judges in righteousness, a judgment which in this instance is expressed by making war on the Beast. With the sword from his mouth he will overpower and conquer the enemy nations, ruling them with a rod of iron (cf. Ps. 2:9, also Rev. 12:5). In doing this, so to speak, he will be treading "the wine press of the fury of the wrath of God the Almighty" (cf. 14:19-20; Isa. 63:1-6).

With the issue between Satan and God so sharply defined in the

[27] a) Faithful and True: cf. Rev. 3-14 where Christ is the faithful and true witness; also 1:5; Ps. 89:35-37.

b) Word of God: cf. John 1:1; Heb. 4:12; and Wisd. of Sol. 18:15-16 for differing and yet related meanings. In the latter reference the Word of God became a "stern warrior."

c) King of kings and Lord of lords: cf. I Enoch 9:4; Dan. 2:47; 11:36; Deut. 10:17, where the title is ascribed to God.

[28] Rist suggests that it might be "Jesus," pointing out that, cryptically speaking, this name contained the numerical equivalent of 888, which would be "a perfect foil to the secret name of the bestial Antichrist which added up to 666." Op. cit., p. 513.

Revelation, and the setting at Armageddon, including the character of both the warrior-Messiah and the Antichrist so graphically presented, one would expect an extended campaign in their struggle-to-the-death. Not at all! The power of Christ is so great that his victory is immediate. The account of the battle is told in these words:

And I saw the beast and the kings of the earth with their armies gathered to make war against him who sits upon the horse and against his army. And the beast was captured, and with it the false prophet who in its presence had worked the signs by which he deceived those who had received the mark of the beast and those who worshipped its image. These two were thrown alive into the lake of fire that burns with brimstone. And the rest were slain by the sword of him who sits upon the horse, the sword that issues from his mouth; and all the birds were gorged with their flesh. (19:19-21.)

Not infrequently the question is raised as to whether the portrait of Christ in the Apocalypse of John is fully Christian. True, he is depicted as possessing great authority and power. And he is also concerned with the suffering of his followers. But there is no grief expressed over the fate of sinners in the final hour. Some have even thought they detected an accent of vengeance in several of the passages we have examined.

Several considerations should be brought to mind before a final evaluation of the portrait in this regard is made. First of all, the Revelation is an apocalypse. Its imagery is highly specialized and more suggestive than other forms of address. Next it customarily borrows pre-Christian Hebrew symbols and sometimes pagan representations, and these are not always disassociated from their original setting. Again, the perspective of the writing places it at the very yonder-edge of history. The gospel of love has been presented over and over again; presented and rejected. Christ has already died for sinners. He stands in heaven as the slain Lamb before he appears again on earth as the warrior-Messiah. And finally, it should be remembered that the times were tense. The author himself saw the visions while a prisoner for the Faith.

### Christ Regnant

Christ emerges from the battle of Armageddon as victor over the Beast and his false prophet. Evil has been routed, and the two are cast into a lake of fire, a place of eternal punishment not unlike the Hebrew Gehenna (19:20). The armies of the Beast have been slain (19:21). Those who served him and bore his wicked mark are later to be raised from death to be finally judged (20:13; 14:9-10). The fiery lake will also receive them (20:15). Satan himself will ultimately be cast into this place of eternal torment, but not until he has been temporarily bound for a thousand years (20:3), while Christ reigns with the martyred saints (20:4-6). Then he will be loosed, captured, and committed (20:7-10).

The portrait of Christ in the final scenes of the Revelation to John shows him in his personal relation to his followers who have remained faithful unto death. These share with him in his victory over Satan, the Beast, his false prophet, and those who worshiped him. There is a tenderness and glory in these relationships which have inspired Christians to anticipate eagerly the day when they shall be joined to their Lord forever.

First of all, Christ is portrayed as reigning with the martyred saints for a thousand years. This is highly appropriate in a writing which has sought to encourage faithfulness unto death. The idea of a millennium has its roots in the Hebrew hope for the coming of God's kingdom on earth where Jehovah's people experience a blessed life with the Messiah. This expectation became increasingly transcendental at the hands of later apocalyptists (II Esdras 7:28-29), and the idea of a temporary rule only of the Messiah on earth to be enjoyed by the righteous, including at least some of those who had already died, was expressed in various forms.[29] In the Revelation the millennium was intended for the martyrs only. As a kind of reward for their loyalty they are singled out for a special reign with Christ. He has not forgotten their sacrifice. It takes place on this earth which will disappear at its close (Rev. 20:11). This will be followed by the final judgment when the dead will be judged according to what was written of them and their deeds in the book of life (20:12-13).

Following the disappearance of the old earth, a new heaven and a new earth come down from above (21:1-2) to become the site for a beatific life forever. John describes this new existence as living in the New Jerusalem (21:9–22:5),[30] and Christ is pictured within this

---

[29] Cf. II Esdras 12:34; Enoch 91:12; Apocalypse of Baruch 40:3.

[30] The description of the New Jerusalem is based largely upon passages in Ezekiel, Isaiah, and Zechariah. For a detailed analysis cf. Charles, op. cit., ad loc.

setting in glorified and exalted terms. As the Lamb, he becomes the groom of the Holy City (21:9-10).[31] And, together with God, he is its temple (21:22) and its light (21:23).

The visions of the Revelation close with Christ sharing the throne of God in the New Jerusalem: "There shall no more be anything accursed, but *the throne of God and of the Lamb* shall be in it, and his servants shall worship him" (22:3).[32] This is the final touch in the transcendent portrait that John draws. All that he has been in this writing—one like a Son of man (1:12-20), he who speaks the authoritative word to the seven churches (chs. 2 and 3), the slain Lamb (ch. 5, *et al.*), and the warrior-Messiah (19:11-21)—all this leads logically to the picture of the regnant Christ. The victory over evil has been God's and Christ's together, and the reign over the saints in the heavenly city is properly theirs also. Although he is not actually identified with God, his function in time and eternity is no less than God's very own.

As has been previously stated, the author of the Apocalypse expected the end of this Age, with its attendant judgment upon evil and ultimate blessedness for the faithful as depicted in his writing, to occur within the very near future. The closing verses of the book repeatedly refer to its immediacy (22:6, 7, 12, 20). This culmination of history was not a question of academic speculation for John. He believed that he was to be a participant in it, and next to his last word was a prayer for Christ's return which would mark the beginning of the End. "Amen," he cries, and then prays, "Come, Lord Jesus!" (22:20).

---

[31] Earlier the church had been named as the Bride of the Lamb (19:6-8). Compare Eph. 5:22-27. Cf. also Mark 2:19-20.

[32] Italics mine.

# FIFTEEN

# In the General and Pastoral Epistles

THE PORTRAIT OF CHRIST IN THE REVELATION TO JOHN WAS DRAWN with bold and dramatic strokes. He is seen there as the leading figure in the denouement of history that is being described. Therefore the approach, more often than not, is direct and delineates both his character and mighty acts. Portraiture is no less present in the writings we are to consider in this chapter, but Christ is not the subject under discussion as immediately as he was in the Apocalypse. The authors of the General and Pastoral epistles were concerned primarily with the problems of Christians within the church. They approach them amidst the tensions and pressures which developed as false teachers, suffering, and unworthy motives bore down upon the Fellowship from within and without. Although there is a lively interest in eschatology and in the return of the Lord in these writings which determines much that is said, they are not apocalyptic documents as such.

## Date—Recipients—Authorship

The time span involved in this group of letters may extend from as early as A.D. 60 to A.D. 150, depending in part upon the date which is assigned to the First Letter of Peter. If it is placed in the 60's,[1] the spread of inclusion is considerable. If, on the other hand, this writing is dated toward the end of the first century, it is not so great.[2] The earlier dating usually carries with it the conclusion that it was written by Peter, the disciple of Jesus. The outer edge of this time span, circa A.D. 150, is set by the date of Second Peter, upon which dating there is a large measure of agreement among modern scholars.[3]

[1] Some early datings are Moffatt, A.D. 60; Hunter, A.D. 62; Bacon, A.D. 64-67; McNeile, A.D. 67. In regard to these and the other dates suggested, the reader should consult the commentaries and introductions to the New Testament.
[2] Some late datings are Goodspeed, in the A.D. 90's; Streeter, A.D. 95; Scott, A.D. 96.
[3] Typical datings are Moffatt, A.D. 150; Scott, A.D. 150; McNeile, shortly before A.D. 150; Barnett, the middle of the second century. Purvis, however, dated Second Peter shortly before the apostle Peter's death in Rome.

A reasonable dating of the remaining writings in this group would be James, A.D. 100 [4]; Jude, A.D. 100-125 [5]; and the Pastorals (First and Second Timothy, Titus), A.D. 125-50.[6] Exactness is exceedingly difficult in matters such as this, and it would take us too far afield to argue the case for the several dates as suggested. With the exception of First Peter, if an early date is assigned to it, the writings in this chapter cover relatively a fifty-year span. And in addition, apart from Second Peter most of them may possibly fall within the same twenty-five years. This is supported by a reading of the epistles themselves, since for all their individualities, they represent a common type of writing in which both preaching and instruction are given as more-or-less similar church needs are found and faced.

In respect to the recipients of these letters, there is also a further commonness which binds them together. They apply to the church in general wherever such problems as persecution, heresy, disunity, and immorality appear. There is not to be found here the specificness of First Corinthians, for instance, which was directed to a single community. Even though the epistles to Timothy and Titus are addressed to individuals, the general church and its officials are in the author's mind. In this connection Moffatt has stated it succinctly: "The three are not private or even open letters to Timotheus or Titus, but general treatises addressed to an age or a circle which was inclined to doubt the validity or to misconceive or misapply the principles of the Pauline Gospel." [7] And the encyclical character of First and Second Peter, James, and Jude is likewise evident. Such statements as "to the exiles of the dispersion . . ." (I Pet. 1:1), "to those who have obtained a faith of equal standing . . ." (II Pet. 1:1), "to the twelve tribes in the dispersion" (Jas. 1:1), and "to those who are called, beloved in God the Father and kept for Jesus Christ" (Jude 1) indicate that their outreach goes beyond that of a limited locality.

Questions of authorship are not finally determinative for a consideration of the portrait of Christ which these books present. If, how-

---

[4] Easton, A.D. 80-100; Scott, A.D. 100; Moffatt, A.D. 100-25. But for an earlier dating, cf. McNeile, A.D. 60-137; Bacon, A.D. 67.

[5] Moffatt, by A.D. 90; Streeter, A.D. 105; Goodspeed, A.D. 125; Barnett, A.D. 125.

[6] Barnett, between A.D. 144-80 (on the assumption that they reflect Marcion's Antitheses); Scott, early part of the first quarter of the second century; Kirsopp and Silva Lake, second century; Goodspeed, about A.D. 150; Bultmann, A.D. 100-50.

[7] Introduction to Literature of New Testament, pp. 412-13.

ever, the author of First Peter is the apostle, then it is interesting to inquire as to what extent his contact with the Jesus of history influenced the conception of Christ in his writing. On the other hand, the fact that the authors of the rest of the books in this group cannot with any certainty be identified does not minimize the significance of the portrait they hold and draw. They are no less informed about Christ or devoted to him because we do not know who they were. And as to the conclusion, widely held, that the apostle Paul did not write the Pastorals, although this fact may carry implications concerning their date, it does not invalidate their conception of the Lord Christ.

### First Peter

The portrait of Christ in First Peter has many facets which relate it to the outlook of the primitive church. Coincidences between the epistle and the speeches of Peter and Acts are numerous. The earliest kerygma can be traced from the beginning to the end of the letter. Although its tenets are not listed in an orderly succession, they underlie and give structure to the practical advice which the author offers his readers. And it is this kerygma which determines the portraiture which the writing contains.

The epistle asserts that it was the prophets of old who foresaw the coming of Christ, particularly his suffering and the glory which would result (1:10-12). The source of these insights into the future, interestingly enough, was regarded as none other than the Spirit of the Messiah himself, indwelling the prophets. They were not to be the recipients of the salvation they envisioned; it was the Christian church upon which the grace would descend. As the one whose coming was prophesied, Christ is the "living stone." Even as the scripture had said, "The very stone which the builders rejected has become the head of the corner" (2:4-8; cf. also Isa. 28:16; Ps. 118:22; Isa. 8: 14-15). Such a use of this Old Testament passage in relation to Jesus had a precedent in the parable of the vineyard where it is found on the lips of our Lord himself (Luke 20:9-18).

Christ's coming as Messiah was not only foreseen by the prophets; his very being was also pre-existent. This point is not argued or developed within the framework of a Wisdom or Logos philosophy as in the Prologue of the Fourth Gospel. It is related, instead, to the religious impulse which was convinced that Christ must be accounted

211

for in terms of the eternal purpose of God: "He was destined before the foundation of the world but was made manifest at the end of the times for your sake" (1:20). A. M. Hunter comments upon this passage by saying, "Only that can be manifested which was in being before it was manifested." [8] And Moffatt makes much of the idea that this view "was natural for readers familiar with the book of Enoch and its messianic theology." [9] Paul's thought upon pre-existence must also have had its influence upon the church, so that it was not necessary to labor the point. The brevity of the reference is a testimony to its congeniality.

The Christ whom the author knew was one who suffered (2:21-24; 4:1-2, 13) and died for the sins of mankind (1:2, 18; 3:18). He was a sinless offering in man's stead. By his dying, men were ransomed from sin, and cleansed through the sprinkling of his blood. Through his death a way of atonement was made possible. The Suffering Servant passages of Isaiah lie just beneath the surface of the several references to the death of Jesus in First Peter:

For to this you have been called, because Christ also suffered for you, leaving you an example, that you should follow in his steps. He committed no sin; no guile was found on his lips. When he was reviled, he did not revile in return; when he suffered, he did not threaten; but he trusted to him who judges justly. He himself bore our sins in his body on the tree, that we might die to sin and live to righteousness. By his wounds you have been healed. (2:21-24.)

The purpose of all this was that Christ might bring men to God (3:18). This is essentially the glory and mystery of atonement. It is God himself who acts to make man's union with the divine possible. Men must act too, but theirs is a response to what God has initiated in the coming of Christ. They will be impelled by their Lord's example to suffer for righteousness also (4:1-2), and through their suffering they will share his glory when it is revealed (4:13), but they cannot do for themselves what God in Christ has already done for them.

First Peter contains a further element in its portrait of Christ which is unique in the New Testament. He is represented as preaching to the spirits in prison (3:19), by which is meant that immediately prior to

[8] The Interpreter's Bible, XII, 84.
[9] The General Epistles, p. 108.

his resurrection he undertook a ministry in Hades. This view ultimately found its way into the Apostles' Creed where it states, "He descended into hell." It is difficult to develop a doctrine on the basis of such a brief reference, and yet, the message implied by the act is so true of the church's conviction concerning the universality of salvation in Christ, that it was accepted at its face value and believed to be a fact.

Modern scholarship has approached this passage variously. It has been argued that it is a textual error which should have read "Enoch" instead of Christ (Rendel Harris, Moffatt, Goodspeed). Again, it has been suggested that the statement means that in his death Christ made a proclamation to the evil powers (Selwyn). Still another view (Hunter) is that the passage intends to say that Christ actually went to Hades during the time between the Cross and the Resurrection to proclaim the gospel, either to the fallen angels (Gen. 6:1-4) or to those who did not obey God in the days of Noah (I Pet. 3:20). Hunter accounts for the tradition on the basis of Ps. 16:10 ("For thou dost not give me up to Sheol . . .") which Peter referred to in the Pentecost Sermon, and also upon Jesus' application of Isa. 61:1 ("to proclaim liberty to the captives") to himself in Luke 4:17-18.[10] In view of the differing conclusions based upon the best scholarship of today, it would be unwise to decide that a final exegesis upon this passage has been reached. Its reflection in the Apostles' Creed indicates, however, that it was believed to refer to Christ, both before and by the time this historic statement was framed. And as such it adds a further dimension to his portrait.

In addition to the lines in portraiture already indicated, reference should be made to the author's presentation of Christ as resurrected (1:3). He is seen also as exalted in heaven at the right hand of God, "with angels, authorities, and powers subject to him" (3:22). Soon he will return as "chief Shepherd" when his glory shall be revealed (1:7, 13; 4:13; 5:4).

Meanwhile, Christ is represented as having an active relationship to his followers. He is referred to as being "the Shepherd and Guardian" (episkopos) of their souls (2:25). As such, he is their overseer or bishop. No special doctrine of church offices is intended in this reference. Instead, it is a picture of Christ as living Lord who guides and

---

[10] Further reading upon suggested solutions to the enigma of this verse may be found in Moffatt, General Epistles, pp. 140-46; and op. cit., XII, 132-33.

213

protects his followers. They should, therefore, obey (1:2) and honor him as such. Although they may be called upon to suffer for righteousness, they should not fear; rather, in their hearts they should reverence Christ as Lord (3:15).

If it is assumed that the author of First Peter was the apostle himself, the question might be raised as to why the epistle does not reflect more of the Jesus of history, as in the case of Mark's Gospel, which tradition also relates through the evangelist to Peter. In replying to this query, it should be pointed out that the writing is a letter and not a gospel. Furthermore, to the extent that the outline of the primitive kerygma can be traced in its statements, the Jesus of history is not missing from the document. And in addition, there is considerable reference to the sufferings of Christ in the epistle. These appear particularly in the fourth chapter where the significant passage relative to the merits of suffering as a Christian occurs (4:16). The main purpose of the writing would seem to be that of admonishing, encouraging, and fortifying those who were about to face social and political persecution and possibly martyrdom because of their faith. It is in this light that the references to the suffering that is required of their brotherhood throughout the world (5:9), and the assurance that after they had suffered a little while, God would restore, establish, and strengthen them (5:10), should be interpreted.

### James

It was noted at the outset of this chapter that the Epistle of James is dated by most scholars today toward the close of the first century. The chief reason that it has sometimes been placed earlier is that the name "James" (1:1) is taken to refer to the brother of Jesus. It is felt that the letter takes a position contrary to Paul on the faith-works issue, one such as James is credited with holding (cf. Gal. 2).[11] Neither external tradition nor internal considerations, however, identify finally the James referred to, nor the exact recipients for whom the letter was intended. Both Syrian Antioch[12] and Ephesus[13] have been claimed as the place where the writing originated.

The epistle has been characterized as a diatribe or a homiletical

[11] For a discussion of this point, see Goodspeed, *Introduction to New Testament*, p. 293.

[12] *Ibid.*, p. 295.

[13] Streeter, *The Primitive Church*, p. 206.

214

exhortation.[14] As an ethical anthology it is Jewish in tone. The name of Christ appears only twice (1:1; 2:1). This has led to the suggestion that it was originally a Jewish work rewritten by a Christian editor. Even so, its spirit is not out of line with accepted Christian teachings. The author may have been acquainted with Hebrews, since he refers to Rahab (2:25), who is singled out as an example of faith in this other writing.

What can one expect by way of a portrait of Christ in such a document? Obviously the epistle is not so complete as it might otherwise be in this regard. And yet the references bring the letter into the historic succession of New Testament tradition concerning our Lord. The two statements in which Jesus is named exalt him to the highest category. He is "the Lord Jesus Christ" (1:1), and "our Lord Jesus Christ, the Lord of Glory" (2:1). As such he is soon to return (5:7), and as the Messiah he is the Judge "standing at the doors" (5:9).[15]

There is also portraiture in the teachings of the epistle at points where one can discover the mind and spirit of Christ, particularly in reflections of the sayings of Jesus which it contains. A. Plummer finds nineteen parallels between James and Matthew, Mark, Luke, and even John.[16] This is probably excessive. Streeter thinks that the author had read Q in the recension of Luke.[17] To single out several passages which may go back to a remembered or quoted word of Jesus, one might include 1:6-8 (advocating faith), 2:8 (urging love of neighbors as oneself), and 5:12 (prohibiting swearing).

If we had only the Epistle of James, our portrait of Christ would be meager indeed. It must be read in the light of the meaning of the traditional phrases it employs, as they occur elsewhere in the New Testament, in order to round out much of a conception. And this was probably what its original readers did. The writing came out of the life of the Christian community for the upbuilding of the faith of the church, whether one concludes that it was the product of a Christian editor, or an original creation of one who was concerned for the ethics of the followers of Christ.

[14] A. H. McNeile, An Introduction to the Study of the New Testament, p. 191.
[15] But cf. B. S. Easton, "Even to the Christian editor the Lord in vss. 7-8 and the Judge in vs. 9 must have meant God, not Christ." The Interpreter's Bible, XII, 66.
[16] The Expositor's Bible, pp. 310-13.
[17] Op. cit., p. 200.

## Jude and Second Peter

In considering the portrait of Christ in Jude and Second Peter together, recognition is being made of the fact that the writer of the latter takes up into his epistle considerable portions of the former short letter of only twenty-five verses. Although from twenty-five to fifty years may probably lie between them, their similarity warrants their being examined together. Both seem to combat the same heresies, presumably at earlier and later stages in their development. Just what these were specifically, it is difficult to say. Certainly an inordinate interest in speculative philosophy (II Pet. 1:16) and the practice of immorality (Jude 5-7; II Pet. 2:4-10) were giving grave concern to the authors. Perhaps the heresy was of the gnostic type, church wide in scope at the time, and later to develop even further. Rome may be considered as a likely site for the origin of these documents, the case being better established for Second Peter than for Jude.

Although the author of Second Peter goes on at great lengths to identify himself with the apostle Peter, even claiming to have been an eyewitness of the Transfiguration (1:1, 14, 16-18; 3:1), his reference to Paul's letters as authoritative for Christians (3:15-16), as well as his use of the words "the predictions of the holy prophets and the commandment of the Lord and Savior through your apostles" (3:2) argue against it. The work should be regarded as pseudonymous, as should also the Epistle of Jude. The character of the contents of the latter places it beyond the date of Judas the brother of Jesus (Mark 6:3; Matt. 13:55) whom Origen regarded as its author.

The place of orthodoxy in meeting false teaching and immorality is the chief preachment in these writings. And, according to them, orthodox teaching is to be found in the words of the prophets and the commandments of the Lord and Savior, as these have been interpreted by the apostles (compare Jude 3 with II Pet. 3:2). This, again, suggests the kerygma, although it is not so developed, point by point, as in First Peter. The recognition given to the words of Jesus provides an element of portraiture where Christ is concerned. He stands supreme between the prophets whose predictions he validated and the apostles whose preaching rested upon his commandments.

Traditional titles are assigned to Christ in these books. He is "our only Master and Lord, Jesus Christ" (Jude 4), "our Lord and Savior Jesus Christ" (II Pet. 1:11). and the "beloved Son" (II Pet. 1:17).

Here again, the content which the church had come to put into these terms must have been intended by the authors and accepted by the readers at this late date in the canonical time-span.

The return of Christ is asserted with considerable emphasis in Second Peter. This was evidently because the parousia was being questioned at the time of its writing. To meet those who were scoffing at this expectation of the Christians because of a seeming delay, the author suggests that with the eternal God time is not as it is with those who live upon the earth. "Do not ignore this one fact," he says, "with the Lord one day is as a thousand years, and a thousand years is as one day." (II Pet. 3:8.) [18] There is no slowness with the Lord; instead he is but giving the people more time in which to repent. But there will be an end one day to this period of forbearance. At such a time, "the day of the Lord will come like a thief, and then the heavens will pass away with a loud noise, and the elements will be dissolved with fire, and the earth and the works that are upon it will be burned up" (II Pet. 3:10).[19]

It must be said that the portrait of Christ appears indirectly in Jude and Second Peter, as is true in so many of the New Testament writings. As problems are discussed and replies to critics and scoffers presented, he emerges as a figure of more-than-human significance, whose ministry, teachings, and coming again are related to the eternal destiny of mankind. One misses the emphasis upon the death of Christ for sin and sinners in these books. But they are acquainted, nevertheless, with the compassion of the Lord Jesus Christ, and they urge his followers to grow in the grace of him who is their Savior (II Pet. 3:18).

### The Pastoral Epistles

In this consideration of the portrait of Christ in the Pastoral epistles, non-Pauline authorship is assumed as the most reasonable interpretation of the data itself.[20] The letters may be regarded as

---

[18] The source of this conception is probably Ps. 90:4, where it says:

> For a thousand years in thy sight
> are but as yesterday when it is past,
> or as a watch in the night.

God lives in the eternal now; time is a human factor.

[19] Compare this picture of the destruction of the earth with the Revelation to John 16:20, and the Sibylline Oracles II. 251-52.

[20] For a discussion of authorship and date the reader should consult the introductions to the New Testament, and the commentaries.

217

pseudonymous, even though they probably contain fragments of genuine words from the apostle Paul.[21] A second-century date (*circa* A.D. 125-50) is also accepted as best suited to the internal picture of church life, the nature of the heresies involved, and the literary resemblances between the letters and other second century writings.

As in all of the New Testament documents there is a relationship in the Pastorals between the portrait of Christ which is presented and the situational background. The main concern of the author is with the responsibilities of church officers or administrators as they function in a time of heretical pressures upon the church. The maintenance of orthodoxy is regarded as essential in meeting gnostic and possibly other (Marcionite if *circa* A.D. 150 be accepted as the date) heresies.[22] The extent to which the author's conception of Christ is involved in meeting heresy will be seen as the portrait he presents is delineated.

The Christ of the Pastoral epistles is descended from David (II Tim. 2:8). This view is broadly held throughout the New Testament. Certainly it was a part of Paul's gospel (Rom. 1:3-4) and testifies to the Hebraic ancestry of the Faith. In Jesus' birth, God had acted openly; he expressed his grace (*charis*) concretely in personal terms (Tit. 2:11). It was his goodness and lovingkindness which were revealed as the Savior appeared (*epiphainō*) in the Advent (Tit. 3:4).

And this appearance was expressed in terms of human flesh. The author stresses this fact quite openly in order to counter gnostic claims as to the unreality of our Lord's fleshly existence. This was one of the heresies against which the Pastorals were directed. The words in which the author asserts the appearance of Jesus in the flesh would seem to have been taken from a lengthier Christian creedal hymn:

> He was manifested in the flesh,
> vindicated in the Spirit,
>   seen by angels,
> preached among the nations,
> believed on in the world,
>   taken up in glory.—(I Tim. 3:16.)

[21] Among these II Tim. 1:15-18; 4:6-8, and Tit. 3:12-15 should be considered as likely Pauline fragments.

[22] The reader is referred to a consideration of the background of the Pastorals by Fred D. Gealy in *The Interpreter's Bible*, XI, 345 ff.

The liturgical character of this statement testifies to its use in the church before its inclusion in First Timothy. It was, therefore, probably not the composition of the author, but was employed by him in accordance with his purpose.

There are some suggestive elements of portraiture in the hymn in addition to its assertion of the reality of Jesus' flesh. A likely interpretation is that the passage declares Christ's exaltation in the realm of spirit, even as he had been known in the flesh. Not only had he been honored on earth as Lord, but he had likewise received recognition in heaven.[23] The final tenet in the hymn implies that after Christ has been preached and believed on among the nations, he will judge the world, set up his kingdom, and be established in glory.

The Pastorals make few references to Jesus' earthly life, even though they take pains to assert its reality. Their main concern was with the Faith in their own day. They do, however, point to Jesus' testimony before Pilate (I Tim. 6:13), and to his teachings ("the sound words of our Lord Jesus Christ . . ." I Tim. 6:3). Note is taken also of the fact that he was risen from the dead (II Tim. 2:8). At the end of the Age he will return to judge both the living and the dead (II Tim. 4:1, 8), appearing in glory as a blessed hope (Tit. 2:13).

Unlike Jude and Second Peter, there is an observable emphasis in the Pastoral epistles upon the death of Christ for sin. It was to save sinners that he came into the world (I Tim. 1:15). In the light of this fact his death is to be regarded as "a ransom for all" (I Tim. 2:6), by which he redeemed mankind "from all iniquity and to purify for himself a people of his own who are zealous for good deeds" (Tit. 2:14). He is the one mediator between God and men in his saving work, unlike the series of emanations between heaven and earth in Gnosticism (I Tim. 2:5).[24] Both the ransom and sacrificial conception of Christ's death are represented in these references, although neither is developed in detail.

Not only did Christ act as Savior in his past death and resurrection,

[23] Scott finds a precedent for the heavenly recognition of Christ in Jewish apocalyptic writings: "In several Jewish apocalypses the Messiah is described as worshipped by angels, and this idea was elaborated in the Early Church; the Christian imagination dwelt on the scene in heaven when Christ returned after His victory and the angels thronged out to acclaim Him." *The Pastoral Epistles*, p. 41. Alternative interpretations are also considered.

[24] This conception may also be set over against the gnostic view of a heavenly being who was temporarily united with the man Jesus, and disunited before his crucifixion.

and will in the future serve as judge and Lord in the Kingdom he will establish; he also is the source of newness of life in the present. The author found strength in Christ for his daily service (I Tim. 1:12) as he experienced the grace of the Lord. And others may know this grace also (II Tim. 2:1). The faith which is in Christ brings both good standing and confidence to those who serve well as deacons (I Tim. 3:13). And in times of persecution they will find salvation "through faith in Christ Jesus" (II Tim. 3:12-15). Indeed, the writer states:

> If we have died with him, we shall also live with him;
> if we endure, we shall also reign with him;
> if we deny him, he will also deny us;
> if we are faithless, he remains faithful—
> for he cannot deny himself. (II Tim. 2:11b-13.)

For this assurance that Christ will bring victory in the lives of his followers as they meet difficulties and even death itself, in the above passage the author has once again turned to a liturgical hymn, selecting a fragment which states the truth he would express.[25] Perhaps this was a baptismal hymn, since it is reminiscent of Rom. 6:3-4 where baptism is the subject under discussion.

All in all, the portrait of Christ which is found in the Pastoral epistles, while not developed in detail, should be regarded as fully in harmony with the significant place which is given to him in the New Testament as a whole. He is pictured as one who came to earth as an expression of God's loving purpose to redeem his children. As a descendant of David, he live a genuinely human life. He was God's Messiah, and in his death he saved his people from their sins. By his resurrection he was exalted to a place of honor in the heavens, and at his return in glory he will judge all men and establish his triumphant kingdom. For the present he is the source of newness of life, and all who live in him are assured of victory both here and hereafter. This delineation is reminiscent of the portrait of Christ in the Pauline epistles, so much so that a relation of the Pastorals to Pauline thought is clearly implied.

---

[25] Cf. previous instance, p. 218.

# SIXTEEN

# One Lord and One Faith

WE HAVE BEEN CONSIDERING THE PORTRAIT OF JESUS CHRIST AS IT IS delineated throughout the twenty-seven books of the New Testament. It has been a journey in developing Christology over a period of approximately one hundred years of documentary history, reflecting the thinking of the church from its inception until about A.D. 150. From the earliest simple kerygma of the primitive Christian community to the more developed metaphysical statements of Philippians, Colossians, the Fourth Gospel, and later writings there was a more-or-less continuous enlargement of portraiture.[1]

It has been evident as we have followed this course of development that new insights concerning Christ were revealed by God as the church undertook its evangelical task and made its witness. A changing cultural milieu when the Faith moved beyond Jerusalem to Syria, and thence to the wider Greco-Roman world contributed an environmental framework within which the revelation was increasingly known, and in terms of which it was expressed. Personality factors were also involved in the formulation of the portrait as authors of various temperaments responded to the impulse of the Holy Spirit, and wrote of these concerns which dealt with the eternal destiny of men and nations. There was never such a story as this.

## Liberalism and Relativism

It could be concluded that a portrait which came out of such a life-process as has been described is too relative to be normative for a final Faith. And, indeed, at the hands of twentieth-century liberalism this conclusion was sometimes implied, if not actually drawn.[2] Such

[1] As has been said previously in this writing, the earliest primitive kerygma contained ontological elements, at least by implication, but they were not developed or presented in terms of metaphysical thought-forms.

[2] Liberalism as employed here refers to the application of contemporary methods of historical study to the biblical documents, together with an acceptance of the twentieth-century world view which modern science has fostered.

questions as these were considered to be in order. Which shall it be —the Jesus of Mark? the Christ of Paul? or the Son of God of John? On this basis the New Testament was a source book in the history of the Christian faith from which it could be learned what succeeding generations thought about Christ. Dogmatic theology might turn to such writings as it constructed its systems of thought, and select such items of belief as were palatable to a twentieth-century world view.

The result was sometimes humanistic or evangelically denatured. In these instances there tended to be a philosophy of the Christian religion but no gospel, no good news in the New Testament sense of what God had done in Jesus Christ for man's redemption. Bernhard W. Anderson has described the situation in these words: "In attempting to bring Christianity up to date, liberals virtually capitulated to the prevailing world-view of the day, so much so that the dividing line between liberal Protestantism and secularism became increasingly dim." [3]

I have taken care to use the words "could," "sometimes," and "might" in this description of the approach of liberalism to the New Testament conception of Christ. The reason for this is that, although these conclusions were drawn by some liberals, this was not always the case. There was a continuing emphasis upon the normative character of the New Testament as a whole in relation to Christ throughout the evangelical communions during the decades when such views were being enunciated. It would take us too far afield from the main consideration of this chapter to develop this situation further; it is sufficient to point out that it existed and to suggest its character as a background for what must yet be said.[4]

It would be a serious error, in my judgment, to conclude that the historical study of the Scriptures which liberalism fostered was finally misleading. Its findings of necessity are too deeply embedded in the structure of any sound analysis of New Testament thought to discredit its tremendous contribution to our understanding. And although liberal scholars sometimes dulled, and on occasion, denied the essential unity of the Scriptures, liberalism itself laid the groundwork for grasping the message of the New Testament documents in

[3] *Rediscovering the Bible*, p. 14.
[4] For further consideration see an article by Clarence T. Craig, "Biblical Theology and the Rise of Historicism," *Journal of Biblical Literature* (December, 1943), LXII, 281-94.

terms of what they meant to their original readers. And without this knowledge any reading of the account would be untrue, misleading, and superficial. As Chester C. McCown has said, "Christianity is rooted in history, in the Old Testament and the New, not hung on the airy nothings of mythological imagination." [5] Liberalism at its best has sought to uncover this history.

### Unity in Variety

In the face of the relativism to which a reading of the New Testament by liberalism has sometimes led, there has been in recent decades a resurgence of interest in biblical theology with its emphasis upon the unity of the Scriptures. At its best, this has built wisely upon the historical understandings which a sound liberalism brought us.[6] Although in the beginning it was the Old Testament which received the greatest study from this vantage point, at present both testaments and the Bible as a whole are being read and interpreted in terms of their unitary message as the word of God.

We are not in a position, in my judgment, to declare what the total message of the Scriptures is until the most painstaking analysis of its parts, in terms of the historical approach, has been made. Unless this is done, a new myth may be imposed upon the Bible by the biblical interpreter rather than its own message drawn from it. Such an analysis will face squarely the evidence for both variety in point of view and growth in conception which the Scriptures contain. Amos, Isaiah, Jeremiah, Ezekiel, Paul, and John will each be viewed in the individuality of their own minds as God spoke through them. And new levels of spiritual insight as the story of God's encounter with man unfolds will be recognized. Mary E. Lyman has expressed a similar conviction in saying, "The view of the Bible which recognizes diversity and change and different levels of value, but which at the same time appreciates the real unities of religious thought and experience is the view which has hope for the future of our world." [7]

[5] Op. cit., p. 305.
[6] Some of the works which have marked the advance in this respect are Otto J. Baab, Old Testament Theology: Its Possibility and Methodology; Amos N. Wilder, "New Testament Theology in Transition," in The Study of the Bible Today and Tomorrow, ed. Harold R. Willoughby; the symposium on biblical unity carried in Interpretation, V, 1951; H. H. Rowley, The Unity of the Bible; Floyd V. Filson, Jesus Christ the Risen Lord, and the series of monographs, Studies in Biblical Theology. Advisory editors of this series are T. W. Manson, H. H. Rowley, Floyd V. Filson, and G. Ernest Wright.
[7] Journal of Bible and Religion, XIV (1946), 11 ff.

It was for this reason that the method followed in the present volume was selected. The portrait of Christ, it was felt, could best be seen in its essential unity throughout the New Testament by following, more or less consecutively, representations of his person and work in the several documents, indicating similarities and differences alike. Unless both are known and recognized, we are deprived of the richness of the full divine revelation.

### The Kerygma and New Testament Unity

In the last analysis, however, the Christian community in the New Testament does not recognize several Christs. It is acquainted with but one Lord Jesus, (1) whose origin was in God, (2) who was the agent of creation, (3) whose advent was prophesied, (4) who came in the flesh, (5) who as the Messiah proclaimed the Kingdom and performed mighty works, (6) who died for man's sin according to the Scriptures, (7) who was raised from the dead, (8) who ascended in glory to God's right hand, (9) who was present in the Spirit as living Lord to bring newness of life to his followers, (10) who established, indwelt, and guided the church, (11) who would return at the end of the Age to judge, bless, and overcome all evil in men, nations, and the spirit world, and (12) who ultimately would reign with God in an eternal kingdom. This might be called the final kerygma of the New Testament church, and *in this message lies the unity of the portrait of Christ in the twenty-seven writings of the canon it produced.*

It is significant to note that throughout the New Testament it is in the kerygma (*preaching message*) rather than in the didache (*ethical instruction*) that this essential unity is to be found. And in this same connection, it should be pointed out that it was the life and ministry of Jesus, together with his resurrection and exaltation, regarded as an act of God in history, rather than a listing and codification of his teachings alone that became the basis of the church's fellowship.

It must not be concluded, however, that the church ignored the teachings of Jesus. They may be traced in word and spirit throughout the entire New Testament. Filson has shown this concerning the primitive church in his significant volume *One Lord—One Faith.* At the close of a careful study on this point, he concludes:

The survey made showed that in the cardinal points of a rounded and effective message Jesus was loyally followed by the first generation of Christians. They faced new tasks of work and thought. They necessarily developed and applied the message which they had received. They did not progress without disagreements and misunderstandings. But in a movement still without written records or standards they were remarkably faithful in their preservation of the essential position of Jesus.[8]

A similar analysis of New Testament writings beyond the primitive period will likewise show that Jesus' teachings continued to be basic in the thinking of Christians.

In spite of this, however, it is the final kerygma and not the teachings of Jesus which binds the several books of the New Testament into a single whole. It is in the light of this fact that the New Testament understands itself. And it is this same kerygma that is basic to the portrait of Christ throughout. Here is true portraiture, including not only the kind of person he was (the Jesus of history), but also what God did, was continuing to do, and would yet do through him (Christ as Lord and Savior).

### Kerygma—Primitive and Developed

In the kerygma of the primitive church there were several major emphases.[9] One was upon the relation of the event which had occurred to the Old Testament, particularly to prophecy (Acts 2:16; 10:43; Rom. 1:2; I Cor. 15:3-4). In many and various ways this theme was developed. It asserted basically that what had happened among them in the coming of Christ was part and parcel of God's continuing purpose for mankind, first expressed and revealed in Israel. Another point that was stressed had to do with the career of Jesus, including his death, resurrection, and exaltation at God's right hand, from whence he would return to judge and save (Acts 2:23, 24, 30, 32; 3:13, 15, 20; 5:30; 10:37, 39, 42; I Thess. 1:10; Gal. 3:13; I Cor. 15:3, 4; Rom. 1:3; 2:16; 4:25; 8:34). A further tenet in the kerygma was concerned with the forgiveness of sins which came through Jesus Christ, the proclamation of which was often accompanied with a call for repentance (Acts 2:38; 3:19; 10:43).

[8] P. 240. Used by permission Although the announced area of study is the primitive period of the church's life, Filson frequently turns to other New Testament writings from later decades to illustrate his thesis.

[9] Cf. a more detailed analysis of this message in connection with the portrait of Christ in the primitive church in Acts, pp. 39-40.

In time, this kerygma of the primitive church was developed or enlarged to include such elements as (1) Jesus' origin in God (Matt. 1:18-25; Luke 1:26-38; John 1:1-18; I Tim. 3:16; Col. 1:15-16; Phil. 2:5-6; I Pet. 1:20). This brings him into the closest possible metaphysical relation to God without, at the same time, identifying him as God; the Father remains the Father and the Son continues to be the Son; (2) his function as agent of creation through whom God created the universe (John 1:3; Col. 1:16; I Cor. 8:6; Heb. 1:2); (3) his presence in the Spirit as living Lord to bring newness of life to his followers (John 14:17-18; Acts 16:6, 7; I Cor. 15:45; Rom. 8:9-10); (4) his relation to the church which he indwells (Eph. 4:12; I Cor. 12:12; Rom. 12:4, 5); (5) his ultimate victory over evil men, nations, and spirits (I Cor. 15:24-25; Rev. 19:11-21); and (6) his reign with God in an eternal kingdom (II Tim. 2:11b-13; Rev. 22:3). It is the kerygma of the primitive church, together with these additional tenets, that constitutes what we referred to earlier in this chapter as the final kerygma. And this, in turn, is the basis for the unity that exists in the New Testament portrait of Christ.

This kerygma is not treated in detail in each of the New Testament writings. It is often implicit rather than explicit. The extent to which it is openly defined depends upon the type of writing at hand (gospel —epistle—homily—apocalypse), the nature of the situation which is being addressed (ethical problems—controversy—heresy—disillusionment—defection), and the personality of the author (mystic—philosopher—theologian—administrator—seer). Rarely is it stated formally (and then only partially) as in a creedal formula (Acts 10:34-43; I Cor. 15:3-8; John 1:1-18; I Tim. 3:16; II Tim. 2:11b-13), and never is it phrased in its entirety in a single reference. Although verses may be cited to indicate its presence, it quite frequently is to be found in the spirit, tone, level, and thought-direction of the documents themselves.

## Variety in Unity

The kerygma as portraiture is not always subject to identical interpretation throughout the New Testament, even when the same tenets are held and stated. This largely accounts for the variety in unity that exists in the several writings. Failure to recognize this may result in a rigidity of interpretation that does violence to the richness of the complete revelation within the Christian community. What we have actually is a dynamic unity in the total New Testament portrait of Christ rather than a static uniformity.[10] To insist upon the latter would be to reduce the the living revelation of God in Christ to a lowest common denominator, which would be a misrepresentation of its true character. Formalized Christology, however necessary, cannot be imposed upon the New Testament without making it something that basically it is not.

Some of the areas in the portrait of Christ where variety in unity exists might be pointed out briefly with benefit. For instance, in interpreting the tenet that the ultimate source of Jesus is in God, the Gospels of Matthew and Luke carry accounts of the virgin birth.[11] The Fourth Gospel [12] and Hebrews,[13] on the other hand, present this truth in terms of a Logos and/or Wisdom thought-form. Again, the conception of the true humanity of Jesus is approached in Hebrews through the similarities of experience between himself and his fellows[14] while the Fourth Gospel asserts this teaching by insisting on the fact that the Word became flesh.[15] Another illustration may be found in regard to the tenet in the kerygma that Jesus' advent was prophesied in the Old Testament. The Gospel of Matthew interprets this largely in terms of parallels between specific events in Jesus' life and verses in the Hebrew scriptures,[16] while Paul frequently regards the relationship as representing earlier and later stages in the revelation of the same God.[17]

To continue this review of variety in unity which appears in connection with the interpretation of tenets in the kerygma, mention may be made of the ways in which Jesus' death for sin is presented. The Fourth Gospel sees it as an example of the lengths to which love will go in order to save, and the application of the principle that a seed must die if it is to germinate and bear fruit. Jesus is also being crucified at the very hour when the Jews are killing the lamb for the Passover meal, suggesting that he is the true Paschal Lamb.[18] Paul

---

[10] Rowley uses the expression "dynamic unity" in relation to the Scriptures as a whole, including both the Old and New Testaments. Cf. op. cit., p. 7.

[11] Cf. reference to the treatment in the Synoptic portrait, pp. 120-23.

[12] Cf. reference to the treatment in the Johannine portrait, pp. 162-64.

[13] Cf. reference to the treatment in the portrait in Hebrews, p. 189.

[14] Cf. reference to the treatment in the portrait in Hebrews, pp. 182-83.

[15] Cf. reference to the treatment in the Johannine portrait, pp. 162-64.

[16] Cf. reference to the treatment in the Synoptic portrait, p. 122.

[17] Cf. reference to the treatment in the Pauline portrait, pp. 64, 90, 102-3.

[18] Cf. reference to the treatment in the Johannine portrait, pp. 174-75.

also finds several areas of illustration by which to interpret Jesus' death for sin. By it sinners are acquitted and declared innocent as before a court of law, ransomed as slaves who are freed with the payment of a fee (not to be taken too literally), and forgiven by possessing faith in Jesus' blood as an expiation.[19] And the author of Hebrews sees in Jesus both the perfect and final sacrifice, as well as the eternal high priest whereby the putting away of sin can be effected.[20]

Yet another illustration of the way in which a tenet of the kerygma may be variously interpreted by New Testament writers may be found in Jesus' relation to the church. In Paul, the church is the community of the true Israel. And at the same time it is the body of Christ, of which he is the head and the *shekinah*.[21] On the other hand, in the Revelation to John the relationship of Jesus to the church is that of the groom to his bride.[22]

Still other examples of varying interpretations might be given in regard to the Kingdom, the return of Jesus, the final judgment, and the ultimate victory of Christ over evil.[23] As was stated at the outset of this section, this is usually variety in unity rather than irreconcilable difference.[24] The one final kerygma is basic throughout so that the New Testament may be said ultimately to know only one Lord and one Faith.

### The Unity of the Bible

The New Testament has consistently been read in the church in terms of its relation to the Old Testament. From the first the Christian community held fast to the Hebrew scriptures. To the extent to which many of them had been Jews before they became followers of Christ, this is understandable. On the other hand, it would not have been illogical for them, psychologically speaking, to have turned their backs completely upon the old as they embraced fully the new. The reason they did not do so is obvious. The very earliest kerygma insisted that what had taken place in Christ had been foreseen in the

[19] Cf. reference to treatment in the Pauline portrait, pp. 70-71.
[20] Cf. reference to the treatment in the portrait of Hebrews, pp. 183-86.
[21] Cf. reference to the treatment in the Pauline portrait, pp. 84-85.
[22] Cf. reference to the treatment in the portrait in the Revelation to John, p. 208.
[23] Cf. the development in Floyd V. Filson's *Jesus Christ the Risen Lord* where the relation of Christ to the Old Testament, the Kingdom, the Cross, the Father, the Spirit, the church, the Christian and the final goal are treated in the light of the unity of the New Testament.
[24] Sometimes what appears to be contradiction in conception and thought will turn out to be a paradox in which both ideas are but logical parts of a larger truth.

Old Testament. This is abundantly clear both in the sermons in Acts and in the epistles. The Gospels and other later writings followed this line of thought. It became normative throughout the New Testament as a whole.

What was the essential basis of the conviction of the early church that what had happened in Christ had been foreseen in the Old Testament? In part, it would seem to have been the status attributed to prophecy among the Jews. It had long since been accepted that under a divine afflatus men had spoken for God of things to come. Prophecy had traditionally been considered as involving both interpretation of current events and prediction. It would have been concluded, therefore, that such an event as the coming of Christ and the new life which attended his ministry, death, and resurrection must not have escaped the prophets. A search of the Scriptures turned up many passages that seemed to suggest certain events in the life of Jesus. Sometimes the connection cited may impress us as tenuous, if not actually coincidental. But again, there are depths of unity between the Old Testament reference and the New Testament event that are self-confirming to the Christian mind and conscience.

In addition to this, there was ample indication in the tradition concerning Jesus that the Hebrew scriptures were important to him personally.[25] On occasion he quoted or referred to passages from many of the writings. Listing these according to the frequency of the reference, they include Isaiah, Deuteronomy, Psalms, Leviticus, Hosea, Zechariah, Genesis, Exodus, Daniel, First Samuel, Numbers, Nehemiah, and Jeremiah. There were times also when he spoke of the significance of the law and the prophets in no uncertain terms (Luke 16:17; Matt. 5:19). They were the thought-world within which he lived and was perfectly at home. Mention should also be made of the place that the Old Testament played in Jesus' personal religious life. In crisis situations such as the period of temptations in the wilderness, the Transfiguration, and the agony on the cross, there are rather clear indications that he turned to his scriptures for wisdom and strength. All of this must of necessity have impressed the early church, impelling them to employ the Old Testament in interpreting Jesus. This would further bind the Old Testament to the New.

Ultimately, and perhaps more significantly than the other factors

---

[25] Cf. my *Life and Teachings of Jesus*, pp. 125-26 for a fuller consideration of this subject.

I have been mentioning, the conviction that the God of Israel and the God of the Christian church were one and the same being did more to tie together the Hebrew and Christian writings into a single whole than any other single element. Here is the final basis of the unity of the Bible. The point is that this one was a revealing God who had made his will known to his own people, both to Israel of old and to the New Israel in Christ. And as Rowley has said, "If God was revealing Himself, then there should be some unity about the revelation, since it was the same Being who was being revealed." [26]

All of this means that the portrait of Christ in the New Testament does not stand apart from the revelation of God in the Scriptures as a whole. The biblical documents are concerned basically, for all their variety, with the same self-revelation of God in creation and redemption. And it is only as we read them in this light that the final significance of Christ can be grasped. Perhaps it should be stated this way. Only as we read the New Testament in relation to God's total revelation in the Scriptures, does Christ in his fullness lay hold of us.

[26] *Op. cit.*, p. 8.

# BIBLIOGRAPHY

GENERAL STUDIES OF THE LITERATURE OF THE NEW TESTAMENT

Angus, Samuel. *The Mystery-religions and Christianity.* New York: Charles Scribner's Sons, 1925.

Baly, Denis. *The Geography of the Bible.* New York: Harper & Bros., 1957.

Barnett, Albert E. *The New Testament: Its Making and Meaning.* Nashville: Abingdon Press, 1946.

Barrett, Charles K. *The New Testament Background: Selected Documents.* New York: The Macmillan Co., 1957.

Buttrick, George A. (ed.). *The Interpreter's Bible,* VII-XII. Nashville: Abingdon Press, 1951-1957.

Dibelius, Martin. *A Fresh Approach to the New Testament and Early Christian Literature.* New York: Charles Scribner's Sons, 1936.

Goodspeed, Edgar J. *An Introduction to the New Testament.* Chicago: The University of Chicago Press, 1937.

Grant, Frederick C. *An Introduction to New Testament Thought.* Nashville: Abingdon Press, 1950.

Heard, Richard G. *An Introduction to the New Testament.* New York: Harper & Bros., 1950.

Hereford, R. T. *Judaism in the New Testament Period.* London: Lindsey Press, 1928.

————. *The Pharisees.* New York: The Macmillan Co., 1924.

Hunter, Archibald M. *Introducing the New Testament.* 2nd edition. Philadelphia: The Westminster Press, 1958.

Kee, Howard Clark, and Young, Franklin W. *Understanding the New Testament.* Englewood Cliffs, N. J.: Prentice-Hall, Inc., 1957.

Loisy, Alfred. *The Origins of the New Testament.* Tr. L. P. Jacks. London: George Allen & Unwin, Ltd., 1950.

McNeile, A. H. *An Introduction to the Study of the New Testament.* 2nd. revised edition. New York: Oxford University Press, 1953.

Metzger, Bruce M. *An Introduction to the Apocrypha.* New York: Oxford University Press, 1957.

Moffatt, James. *Grace in the New Testament.* New York: Harper & Bros., 1932.

————. *An Introduction to the Literature of the New Testament.* New York: Charles Scribner's Sons, 1911.

————. *Love in the New Testament.* New York: Harper & Bros., 1930.

Pfeiffer, R. H. *History of New Testament Times: With an Introduction to the Apocrypha.* New York: Harper & Bros., 1949.

Riddle, D. W. and Hutson, H. H. *New Testament Life and Literature.* Chicago: University of Chicago Press, 1946.

Rowlingson, Donald T. *Introduction to New Testament Study.* New York: The Macmillan Co., 1956.

Scott, Ernest F. *Literature of the New Testament.* New York: Columbia University Press, 1932.

Wright, G. Ernest and Filson, Floyd V. *Westminster Historical Atlas to the Bible.* Philadelphia: The Westminster Press, 1945.

## CHRISTIAN BEGINNINGS

Bultmann, Rudolf K. *Kerygma and Myth.* Tr. Reginald H. Fuller; ed. Hans Werner Bartsch. London: S.P.C.K., 1953.

Burkitt, F. C. *Christian Beginnings.* London: University of London Press, Ltd., 1924.

Burrows, Millar. *The Dead Sea Scrolls.* New York: The Viking Press, 1955.

Cadbury, Henry J. *The Book of Acts in History.* New York: Harper & Bros., 1955.

————. *The Making of Luke-Acts.* New York: The Macmillan Co., 1927.

Cadoux, Cecil J. *The Early Church and the World.* New York: Charles Scribner's Sons, 1925.

Carrington, P. *The Primitive Christian Catechism.* London: Cambridge University Press, 1940.

Craig, Clarence Tucker. *The Beginning of Christianity.* Nashville: Abingdon Press, 1943.

Cross, Frank Moore, Jr. *The Ancient Library of Qumran and Modern Biblical Studies.* New York: Doubleday and Co., 1958.

Cullmann, Oscar. *The Early Church.* Philadelphia: The Westminster Press, 1956.

Dodd, Charles H. *The Apostolic Preaching and Its Development.* Chicago: Willett, Clark & Co., 1937.

Dupont-Sommer, André. *The Dead Sea Scrolls.* Tr. E. Margaret Rowley. New York: The Macmillan Co., 1952.

————. *The Jewish Sect of Qumrân and the Essenes.* Tr. R. D. Barnett. London: Vallentine, Mitchell & Co., Ltd., 1954.

Enslin, Morton S. *Christian Beginnings.* New York: Harper & Bros., 1938.

Foakes-Jackson, F. J. *The Acts of the Apostles* ("The Moffatt New Testament Commentary Series.") New York: Harper & Bros., 1931.

Foakes-Jackson, F. J. and Lake, Kirsopp. *Beginnings of Christianity.* New York: The Macmillan Co., 1920-33.

Goguel, Maurice. *The Birth of Christianity.* Tr. H. C. Snape. New York: The Macmillan Co., 1954.

————. *L'Eglise Primitive.* Paris, 1957.

Hopwood, P. G. S. *The Religious Experience of the Primitive Church.* Edinburgh: T. & T. Clark, 1936.

Knox, John. *The Early Church and the Coming Great Church.* Nashville: Abingdon Press, 1955.

Knox, Wilfred L. *Some Hellenistic Elements in Primitive Christianity.* London: Oxford University Press, 1944.

Mackinnon, James. *The Gospel in the Early Church.* London: Longmans, Green & Co., Ltd., 1933.

Rackham, R. B. *The Acts of the Apostles.* Boston: Gorham Press, 1912. 11th edition, London, 1930.

Rowley, H. H. *The Zadokite Fragments and the Dead Sea Scrolls.* Oxford: Basil Blackwell & Mott, Ltd., 1953.

Scott, Ernest F. *The Nature of the Early Church.* New York: Charles Scribner's Sons, 1942.

Streeter, Burnett H. *The Primitive Church.* The Macmillan Co., 1932.

Weiss, Johannes. *The History of Primitive Christianity.* English translation from the German. New York: Wilson-Erickson, Inc., 1937.

Williams, Ronald R. *Authority in the Apostolic Age.* London: Student Christian Movement Press, Ltd., 1950.

THE SYNOPTIC GOSPELS

Abrahams, Israel. *Studies in Pharisaism and the Gospels.* New York: The Macmillan Co., 1917-24.

Booth, Edwin Prince (ed.). *New Testament Studies.* Nashville: Abingdon Press, 1942.

Branscomb, B. Harvie. *The Gospel of Mark.* ("The Moffatt New Testament Commentary Series.") New York: Harper & Bros., 1937.

Bultmann, Rudolf K. *Die Geschichte der synoptischen Tradition.* Göttingen, 1931.

Cadbury, Henry J. "The New Testament and Early Christian Literature," *The Interpreter's Bible.* Nashville: Abingdon Press, 1951. VII, 32-42.

Creed, John M. *The Gospel According to St. Luke.* London: Macmillan & Co., Ltd., 1930.

Dibelius, Martin. *From Tradition to Gospel.* Tr. Bertram Lee Woolf. New York: Charles Scribner's Sons, 1935.

Dodd, Charles H. *History and the Gospel.* New York: Charles Scribner's Sons, 1938.

Filson, Floyd V. *The Origins of the Gospels.* Nashville: Abingdon Press, 1938.

Gilmour, S. M., "The Gospel According to St. Luke," *The Interpreter's Bible.* Nashville: Abingdon Press, 1952. VIII, 3-434.

Grant, Frederick C. *The Earliest Gospel.* Nashville: Abingdon Press, 1943.

————. *The Economic Background of the Gospels.* London: Oxford University Press, 1926.

———— (ed. and tr.). *Form Criticism: A New Method of New Testament Research.* Chicago: Willett, Clark & Co., 1934.

————. "The Gospel According to St. Mark," *The Interpreter's Bible.* Nashville: Abingdon Press, 1951. VII, 629-917.

————. *The Gospels: Their Origin and Their Growth.* New York: Harper & Bros., 1957.

James, Montague R. *The Apocryphal New Testament.* New York: Oxford University Press, 1950.

Johnson, Sherman E. "The Gospel According to St. Matthew," *The Interpreter's Bible.* Nashville: Abingdon Press, 1951. VII, 231-625.

Lightfoot, Robert H. *The Gospel Message of St. Mark.* New York: Oxford University Press, 1950.

————. *History and Interpretation in the Gospels.* London: Hodder & Stoughton, Ltd., 1935.

Major, Henry and others. *The Mission and Message of Jesus.* New York: E. P. Dutton & Co., Inc., 1948.

Manson, William. *The Gospel of Luke.* ("The Moffatt New Testament Commentary Series.") New York: Harper & Bros., 1930.

Montefiore, Claude G. *Rabbinic Literature and Gospel Teachings.* New York: The Macmillan Co., 1930.

———— (ed.). *The Synoptic Gospels.* New York: The Macmillan Co., 1927.

Rawlinson, A. E. J. *The Gospel According to St. Mark.* London: Methuen & Co., Ltd., 1931.

Redlich, E. B. *Form Criticism.* New York: Charles Scribner's Sons, 1939.

Richardson, Alan. *The Miracle-stories of the Gospels.* New York: Harper & Bros., 1942.

Robinson, Theodore H. *The Gospel of Matthew.* ("The Moffatt New Testament Commentary Series.") London: Hodder & Stoughton, Ltd., 1947.

Scott, Ernest F. *The Purpose of the Gospels.* New York: Charles Scribner's Sons, 1949.

————. *The Validity of the Gospel Record.* New York: Charles Scribner's Sons, 1938.

Streeter, Burnett H. *The Four Gospels.* New York: The Macmillan Co., 1952.

Taylor, Vincent. *Formation of the Gospel Tradition.* New York: The Macmillan Co., 1933.

————. *The Gospel According to Mark.* London: Macmillan & Co., Ltd., 1952.

## STUDIES OF JESUS

Barnett, Albert E. *Understanding the Parables of Our Lord.* Nashville: Abingdon-Cokesbury Press, 1940.

Beck, Dwight M. *Through the Gospels to Jesus.* New York: Harper & Bros., 1954.

Bosworth, Edward I. *The Life and Teachings of Jesus.* New York: The Macmillan Co., 1939.

Bousset, Wilhelm. *Kyrios Christos.* Göttingen, 1913.

Branscomb, B. Harvie. *The Teachings of Jesus.* Nashville: Abingdon Press, 1931.

Burney, C. F. *The Poetry of Our Lord.* New York: Oxford University Press, 1925.

Cadbury, Henry J. *Jesus: What Manner of Man?* New York: The Macmillan Co., 1947.

———. *The Peril of Modernizing Jesus.* New York: The Macmillan Co., 1937.

Cadoux, Cecil J. *The Historic Mission of Jesus.* New York: Harper & Bros., 1943.

Dalman, Gustaf. *The Words of Jesus.* Translated into English. Edinburgh, 1909.

Deissmann, Gustav A. *The Religion of Jesus and the Faith of Paul.* Tr. William E. Wilson. London: Hodder & Stoughton, Ltd., 1923.

Dodd, Charles H. *The Parables of the Kingdom.* New York: Charles Scribner's Sons, 1936.

Duncan, George S. *Jesus, Son of Man.* New York: The Macmillan Co., 1949.

Goguel, Maurice. *The Life of Jesus.* Tr. Olive Wyon. New York: The Macmillan Co., 1933.

Goodspeed, Edgar J. *Life of Jesus.* New York: Harper & Bros., 1950.

Guignebert, Charles A. *Jesus.* Tr. S. H. Hooke. New York: Alfred A. Knopf, Inc., 1935.

Jeremias, Joachim. *The Parables of Jesus.* Tr. S. H. Hooke. New York: Charles Scribner's Sons, 1956.

Johnson, Sherman E. *Jesus in His Homeland.* New York: Charles Scribner's Sons, 1957.

Kepler, Thomas S. (ed.). *Contemporary Thinking About Jesus.* Nashville: Abingdon Press, 1944.

Klausner, Joseph. *Jesus of Nazareth.* New York: The Macmillan Co., 1929.

Knox, John. *The Man Christ Jesus.* Chicago: Willett, Clark & Co., 1942.

Laymon, Charles M. *The Life and Teachings of Jesus.* Nashville: Abingdon Press, 1955.

Manson, Thomas W. *The Servant-Messiah.* London: Cambridge University Press, 1953.

———. *The Teaching of Jesus.* London: Cambridge University Press, 1935.

Manson, William. *Jesus the Messiah.* Philadelphia: The Westminster Press, 1946.

McCasland, Selby V. *By the Finger of God.* New York: The Macmillan Co., 1951.

McCown, Chester C. *The Search for the Real Jesus.* New York: Charles Scribner's Sons, 1940.

Oesterley, W. O. E. *The Gospel Parables in the Light of Their Jewish Background.* New York: The Macmillan Co., 1936.

Otto, Rudolf. *The Kingdom of God and the Son of Man.* Grand Rapids: Zondervan Publishing House, 1938.

Ramsey, Arthur Michael. *The Resurrection of Christ.* Philadelphia: The Westminster Press, 1946.

Rollins, Wallace E. and Rollins, Marion J. *Jesus and His Ministry.* Greenwich: The Seabury Press, Inc., 1954.

Schweitzer, Albert. *Quest of the Historical Jesus.* New York: The Macmillan Co., 1948.

Scott, Ernest F., *The Lord's Prayer*. New York: Charles Scribner's Sons, 1951.

Stewart, James S. *The Life and Teaching of Jesus Christ*. Nashville: Abingdon Press, 1957.

Strachan, Robert H. *The Historic Jesus in the New Testament*. London: Student Christian Movement Press, Ltd., 1931.

Taylor, Vincent. *Jesus and His Sacrifice*. London: Macmillan & Co., Ltd., 1937.

_____. *The Life and Ministry of Jesus*. Nashville: Abingdon Press, 1955.

_____. *The Names of Jesus*. London: St. Martin's Press, 1953.

Warschauer, Joseph. *The Historical Life of Christ*. New York: The Macmillan Co., 1926.

Wrede, William. *The Messianic Secret in the Gospels*. 1901.

Zeitlin, Solomon. *Who Crucified Jesus?* New York: Harper & Bros., 1942.

## THE JOHANNINE WRITINGS

Barrett, C. K. *The Gospel According to St. John*. New York: The Macmillan Co., 1955.

Bernard, J. H. *The Gospel of St. John*. 2 vols. ("International Critical Commentary.") Ed. A. H. McNeile. New York: Charles Scribner's Sons, 1929.

Bultmann, Rudolf K. *Das Evangelium des Johannes*. Göttingen, 1941.

Colwell, Ernest C. *John Defends the Gospel*. Chicago: Willett Clark & Co., 1936.

Colwell, Ernest C. and Titus, Eric L. *The Gospel of the Spirit*. New York: Harper & Bros., 1953.

Dodd, Charles H. *The Interpretation of the Fourth Gospel*. London: Cambridge University Press, 1953.

_____. *The Johannine Epistles*, ("The Moffatt New Testament Commentary Series.") New York: Harper & Bros., 1946.

Drummond, James. *An Inquiry Into the Character and Authorship of the Fourth Gospel*. London: Williams & Norgate, Ltd., 1903.

Gardner-Smith, Percival. *Saint John and the Synoptic Gospels*. London: Cambridge University Press, 1938.

Grant, F. C. *The Gospel of John in the King James Version*. 2 vols. New York: Harper & Bros., 1957.

Hoskyns, Edwyn C. *The Fourth Gospel*. Ed. Francis N. Davey. London: Faber & Faber, Ltd., 1940.

Howard, Wilbert F. *Christianity According to St. John*. Philadelphia: The Ryerson Press, 1946.

_____. "The Gospel According to St. John," *The Interpreter's Bible*. Nashville: Abingdon Press, 1952. VIII, 436-811.

Macgregor, G. H. C. *The Gospel of John*. ("The Moffatt New Testament Commentary Series.") New York: Harper & Bros., 1929.

Scott, Ernest F. *The Fourth Gospel: Its Purpose and Theology*. Edinburgh: T. & T. Clark, 1908.

Smart, Wyatt A. *The Spiritual Gospel*. Nashville: Abingdon-Cokesbury Press, 1946.

Strachan, Robert H. *The Fourth Evangelist: Dramatist or Historian?* New York: George H. Doran Co., 1925.
————. *The Fourth Gospel.* New York: The Macmillan Co., 1952.
Titus, Eric L. *The Message of the Fourth Gospel.* Nashville: Abingdon Press, 1957.
Wilder, Amos. N. "The First, Second, and Third Epistles of John," *The Interpreter's Bible.* Nashville: Abingdon Press, 1957. XII, 209-313.
Windisch, Hans. *Johannes und die Synoptiker.* Leipzig: J. C. Henrichsche Buchhandlung, 1926.

### THE PAULINE WRITINGS

Andrews, Elias. *The Meaning of Christ for Paul.* Nashville: Abingdon Press, 1949.
Bailey, John W. "The First and Second Epistles to the Thessalonians," *The Interpreter's Bible.* Nashville: Abingdon Press, 1955. XI, 245-339.
Beare, Francis W. "The Epistle to the Colossians," *The Interpreter's Bible.* Nashville: Abingdon Press, 1955. XI, 133-241.
————. "The Epistle to the Ephesians," *The Interpreter's Bible.* Nashville: Abingdon Press, 1953. X, 597-749.
Craig, Clarence T. "The First Epistle to the Corinthians," *The Interpreter's Bible.* Nashville: Abingdon Press, 1953. X, 3-262.
Dodd, Charles H. *The Epistle of Paul to the Romans.* ("The Moffatt New Testament Commentary Series.") New York: Harper & Bros., 1932.
Duncan, George S. *The Epistle of Paul to the Galatians.* ("The Moffatt New Testament Commentary Series.") New York: Harper & Bros., 1934.
Easton, B. S. *The Pastoral Epistles.* New York: Charles Scribner's Sons, 1947.
Edman, Irwin. *The Mind of Paul.* New York: Henry Holt & Co., Inc., 1935.
Filson, Floyd V. "The Second Epistle to the Corinthians," *The Interpreter's Bible.* Nashville: Abingdon Press, 1953. X, 265-425.
Gealy, Fred D. "The First and Second Epistles to Timothy and the Epistle to Titus," *The Interpreter's Bible.* Nashville: Abingdon Press, 1955. XI, 343-551.
Glover, Terrot R. *Paul of Tarsus.* New York: George H. Doran Co., 1925.
Goodspeed, Edgar J. *The Meaning of Ephesians.* Chicago: University of Chicago Press, 1933.
Hunter, A. M. *Interpreting Paul's Gospel.* Philadelphia: The Westminster Press, 1955.
Kennedy, H. A. A. *St. Paul and the Mystery Religions.* London: Hodder & Stoughton, Ltd., 1913.
Klausner, Joseph. *From Jesus to Paul.* New York: The Macmillan Co., 1943.
Knox, John. *Chapters in a Life of Paul.* Nashville: Abingdon Press, 1950.
————. "The Epistle to Philemon," *The Interpreter's Bible.* Nashville: Abingdon Press, 1955. XI, 555-73.
————. "The Epistle to the Romans," *The Interpreter's Bible.* Nashville: Abingdon Press, 1954. IX, 355-668.

Lightfoot, Joseph B. *St. Paul's Epistle to the Philippians.* London: Macmillan & Co., Ltd., 1868.

McNeile, Alan H. *New Testament Teaching in the Light of St. Paul's.* New York: The Macmillan Co., 1923.

Michael, John H. *Philippians.* ("The Moffatt New Testament Commentary Series.") Garden City: Doubleday & Co., Inc., 1929.

Moffatt, James. *The First Epistle of Paul to the Corinthians.* ("The Moffatt New Testament Commentary Series.") New York: Harper & Bros., 1938.

Neil, William. *The Epistle of Paul to the Thessalonians.* ("The Moffatt New Testament Commentary Series.") New York: Harper & Bros., 1950.

Porter, Frank C. *The Mind of Christ in Paul.* New York: Charles Scribner's Sons, 1931.

Rall, Harris F. *According to Paul.* New York: Charles Scribner's Sons, 1944.

Schweitzer, Albert. *The Mysticism of Paul the Apostle.* New York: Henry Holt & Co., Inc., 1931.

Scott, C. Anderson. *Christianity According to St. Paul.* New York: The Macmillan Co., 1927.

Scott, Ernest F. *The Epistles of Paul to Colossians, to Philemon and to the Ephesians.* ("The Moffatt New Testament Commentary Series.") New York: Harper & Bros., 1930.

————. "The Epistle to the Philippians," *The Interpreter's Bible.* Nashville: Abingdon Press, 1955. XI, 3-129.

————. *The Pastoral Epistles.* ("The Moffatt New Testament Commentary Series.") New York: Harper & Bros., 1936.

Stamm, Raymond T. "The Epistle to the Galatians," *The Interpreter's Bible.* Nashville: Abingdon Press, 1957. X, 429-593.

Strachan, Robert H. *The Second Epistle of Paul to the Corinthians.* ("The Moffatt New Testament Commentary Series.") New York: Harper & Bros., 1935.

## HEBREWS

Andrews, Herbert T. "Hebrews," *The Abingdon Bible Commentary,* ed. Frederick C. Eiselen. Nashville: Abingdon Press, 1929.

Barrett, C. K. "The Eschatology of the Epistle to the Hebrews," *The Background of the New Testament and Its Eschatology,* ed. William D. Davies and David Daube. London: Cambridge University Press, 1956.

Moffatt, James. *Epistle to the Hebrews.* ("International Critical Commentary.") New York: Charles Scribner's Sons, 1924.

Purdy, Alexander C. "The Epistle to the Hebrews," *The Interpreter's Bible.* Nashville: Abingdon Press, 1955. XI, 577-763.

Robinson, T. H. *The Epistle to the Hebrews.* ("The Moffatt New Testament Commentary Series.") New York: Harper & Bros., 1933.

Scott, Ernest F. *The Epistle to the Hebrews.* Edinburgh: T. & T. Clark, 1922.

## THE GENERAL EPISTLES

Barnett, Albert E. "The Epistle of Jude," *The Interpreter's Bible.* Nashville: Abingdon Press, 1957. XII, 317-43.

―――. "The Second Epistle of Peter," *The Interpreter's Bible*. Nashville: Abingdon Press, 1957. XII, 163-206.

Case, Shirley Jackson. "Jude," *The Abingdon Bible Commentary*, ed. Frederick C. Eiselen. Nashville: Abingdon Press, 1929.

―――. "Second Peter," *The Abingdon Bible Commentary*, ed. Frederick C. Eiselen. Nashville: Abingdon Press, 1929.

Easton, Burton Scott. "The Epistle of James," *The Interpreter's Bible*. Nashville: Abingdon Press, 1957. XII, 3-74.

Hunter, Archibald M. "The First Epistle of Peter," *The Interpreter's Bible*. Nashville: Abingdon Press, 1957. XII, 77-159.

Moffatt, James. *The General Epistles*. ("The Moffatt New Testament Commentary Series.") Garden City: Doubleday, Doran, & Co., Inc., 1928.

Robinson, Benjamin W. "First Peter," *The Abingdon Bible Commentary*, ed. Frederick C. Eiselen. Nashville: Abingdon Press, 1929.

Selwyn, Edward G. (ed.). *The First Epistle of St. Peter*. London: Macmillan & Co., Ltd., 1946.

Sugden, Edward H. "James," *The Abingdon Bible Commentary*, ed. Frederick C. Eiselen. Nashville: Abingdon Press, 1929.

## REVELATION TO JOHN AND APOCALYPTICISM

Barclay, William. *Letters to the Seven Churches*. Nashville: Abingdon Press, 1957.

Beckwith, Isbon T. *The Apocalypse of John*. New York: The Macmillan Co., 1919.

Bousset, Wilhelm. *Die Offenbarung Johannis*.

Bowman, John Wick. *The Drama of the Book of Revelation* (a new translation in modern idiom). Philadelphia: The Westminster Press, 1955.

Charles, Robert H. *The Apocrypha and Pseudepigrapha of the Old Testament*. London: Oxford University Press, 1913.

―――. *The Revelation of St. John*. ("International Critical Commentary.") 2 Vols. New York: Charles Scribner's Sons, 1920.

Cullmann, Oscar. *The State in the New Testament*. New York: Charles Scribner's Sons, 1956.

Davies, William D. and Daube, David (eds.). *The Background of the New Testament and Its Eschatology*. London: Cambridge University Press, 1956.

Guy, Harold A., *The New Testament Doctrine of the Last Things*. London: Oxford University Press, 1948.

Kepler, Thomas S. *The Book of Revelation*. New York: Oxford University Press, 1957.

Kiddle, Martin. *The Revelation of St. John*. ("The Moffatt New Testament Commentary Series.") New York: Harper & Bros., 1941.

Lilje, Hanns. *The Last Book of the Bible*. Tr. Olive Wyon. Philadelphia: Muhlenberg Press, 1957.

Minear, Paul S. *Christian Hope and the Second Coming*. Philadelphia: The Westminster Press, 1954.

Rist, Martin. "The Revelation of St. John the Divine," *The Interpreter's Bible.* Nashville: Abingdon Press, 1957. XII, 347-613.

Rowley, H. H. *The Revelance of Apocalyptic.* London: Lutterworth Press, 1944.

Scott, Ernest F. *The Book of Revelation.* New York: Charles Scribner's Sons, 1940.

Simkhovitch, Vladimir G. *Toward the Understanding of Jesus.* New York: The Macmillan Co., 1947.

Swete, Henry B. (ed.). *The Apocalypse of St. John.* New York: The Macmillan Co., 1907.

Wilder, Amos N. *Eschatology and Ethics in the Teaching of Jesus.* New York: Harper & Bros., 1939.

## NEW TESTAMENT THEOLOGY

Albright, William Foxwell. *From the Stone Age to Christianity.* Baltimore: The Johns Hopkins Press, 1940.

Anderson, Bernhard W. *Rediscovering the Bible.* New York: Association Press, 1951.

Andrews, Herbert T. *The Christ of Apostolic Faith,* ed. Wheeler Robinson. London: James Nisbet & Co., Ltd., 1929.

Argyle, Aubrey W. *The Christ of the New Testament.* London: Kingsgate Press, 1952.

Aulén, Gustaf. *Christus Victor.* Tr. A. G. Hebert. London: The Sheldon Press, 1931.

Baillie, Donald M. *God Was in Christ.* New York: Charles Scribner's Sons, 1948.

Bowman, John Wick. *Prophetic Realism and the Gospel.* Philadelphia: The Westminster Press, 1955.

Bultmann, Rudolf K. *Theology of the New Testament.* 2 vols. Tr. Kendrick Groble. New York: Charles Scribner's Sons, 1951, 1955.

Burrows, Millar. *Outline of Biblical Theology.* Philadelphia: The Westminster Press, 1946.

Case, Shirley Jackson. *Jesus Through the Centuries.* Chicago: University of Chicago Press, 1932.

Clark, Neville. *An Approach to the Theology of the Sacraments.* Naperville: Alec R. Allenson, Inc., 1956.

Cullmann, Oscar. *Baptism in the New Testament.* Tr. J. K. S. Reid. London: Student Christian Movement Press, Ltd., 1950.

————. *Christ and Time.* Tr. Floyd V. Filson. Philadelphia: The Westminster Press, 1950.

————. *Early Christian Worship.* Tr. A. Stewart Todd and James B. Torrance. Chicago: Henry Regnery Co., 1953.

Dibelius, Martin. *Gospel Criticism and Christology.* London: Ivor Nicholson & Watson, Ltd., 1935.

Easton, Burton Scott. *Christ in the Gospels.* New York: Charles Scribner's Sons, 1930.

————. "The Epistle of James," *The Interpreter's Bible.* Nashville: Abingdon Press, 1957. XII, 3-74.

Elliott-Binns, Leonard E. *Galilean Christianity.* Chicago: Alec R. Allenson, Inc., 1956.

Filson, Floyd V. *Jesus Christ the Risen Lord.* Nashville: Abingdon Press, 1956.

————. *The New Testament Against Its Environment.* London: Student Christian Movement Press, Ltd., 1950.

————. *One Lord, One Faith.* Philadelphia: The Westminster Press, 1943.

Fridrichsen, Anton and Others. *The Root of the Vine; Essays in Biblical Theology.* New York: Philosophical Library, Inc., 1953.

Goppelt, L. *Die typologische Deutung des Alten Testaments im Neuen.* Gütersloh, 1939.

Henderson, Ian. *Myth in the New Testament.* Chicago: Henry Regnery Co., 1952.

Higgins, A. J. B. *The Lord's Supper in the New Testament.* Chicago: Henry Regnery Co., 1952.

Hunter, Archibald M. *The Message of the New Testament.* Philadelphia: The Westminster Press, 1944.

————. *Introducing New Testament Theology.* Philadelphia: The Westminster Press, 1958.

Knox, John. *Christ the Lord.* Chicago: Willett, Clark & Co., 1945.

————. *The Death of Christ.* Nashville: Abingdon Press, 1957.

Kümmel, Werner G. *Promise and Fulfillment.* Tr. Dorothea M. Barton. Naperville: Alec R. Allenson, Inc., 1957.

Lampe, Geoffrey W. H. and Woollcombe, Kenneth J. *Essays on Typology.* Naperville: Alec R. Allenson, Inc., 1957.

Minear, Paul S. *Eyes of Faith: A Study in the Biblical Point of View.* Philadelphia: The Westminster Press, 1948.

Nygren, Anders T. S. *Agape and Eros.* Tr. A. G. Hebert. New York: The Macmillan Co., 1932.

————. *Christ and His Church.* Tr. Alan Carlsten. Philadelphia: The Westminster Press, 1956.

Rawlinson, A. E. J. *Christ in the Gospels.* New York: Oxford University Press, 1944.

————. *The New Testament Doctrine of the Christ.* New York: Longmans, Green & Co., Inc., 1949.

Robinson, James M. *The Problem of History in Mark.* Naperville: Alec R. Allenson, Inc., 1957.

Rowley, H. H. *The Unity of the Bible.* Philadelphia: The Westminster Press, 1955.

Stauffer, Ethelbert. *New Testament Theology.* Tr. John Marsh. London: Student Christian Movement Press, Ltd., 1955.

Strachan, Robert H. "The Gospel in the New Testament," *The Interpreter's Bible.* Nashville: Abingdon Press, 1951. VII, 3-31.

Tasker, R. V. G. *The Old Testament in the New Testament.* 2nd revised edition. London: Student Christian Movement Press, Ltd., 1954.

Taylor, Vincent. *The Atonement in New Testament Teaching*. London: The Epworth Press, 1940.

————. *Forgiveness and Reconciliation*. London: Macmillan & Co., Ltd., 1946.

Wright, G. Ernest. "The Faith of Israel," *The Interpreter's Bible*. Nashville: Abingdon Press, 1952. I, 349-89.

————. *The Old Testament Against Its Environment*. London: Student Christian Movement Press, Ltd., 1950.

Zenos, Andrew C. *The Plastic Age of the Gospel*. New York: The Macmillan Co., 1927.

Zimmerli, Walther and Jeremias, Joachim. *The Servant of God*. English translation. Naperville: Alec R. Allenson, Inc., 1957.

# INDEX OF REFERENCES

## Old Testament

## New Testament

243

# Early Noncanonical Writings

# INDEX OF SUBJECTS

253